THE BACK OF THE BUS

THE LIFE AND TIMES OF MILITARY MUSICIANS

a love story by

Fred J. Robinson

& the usual bunch of idiots

Special Thanks

Contributing Editor:
Tom Porter

Major Contributors:
Stephanie Franks and Chris Hudson

Cover Handwriting:
Lisa Jones

Contributors:
**Bill B., Bill C., BJ, DL, Jim, Jon, KF,
Michelle, Mickie, Mike, Rick,
Sgt. Flattop, Shep . . .**

And of course:
Anonymous

Table of Contents

4TH MOVEMENT: A MUSICAL LIFE

Introduction

It is a fairly simple maneuver to grasp the essence of a rigid military milieu dedicated to a skill set aimed at perfecting the technique of controlled violence; a state inculcated with great potential to lay waste to significant numbers of people and vast amounts of property.

Nor is it difficult to imagine the fundamental concepts that lay at the base of a creative musical spirit obsessed to draw from the raw material of nature to make manifest the inspiration of a composer or, in the case of the jazz or blues or country soloist, to instantly create that with has never-to-fore existed.

No, it is not difficult to know either of these polar opposites on the vast spectrum of humanity. But when you jam the two together and light a match, well...

Names have been changed to protect the innocent and the guilty. The adventures and tales concerning the lives of military musicians herein are based on the Fred Robinson web blog "The Back of the Bus." The events occurred in the years roughly spanning 1975 to 1995 and have been distributed among three fictional bands: the Air Force Band East, the Air Force Band West and the Air Force Band Overseas.

Overture

Is This Thing On, Witcataw?

Well, it's a start...

Yesterday I sent out invitations to 47 prospective Contributing Editors. The responses have been underwhelming but positive - in a less than negative sense. So I guess we are moving forward.

Actually, I have heard back from five or six folks already and had a couple of folks ask in, that were not on the original invitee list as I did not have their current contact information. So things are looking good.

I guess this is the place for our Mission Statement, if I may be so GI, or Government-Issue, about all this.

I am Fred, and I will be your emcee for the night (which has a thousand eyes, a moon that never sets, is only half the day, is my time of day, but I digress) though there will be plenty of guest speakers - at least I hope so.

When referring to contributors here, I will use only first names and would encourage y'all to do the same. When necessary I will deploy initials to distinguish between multiple Bills, Bobs, etc. I hope that will promote unguarded language while maintaining some sort of anonymity for the posters and those being humiliated, oops, I mean spoken of in a loving and caring manner.

And so, brush off your short and long-term memory cobwebs, and get ready to contribute your recollections of life on the road, in rehearsals, practice rooms, post-gig shenanigans, whatever. This is the place to share things that probably should not be shared, without getting an STD.

Soon...

Posted by Fred

A Rigged Audition?

So one day my buddy Rich calls me up in Denton, where I was a music undergrad at North Texas State University, and tells me that his old High School Band Director needs a couple of Big Band charts. He wanted an instrumental version of the George Benson version of "This Masquerade" and a vocal chart on the Rita Coolidge version of "The Way You Do The Things You Do."

While pop tunes were certainly not my specialty and although I had only done one other vocal chart I figured that making some bucks would be better than not making some bucks, so I cranked out the charts and sent the scores to Rich, best damn left handed copyist I ever met, to do the copy work and negotiate the transaction where he was stationed as a musician with the Air Force Band West, which I will hereafter refer to as AFB West.

I didn't hear anything from Rich for a few weeks but that was okay. Hey, it was 1978 in Denton, Texas. I was in love, I had a job - so beer money was available - and it was still spring so the weather was nice.

Then one day, it was a Monday, I remember because that was my sleep-in day, late shift at the gas station after opening on Saturday and Sunday – 6:00 AM if you can believe it, I got a phone call. Oh, the phone call was not at 6:00 AM, it was more about 8:00 but the time still pissed me off.

The house I was living in at the time had one phone. It was a 1920's vintage replica, you know with the earpiece and you picked up the body of the phone and spoke into it – not sure who came up with that and it sat in this little phone nook in the downstairs hallway.

My roommates did not seem interested in answering the call and my girlfriend had already responsibly departed to attend her 8:00 class, so I stumbled, literally, down the stairs and answered the phone. This was before answering machines had been invented. On the other end was this shrill male voice speaking with an accent that could only have been acquired in an insane asylum so quickly that I had trouble following him, though I did understand enough to acknowledge that

I was who I am. So, I asked him if he could slow down and repeat his opening barrage. It turned out that I had followed him, I just could not believe what he was saying.

He more calmly stated that he was Technical Sergeant Joe... calling from the AFB West and that he had just gotten off the phone with "my recruiter" and fixed up the problem that was holding up "my enlistment" processing. WTF?!? I told him he had the wrong guy, even if he had said my name, and hung up on him. A little while later Rich called to fill me in.

It turned out that the charts I sent him never made it over to that old high school; they made it to the AFB West instead. I don't know exactly what Rich did to get the ball rolling on the Air Force side, though I was fully aware of the wool pulling he had pulled on me. But, it was true, all I had to do was go down to the local recruiter, sign a few papers (a few papers means something different to the U.S. Air Force than it does to other people) and I would have a steady gig. Rich then asked how soon I could do it. I don't remember if I actually said "Hell no!" or if he just interpreted my silence, but he added, "Man, they will pay you to do what you do at NTSU. So what's the problem?" I pointed out Basic Training and an iron-clad four year contract. We left it at that.

A few days later I was retelling that story to somebody with a knowledge of the NTSU Lab Band designation system and after I finished up with a "Hell No!" he delivered the kicker and said "How many cats do you know who are playing at the 8 O'clock level that have a steady gig, booked up for four years?" I saw the Air Force recruiter the next day. So, while the audition had not been rigged in the traditional manner,it did get me to do something I probably never would have even seriously considered, let alone do. It begin what turned out to be a charmed existence for me over the next 14 years, 5 months and 22 days (TADMST). The dumbest thing I ever did was split that gig!

Posted by Fred

1 comment:

Chris said...

> Told ya so!

Buddy's Back

July 1978, Lackland Air Force Base, San Antonio, Texas, Basic Military Training Squadron 3704, Flight 528, Bay 1, Bunk 12. About halfway through Basic Training we got Base Liberty. This was not like in the movies where you went to town, found a hooker, got drunk and made eggs in the Base Commander's kitchen with a couple of cute MP's. This meant we could go to the Base Exchange and buy shoe polish and stamps. OK, you could get other stuff, but it all had to fit in one drawer in your locker, about the size of two shoe boxes.

One of the popular purchases that day was a little pre-Walkman JVC Boom-Box that was about the size of one shoe box. I don't know if they came free with the box, but it seemed to me that everybody in my flight, comprised mostly of 17 year-olds, also came back with the Donna Summer "Last Dance" cassette. By the time I got out of basic training, I swore I would go postal if I ever heard that song again. My first chart arranging assignment after basic: "Last Dance" for vocal and concert band...

The cassette selection was almost all Pop, Disco and C&W, but the LP selection included some Jazz. That's where I found "Buddy Rich and Mel Torme Together Again for the First Time." Wow, a Buddy album I didn't have and at $4.00 BX prices. Gotta have it... That, a couple packs of smokes, black shoe polish and stamps and I was out of there.

Time to stow the gear. Oops, the LP does not fit in the drawer. Panic. The best I could do was slide it to the back of the hanging section of the locker and hope that my uniforms would cover it during inspections. Yeah right...

The very next day, Staff Sergeant Barns, the non-musician Training Instructor of my flight, found it first thing. Again, remember this was not a movie, and it was AF basic in 1978 so the language Sgt Burns used was somewhat civil, and I was not struck or poked. Humiliated, embarrassed? Oh yeah. I don't know what got a hold of me but as soon as he finished his rant, I just came to a slouch and blurted out something like, "But at least it's not Disco, sarge."

I quickly attempted to get back to attention, but I don't know if I ever really made it. Having just performed two major screw-ups, I expected an explosion from the TI. Instead, he screwed up a bit himself. Cracking a tiny smile he simply walked away to his office leaving the whole flight at attention. He returned a few minutes later, composure regained and the day continued as normal.

Coda: The only repercussion, if I can call it that, from that incident was from that day forward I was called "Buddy!" rather than "Robinson!!!" by both SSgt Barns and Master Sergeant Ramirez.

Posted by Fred

Basic Training?

ATTENTION all those who served ably with and under General in the United States Air Force, as musicians or otherwise: A civilian inquiry into the Basic Training of the future USAF bandsmen who contribute to this web blog. Interested in stories of 20-mile hikes with full sousaphones, surviving in the wilderness for a month with nothing but a penknife and some cork grease, endless push-ups, weapons training (did they REALLY let any of you have guns!?); in short, the making of an aerial warrior/jazz hipster...

Posted by Bill C.

1 comment:

Tom P. said...

> After successfully auditioning for the Air Force band
> program as a raggedy-haired, sneaker-wearing jazz-hipster all
> that is left to do to complete the transformation is run the
> victim through the standard, yet rigorous, martial
> indoctrination program at Lackland Air Force Base in San
> Antonio, Texas. How rigorous you say? During a light
> afternoon outdoor training activity I found myself compelled
> to pose a pertinent and legitimate question to my hollow
> cheeked,iron-jawed drill instructor. He lit into me like I had
> just murdered his dog. The resulting volcanic display was so
> outrageous and over-the-top that I could only observe the
> carnage with a kind of detached bemusement (or bemused
> detachment whichever you prefer). Later the sergeant pulled
> me aside and said:
>
> "I'm really sorry about that but my girlfriend was standing
> nearby and I wanted to impress her. I owe you one."

Leave It To BEVR

This was intended to be a comment to Bill C.'s "Basic Training"
post, but it was too long so here goes: I have no psychotic Basic
Training stories. In fact, I thought of Basic more like an annoying
Summer Camp experience; not that cool, but it actually had some
moments. Playing "Army Guy" can be fun.

At the end of day two my Head Training Instructor, Master Sergeant
Ramirez, called me into the office. After glancing at my personnel
file for a moment he must have noticed that I had a guaranteed job
complete with orders to the band at McChord AFB. He suggested
that I not mention that I was going into the band to anyone around
there. He pointed out that "Band Queer" was still a popular redneck
term in those days. "So, if anybody asks just tell them you are going
to be an 871." OK, an 871 (whatever that was).

He went on to say, "They are short on Spooks and S.P.s right now,"
he said, referring to Cryptographers and Security Police, "so you are
not going to want to do too good on the Crypto test. And, don't shoot

too good on the range." Messing up tests had been a specialty of mine for years, and considering I had never held a gun other than ones that shot rubber tipped darts or BB's, I didn't think I was apt to pull a William Tell either. Basically, that was my Basic. Now to the interesting stuff.

I never got to McChord, though I had orders three different times, but that's a different story. Instead, I reported directly to the AFB West. Most Permanent Party Squadrons were on the other side of the base, but the Band Hall was near the Basic Military Training Squadron (BMTS) buildings. For me it was kind of creepy being in a place where I had just spent six weeks as a "Pickle", while at the same time it was kind of cool. Watching the Pickles from afar made some of the crap that I had endured in basic make more sense.

Then one morning in September, I came in through the back gate and was driving past my old BMTS building when I noticed a bunch of Pickles raking leaves. I found that odd for two reasons. First, the leaves on the trees were still green, so why were they falling off? Second, the amount and types of leaves did not match up. That bugged me.

A few days later, I was playing pool in the Day Room when in walked MSgt Ramirez. I snapped to attention and he got this big old grin on his face and laughed. Then he said, "Relax Fred, I'm just here to sit in with the Critters" and strolled around the corner carrying a Gibson guitar case. Turned out that "Tito" was a pretty damn good country type guitar player, the Country Critters were the band's Country Music contingent. He had been attempting to cross train into the Critters for years, but there was never an opening at the right time.

As he was leaving, he shouted to somebody back in the rehearsal room that he had to get back to work "rearranging leaves." The leaves! He might know something about the leaves!!! I put down my stick and raced to catch up with him at his car. So, I asked him what was up with all the leaves and so few trees? At first he had one of those TI looks on his face, then he smiled, extended his hand, introduced himself as Tito and filled me in. It turns out that during the days, starting after Labor Day and running through Thanksgiving, the BMTS grunts would rake up all the leaves and carefully pack them into these big semi-cloth, semi-plastic bags that I can only remember seeing in the Air Force, and loaded them into the back of a deuce-and-a-half to be carted off somewhere. The somewhere turned out to be a hanger type building on the other side of the base for storage.

Then, about dusk, while the Pickles were readying for their insanely early lights-out, the BEVR's (pronounced Beavers) would pick up the leaves and cart them back to the BMTS areas and spread them out around the few trees there. By the way, the Beavers were made up by those on Casual Status, fresh out of Basic, but without an assignment.

To top this whole thing off, sometime after Thanksgiving, when the leaf game came to an end, the BEVR's would sort through the remaining leaves eliminating those too shabby to meet AF standards. Yes, there was a regulation for that in some book, spray them down with some kind of preservative, bundle them back into those bags and lock them in that building until the start of the next leaf game season.

Ladies and gentlemen, your tax dollars at work!

Posted by Fred

1 comment:

Fred said...

> OK, I dug out this pamphlet from either Basic or maybe from my recruiter from before I enlisted. It turns out that BEVRS stood for "Basic Enlisted Variety Resource Squadron," the Officer equivalent was BOVRS. I cannot find any reference to either of those acronyms on the Internet, so I assume they are no longer used.

1st Movement:

Before The Show

Pleased to Meet You

Mid August, 1978, AFB West. I had been out of Basic for maybe two weeks when this all came down. I was so new that I was still VERY impressed that I had my own office, me a no-striper when Master Sergeants in the squadron had none – another perk of being the Music Arranger. It was a simple room, I think it was supposed to have been a closet actually, which was tucked away behind the band's library. It had only four pieces of furniture; a GI locker, a Baldwin Hamilton Studio Upright Piano, a stock GI desk and a really cool roll-around chair. Oh, and I had added a coffee pot, percolator, I didn't know about drip machines yet.

So that particular morning I was sitting there in my office attempting to put off as long as I could my first arranging assignment: Donna Summer's "Last Dance" for Concert Band and female vocal. The Air Force had given me a month to do what would have been a three-day assignment at NTSU so I was just grinning at the room when this guy I had not met walked in.

He was in civvies and me in my Pickle outfit. As he walked in he was checking his watch, I remember that because he wore it face down, below his wrist, rather than the traditional way with the face up, I thought that was cool. He extended his hand and said, "So, you're the new arranger..." we shook hands. "Yeah, that would be me" or something like that, I replied. Before I could ask he said, "I am so new I am not even here yet." I smiled, I think I like this guy... "Yeah, I don't report for another three or four days" he said. Three or four? You get an option?

Then he mentioned that he had heard I went to North Texas, and he asked if I knew "LEW." "Oh, yeah, he was my teacher." Actually he was more my Guru or Rabbi, and the single name recognition of "LEW" was reserved for him. There were some other famous Lew's/Lou's, like Lou Marini Jr. and Lou Solof from NTSU, but when you spoke of them you always used their last name. "LEW" was always, just LEW. "Me too, at TCU..." We chatted for a few minutes and then he had to go. As he was leaving he said, "Look me up next week when I'm official." "I will" or something like that...

It was not a Monday, I remember that because that band used to have staff meetings every Monday and it was not a staff meeting day, so it had to be like Tuesday or Wednesday. I was in the latrine filling my coffee pot for my morning brew when my supervisor came in and said, "Hey, let me introduce you to the new boss when you get finished with that" as he discreetly did his business. "OK, I'll be right over" or something like that. A few minutes later I came up to my supervisor's desk, in the Orderly Room and plopped myself in the chair next to his desk. "OK, Robbie, lets go meet the Captain" and we started out of the orderly room.

As we wove our way between desks here came that guy I met in my office a few days before, only this time he was in uniform but I did not pay much attention to it. Instead I just blurted out something like, "Oh, hi!" Before anyone else could say anything, my supervisor said, "So you have meet the Captain?" The Captain followed with, "Yes, but not officially until now" we shook hands again. In one of the few militarily correct moments of my career I actually said, "Pleased to meet you, Sir" and that was that.

Coda: I quickly glanced at his uniform and indeed, there were the bars. Then I glanced down to his left wrist and there was the same inverted watch. How could this be? I had been in the United States Air Force for less than three months and I had already met an officer and a gentleman (though that movie would not come out for some time). Let me tell you, they were few and far between, but yes, I had met one.

Posted by Fred

Fred's War Story #1

Like I was telling a friend, "If you are going to have a Blog, you are going to have to post something EVERY DAY." Fortunately; I have no life, am full to the brim with worthless information and willing to comment on just about anything, warranted or not. So here goes. My first Bus Ride with the Air Force Band West: 1978 – The ride was relatively short. The guys started playing poker even before we got out of the parking lot.

Somehow, even being the new guy and a no-striper, I found myself in the game. Having fancied myself a card player, in Denton, I thought I would be able to hold my own. As we were pulling in to Waco, we started to settle up. I had lost all but a few bucks of my per diem check which was supposed to last me a week. As we were stepping off the bus, Gerry, the guy I lost most of my money to in just a few hands, handed me back everything he won from me and asked if I had learned anything today. I said, "Yes Sir" In a rather fresh out of basic training manner. To that Gerry said, "Then learn something else; NEVER call me sir again!" He gave me Noogies and we checked in to the motel.

I never played poker again for more than nickel and dime stakes. I never called Gerry sir. We remained good friends until he passed, not that long ago.

Posted by Fred

Sociology

Military bandsman are not immune to the basic tenets of musician sociology, to wit:

If you put five trombone players in a room they will get together to play cards and tell jokes and stories.

If you put five saxophone players in a room they will go off by themselves to read or play solitaire.

If you put five trumpet players in a room - there'll be a fight.

Statements that purport to lay claim to the behavior patterns of five drummers in a room are thought to be urban legends or apocryphal at best. A survey of the academic literature on contemporary human phenomena indicates that numerous studies to document the interactivity of drummers had to be abandoned because drummers could never find the room.

Posted by Tom P.

Crime Scenes

The First Sergeant was conducting the morning meeting and things did not start well.

"Okay, who dropped the jelly doughnut on the floor near the office, stepped in it and left it there?"

Silence.

"Fine. Then does anyone want to 'fess up to leaving the window open in Practice Room One last night?"

Mitchell raised his hand.

"That was me. Sorry about that."

"Sorry!? Boy, was I cursing you out at four o'clock this morning when the Air Police got me out of bed to deal with an unsecured window. That doesn't make it, Man. That doesn't make it at all."

The sergeant went on to rant about that for awhile but eventually stopped to compose himself. It was then that a voice from the back offered Mitch some belated advice:

"You should have confessed to the doughnut."

Posted by Tom P.

4 comments:

Fred said...

>   When did you go in? They changed AP to SP in '66. Lol.

Tom P said...

>   Just quoting the old guy.

Fred said...

Just stirrin', stirrin'...

Tom P said...

Troublemaker. Go play in the street.

What To Wear

Back in the day, the AFB West was issued very sharp black uniforms that we wore to our jobs at the highest echelon. We broke them out only a few times a year although it was never always clear which gigs were worthy of this particular uniform choice. During a morning meeting to discuss that night's high-profile concert band performance the Major was asked if we were going to wear our most formal attire."No, we're not going to use the blacks tonight."At that point three African-American bandsmen whooped it up as they headed for the door.

Posted by Tom P.

2 comments:

Fred said...

I too had the experience of doffing the "Blacks" for two plus gigs. While sharp in appearance, they lacked much versatility as far as addressing temperature.

The first gig I did in them was some marching band ceremony. The band stood in the middle of this river bridge of what I want to say was over the Rio Grande but I guess it could have been the Brazos. What I am sure about is that there were both American and Mexican dignitaries, and there speeches all had to be delved twice, the second being the translation that nobody in the band gave a hoot about. Finally, it was the middle of the Winter - or at least a day where it was cold enough to be associated with a part of a

Fred said . . . (cont.)

witch's anatomy in a rather uncomfortable undergarment.

The "Blacks" had obviously been designed for the more normal San Antonio scorching heat, so they offered little protection on that blustering bridge that day. Oh, I had a pretty good vibrato that day because of it though. I swore if I ever had to wear those uniforms again I would go AWOL!

Men In Black, the sequel (no, I didn't go AWOL), Part One. April 27th 1979. I only remember the date is because it was my Birthday and I was pissed that God would punish me by making me march a 600 mile parade on my Birthday; well, OK, 60 blocks maybe, I just hated marching gigs where we actually marched. The band reported around 9:00 AM for a 10:00-ish form-up for the parade. As we were getting on the bus, the commander called us back to run down a chart I had just done on "Cotton-Eyed Joe" just for that gig. We stood in the parking lot on a slightly nippy morning and played it through a few times. All the time I was thinking, here we go with these summer weight uniforms... I'm freezing my (choose your favorite body part) off!

We got to the parade site a little late because of that little rehearsal only to find that there had been a sniper incident that was in the process of being quelled by a few Texas Rangers, and I'm not talking about the Baseball team. There will be more about that in a later post. Needless to say, that gig got canceled. Off the hook? Nope, there was a second parade scheduled for the following night in the continuation of Fiesta time in San Antonio.

Gig two, take two. This was a night parade, so when we reported in mid afternoon it was San Antonio HOT! I looked at the uniform, which had gotten a little crumpled because of the back to back use, and looked up to the sky and said, out loud, "Pretty good choice of uniforms for today!"

Tom P. said...

> Reminds me of the park re-dedication ceremony we played on a sweltering Texas summer day. The speeches, although interesting, seemed interminable and the band complaint department kicked in:
>
> "I thought when you re-named a park all you had to do was change the sign."
>
> "Why don't they just throw a bottle of champagne on the sidewalk and let us go home."

Nothing But The Best

The Major seemed subdued and thoughtful after we breezed through an intricate and difficult composition during a stage band rehearsal. Finally he looked up to tell us what was on his mind:

"Have you been practicing or did you just get lucky?"

Posted by Tom P.

1 comment:

Fred said...

> Cute! I'd rather be lucky...

Sorry Chief . . .

The AFB East Jazz Ensemble had one final rehearsal day for a tour in South Florida during the mid 80's, and the charts on the program were OBSCENELY entertaining, yet OBSCENELY difficult. Fred had composed a chart entitled, "Smilin' Out Loud" and there were several other selections including a Rob McConnell chart and some other chart subtitled, "Let's see how much the sax and trumpet sections can endure before their chops and brains bleed simultaneously." The jazz band had been rehearsing said charts for a couple of weeks and they were still in need of some fine tuning. Needless to say, tension was building about preparation for the show. It was 9:15-ish and rehearsal start-time was 9:00 sharp and the Chief Master Sergeant, our illustrious conductor, was not amused if you were late to rehearsal, especially if we were on the brink of a tour departure and the charts were not ready to be .... immaculately performed.... in your sleep.... or in a coma.... (even if you had a valid excuse for being late, like you had double pneumonia, chronic diarrhea or you had been in a car accident and lost an appendage and had a near death experience....), sorry.... don't expect any sympathy.....

Our lead trumpet player picked this day, of all days to be late to rehearsal.

At approximately 9:35 am, he strolled into the band hall and the Chief exploded.... "You better have one #$@& of an incredible excuse for being late to this %^$#@ rehearsal or I'll have your %^$#-ing head on a $#@%% plaque on my $%#@*# wall this very &$##@ing day!....To which our hero replied, "Sorry I'm late Chief, ...but my dog blew up!...."

At that moment, you could have heard a pin drop.... everyone was, of course, scared shitless!!!!! because Chief was so insanely mad.... but, yeah!.. it was funny as hell!, we could barely hold it together! Within those few seconds, Chief turned around and faced the wall to hide his grin.... and the band burst into laughter for about 20 seconds, while Chief howled with laughter while facing the wall...... Then,........ silence...... then..... Chief turned around, stone-faced, and said, "Take it at the head....." and it was just another day at the office....

By the way, that tour was a blast and the band played it's ass off! I guess that just proves that a dog is man's best friend, even when he explodes... and that laughter is the best medicine.... and that laughter makes us better musicians, too!

Posted by Stephanie

4 comments:

Fred said...

> Yup. I can stop posting now. Stephanie is in charge.

BJ said...

> It was his electric dog. He had a problem with the electric dog charger... I remember it well. d;-))

KF said...

> Or was it an electric dog polisher?

Chris said...

> I do remember trying (in vain) to keep from falling off my chair... He could deliver a line straight-faced that would literally slay everyone else... remember "how'd ya like your eggs cooked?"

Anatomy of a Rehearsal

It was all hands on deck for a 17-piece Air Force Band Overseas stage band rehearsal but before the first downbeat the Chief made an announcement.

"I've got a lot of work to do in the office so I'm turning the rehearsal over to the Operations NCO."

After the Chief was safely in his office the Operations NCO said: "We've got to finish final preparations for the upcoming tour so I want the Personnel NCO to take the rehearsal from here."

Fair enough and after a remarkably quick change-of-command ceremony the Personnel NCO told us:

"I've got just as much work to do as those guys - if not more - so I want you to break up into sections and run the charts on your own. Horn players can use the downstairs practice rooms. Rhythm section can stay here in the main room."

With that he was gone and the horn sections migrated to the lower regions leaving the three men of the AFB Overseas rhythm department staring at each other.

The first said:

"I'm not feeling that well so I'm going to check in at the base infirmary."

The second said:

"My best practice books are at home so I'm going to work out there."

The third said:

"I'm great and I don't need to practice so I'm going to play golf."

Ten minutes later the Chief returned to see how the rehearsal was going and found an empty room.

Posted by Tom P.

1 comment:

Fred said...

> I bet some people didn't understand why the Major, in one of your previous posts, asked about being lucky. As always, the best part of a rehearsal is remembering them, not participating in them.

Plato's Rock

Sometimes the Major went into teaching mode and would pose music theory questions. One query involved a certain section of a piece and whether it was written in a Major or a Minor key:

"E-flat," said a trombone player.
"E-flat - what?" the Major responded.
"E-flat . . . sir!"

Posted by Tom P.

1 comment:

Fred said...

> I "see minor" problems with the way the "Major" composed his question. I think it was part of his "signature."

Critiques

At any level of musical performance you want to discuss sometimes the initial rehearsal of a piece does not go as smoothly as what one might have hoped. Band leaders have a way of expressing their disappointment at these results:

"Is anybody hurt?"

"That sounded like dinner music for people who aren't very hungry."

"You missed enough notes to play a whole 'nother concert."

"Each of you is playing like you're trying to save the gig yourselves. Knock it off."

"Milt has some extra flats if anyone needs some."

Of course sometimes we tried to repair the damage ourselves:

"We need some soul in this household"

"It's more than soul we need, brother, I think you're rushin'."

"He's one of them Black Russians."

"Like in Russian hands and Roman fingers."

"Lenny's a Red brother."

"From the Russian Mob."

"All right. All right. Gimme a pencil. I'll make a note. I don't want to be different just because I'm black."

Posted by Tom P.

I Toucan Tell Caribbean Tales . . .

I was also one of those lucky ones to have made some of those trips to St. Croix with the AFB East. I think it was my second trip, when our head Ops guy invited me to come on a scouting trip to St. Thomas the following day. I am not sure why I was invited. I was not particularly friends with this guy and didn't work in Ops. But, I had done a pretty good chart on the tune St. Thomas, so maybe he just figured I would like to go. I did, even though it meant Bows-up at O-Dark-Thirty. I played lackey, being substantially out ranked, and we walked around a bit in St. Thomas checking out some possible gig sites. Then we took a cab - not something I would recommend to the faint of heart - to the port so he could see some BIG BOATS.When we got there he was disappointed, no ships evenclose to the port. They were doing some dredging so all the cruise ships had either altered their routs, skipping St. Thomas, or were parked a mile or so out, behind the break water, and the passengers had to be brought in on launches. So we had some lunch at this Pizza place there near the docks. Like the absent minded airhead I can be before the sun goes down, I left the Ops folder and this little fanny-pack thing I had just bought in St. Croix at the Pizza joint and didn't realize it until we were getting off the boat back in St. Croix. I got much shit about that, but was mostly pissed off because my fanny-pack had some cash in it!

Fast Forward almost 10 years. My second Royal Caribbean cruise ship ported out of Miami and stopped in St. Thomas every Tuesday.In cruise ship parlance Tuesday this made Tuesday "St. Thomas Day." Walking down the crew ramp I spotted that same Pizza joint. So I headed directly there. At that place you ordered at the counter but they did bring your orders to your table. They did not use the little number things or shout out your order to find you, they simply remembered you. I ordered a couple of slices of cheese pizza and a local beer. $9.50!!! ($2.00 for the pizza and $7.00 for the not very good beer.) What's with that? Oh, yeah, tourist trap. My bad. So I went out to the patio and found a small table. I had not net connected with the band guys yet on that ship, I was lunching alone.

After a few minutes, out came the waiter, an older, local type, with a plate the beer and a Walgreens shopping bag. He set the plate and beer down and handed me the bag and asked if I had left that stuff here the last time I was in. So, I opened the bag and inside was the Ops folder and my fanny-pack, complete with over $20.00 in cash. I looked up at the guy and didn't know what to say. He smiled and said, "You're pretty forgettable, but not that shirt. I have been looking for one like it for 10 years or so now."

For those of you from AFB East who remember my VERY LOUD red Hawaiian shirt with the big Toucan on the back, that's what I had on. And I assume I had been wearing it that day a long time ago. I took off the shirt and handed it to him. He removed his gray t-shirt with, "St. Thomas, Birth Place of Sonny Rollins" written across the front and handed it to me. I still have that St. Thomas shirt.

Coda: As I was leaving, I reached into the bag, dug around in the fanny-pack and grabbed the cash that he had not touched for 10 years and left it as a tip. Oh, I did eat there every St. Thomas-day from then on, though I never drank beer there again. Instead I drank my port beer at a place that my pizza friend - I don't think we ever exchanged names - recommended where the beer was MUCH cheaper.

Posted by Fred

Shirt-Tales

Stephanie asked a good question in a comment about my Caribbean story, how did that shirt last so long? Well, I actually do know the answer to that.

Since I was in junior high school shirts, normally t-shirts or sweatshirts, have been my favorite gifts. That came from getting my first college sweatshirt from my sister in like 1971, Colby College, Waterville, Maine. From that point on I paid special attention to special shirts.

In the late 80's the AFB East sent a small band to Key West, FL for some sort of gig, I was running sound. They flew us down on some small Navy jet, something I thought was cool until it started bouncing around – give me a C 130 any time - and we had some down time between gigs.

Though I am not well read, I did know about Key West as a favorite place of Ernest Hemingway so I thought I would try to find that bar Papa used to hang out during one afternoon while the band was rehearsing and I had nothing to do. This is one benefit of being on a gig as the sound guy.

I asked at the hotel desk, and got the name of the place and directions. I was told that it's about the most famous "straight" bar on the island and was only about five blocks away. With that in mind I changed from my rather stylish completely red shirt, kind of a bowling-shirt thing, to my Toucan shirt and proceeded to head down the street. That bar also turned out to be nothing but a tourist trap at that point, 1988, so I spent all of about ten minutes there.

As I was wondering back up the street, I saw a Bar Sign that looked exactly like the back of the shirt I was wearing, though I found out later that my shirt was a replica of that sign. I thought for a moment about going in, but then remembered the lady at the hotel pointing out "straight bar" so I just stood there and looked at the sign for a minute. While I was standing there a guy came up behind me and said, "Dude" (remember this was the 1980's and "Dude" was not yet a cool universal word) cool shirt. I bet if you went in to Jimmy's he would let you drink all night for free if you walked around in that thing." I turned around and asked this rather sharply dress Afro-American gentleman, how he would know that. He replied, "Because I am Jimmy." So, we went in.

They insisted that I do Tequila shooters . This is not something I am good at – but at the price, heck. In like 15 minutes I was screwed to the wall and loving it. People took pictures of me, showing my best side, my back with the famous bird, and they all kept buying me drinks. I finally puked and the bartender asked where I was staying so he could call me a cab. Fortunately I had a matchbook from the hotel I was staying in so I handed that to him and I guess I made it back OK.

I don't know if I missed a formation/gig that night. I do know I slept on the floor of my room though. Fortunately the Band's Commander at that time understood partying so I guess I was pretty OK.

When I got back to our home base after that trip, I placed that shirt in a plastic bag where it sat until I did my second ship thing with RCCL. You know the rest of the story.

Posted by Fred

Bring a Hat

Air Force musicians dislike rain as much as Air Force pilots. It rains a lot in Germany. A lot. Shortly after arriving at AFB Overseas one of the flute players brought me up to speed on the weather conditions I could expect during my assignment there:

"If you can see the sky it means it's going to rain. If you can't see the sky it means it's already raining."

As an aside, that summer the Weather Recon Squadron had their annual picnic rained out three times.

Posted by Tom P.

1 comment:

Fred said...

> After about a month in Germany I chopped 5 minutes off my
> get ready for work time, by not drying my hair. It was going
> to be wet, 99% of the time when I got to the squadron any
> way...

Career Move

A piano-playing sergeant grew weary of military life and seemed
disinclined to participate in accepted military courtesies. One day he
was berated by his commanding colonel for not saluting as they
passed in a hallway. The sergeant quickly popped a salute but
wanted to explore the issue further.

"Permission to ask a question, sir."

"What is it?"

"I know it would be insubordinate and disrespectful if I called you
an asshole but would it be insubordinate and disrespectful if I just
THOUGHT you were an asshole?"

Twenty four hours later the sergeant was airborne to his new
assignment with AFB West.

Posted by Tom P.

2 comments:

Fred said...

> You win the ceremonial Zircon Encrusted Tweezers for this
> post! This is exactly the way I remember this story, from 30
> years ago.

Tom P. said...

Thank you, Grand Pooh-Bah, I hope I don't put out an eye.

Salvation

The good humor of the sergeant from "Career Move" may not have improved much at his new assignment.

He was asked to play the big bass drum in a marching band job. Not having attempted this instrument before he asked to take it for a spin in the band hall parking lot.

Minutes later he could be seen and heard stomping around the lot wailing-away on the drum and singing in his best Salvation-Army voice:

"We have a friend in Jesus . . . Christ Almighty, what a pal!!"

Posted by Tom P.

Neither Rain Nor Sleet . . .

We had an Operations sergeant who didn't like to book us on certain jobs. One day he was overheard on the phone trying to get us out of a military air show.

"We don't get two friggin songs played before they do the damn inspection. Then they start warming up the g-ddamn jets and no one can hear the f-cking band anyway . . . . sir."

Posted by Tom P.

1 comment:

Fred said...

I only had to do a couple air shows. But, one has a story.

Fred's War Story #5:
"What Tom Said . . ."

Sticking with Tom's military theme, and contemplating such non sequiturs as Jumbo Shrimp and Military Intelligence, I offer you this:

The day before the trip to Turkey immortalized in FWS #4 I got promoted so I had to go to Consolidated Base Personnel Office (CBPO – pronounced Cee-Bow) to get my travel orders changed.

When I got to the CBPO I chose the short line. At the counter there was a Senior Master Sergeant there to help me. She asked for my name, rank, last-four of my social security number and my Air Force Specialty Code (AFSC). She quickly scribbled my name, rank and number and then was carefully placing the AFSC in those wonderful little boxes on the AF Form XYZ she was filling out. 8-7-1-5-0-P. Then she paused and asked, what's the "P" stand for?

Perhaps I contributed to the confusion that followed by attempting to explain the whole AFSC by stating "Band Career Field, 5 Level, Arranger."

She calmly looked me straight in the eye and asked "Do you get combat pay for that?"

Before I could reply she pulled out a different form, one I had never seen before and would never see again, and quickly filled out three copies by hand - as there were not many copy machines around in those days. She then handed me my new Combat Travel Orders.

She had obviously heard "A Ranger" rather than "Arranger." But there I was in my favorite uniform, Combo 3, with the cool long-sleeve dark blue wool shirt with my brand new Air Force chevrons, so how could she have confused me for being Army?

In an attempt to lighten the moment (she now had one of those grumpy 'lifer' expressions on her face) I said, "Well, at times Beer Tent crowds can get ugly, but, no, I don't get Combat Pay."

To that all she had to say was, "Next!" and waved me away.

A bit dazed, I realized that I would probably get in trouble if I attempted to use those orders, so I looked around and noticed that the lady tending to the people in the long line was a one-striper. The wait in line was substantially longer but once I got to the counter, she simply asked for my last-four and AFSC. Clearly she had already noted my Name and Rank from LOOKING at my UNIFORM.

Head down, pen flying she commented that she had heard the band a few weeks before at a local beer tent and liked us. Then she handed me three copies of the appropriate travel orders. Noticing the other papers in my hand she asked if she could see them. Her brow rose just a bit, and said calmly "I will take care of these for you. SMSgt M***** is my supervisor. Is there anything else I can do for you sir?"

From that point on, I always looked for the lowest ranking person when dealing with anything official with the military.

Posted by Fred

2 comments:

Tom P. said...

> My grasp of the 1980's rules of engagement is a little cloudy but I can tell you with absolute certainty that a certain AFB West member would have kept the combat orders and thrust them into the face of anyone who dared question why he was boarding a C-9 with a .45 strapped to his hip.

Stephanie said...

> Fred, this story brings Sue B,'s desk plaque to mind: "Do you want to speak to the officer in charge or the woman who knows what's going on......?"

The Great Haircut Mutiny

To ease the Major's workload a second-lieutenant and recent graduate of the Air Force Officers Training School was assigned to lead the AFB West's 17-piece stage band.

After "Hello" practically his first words to us were: "I intend to be the sharpest-looking person here and I'll be the model I want you to follow."

We knew we were in trouble.

Things deteriorated quickly as his complaints against the length of our hair grew more agitated and vociferous with each passing week. I vaguely remember threats of administrative action against us if we did not conform to his interpretation of military regulations.

This was happening just after the Vietnam War ended and recruiters were having a nearly impossible time landing new recruits. It was perhaps our primary mission at that time to support Air Force recruiters in their efforts; most notably by performing at Texas high schools prior to a big recruiting pitch.

A few days before we were to leave on a major Dallas-area recruiting tour the lieutenant lit into us big time over our hair length. He was in such a ferocious rage that we submitted:

"Okay, lieutenant, we'll get haircuts."

Throughout the course of that afternoon we went over to the base barber shop to get skin-head, basic training haircuts. In any other military organization it would have been a senseless and futile display of defiance but our primary mission, as the reader will recall, was to entice long-haired 1970's teenagers to join the Air Force family.

To this day I can see the Major doubled-over laughing as we walked in through the back door of the band hall with our new haircuts. He knew that his overly-rigid second-officer was twelve kinds of screwed and that there was going to be Hell to Pay from the Dallas-

Fort Worth recruiting squadron.

When the recruiters saw us they went absolutely stone ape-shit and the tour was nearly canceled. Many potential recruits were lost that week out of fear that they would be forced to wear their hair as short as ours.

The colonel in charge of recruiting ordered the lieutenant to order us to grow our hair out and we said:

"No."

We pointed out that our hair was completely within regulations, that we liked it as it was in this hot Texas climate and that we were going to wear it like that forever - oh, and that if he decided to take action against us our military lawyer would probably beat him like a gong.

A few days later the lieutenant said:

"Guys, will you please grow your hair out?"

We thought about it. "Okay but only because you said 'please'."

God, we could be little stinkers.

Posted by Tom P.

Fly the Friendly Skies . . .

One of the great ironies of serving Uncle Sugar as a musician in his Flying Circus was that we actually spent a considerable time flying, of all things. At least in the AFB East Musical Maintenance Squadron...

Some of us became intimately familiar with the interiors of the workhorse of the latter part of the 20th century, the C-130 Hercules. I once counted as well as I could, and figured that in 15 years, 1 month, and 26 days, I had spent more than 5,000 hours in a 130. For a guy who spent his entire youth wanting to be a pilot, this was sweet agony - at least I was flying, even though I wasn't in control of the aircraft.

This is not to say that I didn't enjoy flying, though... I loved every minute of it! But sometimes... things just had to go crazy.

Case in point:

For those of you who flew aboard the Herc, you will remember the support members that were located on the sides of the fuselage right where the ramp met the rear upper door - they were painted bright yellow, and were next to the handy-dandy urinal in the port side, and the honey bucket on the starboard side. For those of us lazy bums, these proved to be THE place to fasten the ends of your fancy fishnet survival hammock for those extended flights longer than a couple of hours. Among the AFB East, there were usually a couple or two geniuses who fought over the stanchions every flight. This led to an opportunity too good to pass up. I had scored the coveted position on a flight to somewhere in the Caribbean or Central America - I don't remember where, exactly, just that it was going to be an 8-hour flight -and had settled comfortably in for a snooze free of bumps and web bruises, when the loadmaster, a friend of many flights with the band, called me up to sit in the Instructor Pilot seat on the flight deck for a while. To say that I jumped at the chance was not quite accurate; more like I flopped around for a moment until I could get clear of the hammock, then staggered up the port side spaces between legs until I reached the flight deck, whereupon I enjoyed an hour or so digging the view through the windscreen and chatting up the crew. When I reluctantly gave up my position to another eager beaver, I returned back to the aft lounge (hammock) only to find another of the DFs (you know who you are!), a great bass player, clarinet picker, and sound tech nonpareil, occupying the said lounge area, sound asleep. This particular troop could sleep through a takeoff and landing in a Herc, so he was down for the count, and would not be roused, no matter how much I tried. After a moment's thought, I decided that if he wanted the hammock so much, he could damned well keep it, but under my conditions. I carefully drew the sides of the hammock together over him - those things could stretch quite a bit, you know until I could lace them together with the nylon cord that was intended for the survival knife in the flight suit inner thigh pocket.

After trussing him up like a Christmas goose - still asleep, mind you - I slipped my flight jacket over and around him and the hammock, and zipped it up tightly. Then the trespasser was flipped over so that he was face-down in the hammock, and allowed to stay that way for the better part of two hours, until he began bellowing that he needed to use the evacuation station. I let him hang there for only a few minutes before I took pity on him and released him, whereupon he promised death and gooey dismemberment while I rolled on the deck laughing at him.

Funny thing was, we roomed together that trip, and I never quite slept soundly, waiting for payback...

Posted by Chris

6 comments:

Fred said...

> Just you wait, 'enry 'iggans, just you wait! LOL I love you, man!

Chris said...

> There are enough stories on C-130s to make an entire chapter...

Michelle said...

> These trips posed a significant challenge to the females. How long could we go without using the restroom? Always dreaded having to use those portable potties!!!

Fred said...

> To call them porta-potties would be an overstatement. As I recall it was more like a shower curtain and a 5 gallon lard bucket with a piece of plywood with a whole cut in it sitting on top. No $600.00 toilet seats on a 130. Then there was that mystery urinal?!? Was that just a tube that went right out the

Fred said . . . (cont.)

> side of the plane?

Chris said...

> Yep...just a right angle 1/4 inch tube that was connected to a funnel...for those guys with no sense of aim, I guess.
>
> The bad thing for the girls was the tradition of "You use it, you clean it" when it came to the honey bucket. At least the urinal cleaned itself if you left the flap open a few seconds...

Fred said...

> "Honey Bucket" that's what I couldn't remember... Lol.

The Lion's Den

Sometimes, not often, the driving requirements of an AFB West road tour necessitated that a second driver be assigned to share the driving duties. Among other things, this meant that trumpet player Billy Bob, a trained commercial driver, had a second target from which to coax an opportunity to drive the bus. For Bob this had become a kind of unrequited Don Quixote mission destined for failure due to the fact that, for the driver, this was tantamount to leaving their post at best and desertion at worst. Depending on the state of world affairs it was, theoretically, a capital offense for which the lieutenant could be justified in shooting them so, no, Billy Bob, you can't drive the bus.

While not generally a sentimental bunch, we were always touched by the real human tragedy of seeing Billy Bob rebuffed yet again.

Then something happened that was far more rare than a second driver - the lieutenant paid a visit to the back of the bus.

"I feel like Daniel in the Lions Den."

"Daniel? Was he that fool that got swallowed by a whale?"

"Don't you guys know the story of Daniel?"

We stared blankly.

"Geez, what a bunch of heathens. All right, I'll tell you the tale of Daniel."

Roger, a sax-playing sergeant with career aspirations assumed a command presence.

"Gather 'round, men, the lieutenant's going to tell a story."

Then - a miracle - bus driver Sid, in an act of compassion not to be seen again until Mother Teresa, let Billy Bob take the wheel.

Sid joined the exodus to Storyville and sat himself down next to relief driver Ollie in the two seats facing the lieutenant so that the three men were almost touching knees. This was where the poker games took place but for an important event like the lieutenant telling a story the poker was put on hiatus.

To his polite, rapt and unblinking audience and with a fervor usually reserved for, and attained by, the True Believer, the lieutenant weaved the Biblical story of Daniel.

When he was finished Roger, who continued to wear the mantle of enlisted command, spoke for us all:

"Lieutenant, until now we didn't know what a cool and laid-back guy you were."

We nodded. The lieutenant beamed. Roger continued.

"I mean, here we are booming down this superhighway at seventy miles an hour - and here you are responsible for all our lives and all this equipment and this hundred-thousand dollar bus . . . and you don't know or care who's driving."

It was only then that the young officer noticed the two grinning bus drivers sitting directly across from him.

Blood drained from the lieutenant's face as he looked up the aisle to see Billy Bob waving and laughing.

"Hey lieutenant! How'm I doing?! Woo-Hoo!!"

Posted by Tom P.

1 comment:

Fred said...

> Now that's a Bible story worth wading through. Good old BB!!!

The Bees and the Birds

A generation ago the average score of Air Force musicians on the military's Basic Aptitude Test was second only to the cryptographers. So it was not unusual to see bandsmen absorbed in the daily newspaper in order to keep their fingers on the pulse of local, state, national and world affairs.

On one morning bus ride the quiet sounds of coffee slurping and news page turning was interrupted by a female player reacting to a published communication:

"Hey, let's stop at Penny's. It says here that men's clothes are half off."

Posted by Tom P.

2 comments:

Fred said...

> Denton, TX, 1975: One day my Girlfriend mentioned that the

Fred said . . . (cont.)

> Dallas Morning News had an ad for a sale on Seersucker
> Suits at Cox's (a local Dallas/Ft. Worth clothing chain). Then
> she added, "I wonder what they have on sale at Sears?"
> Could these two ladies have been related?

Stephanie said...

> I think that all said locations probably had the same MUSAK
> piped in over the department store speakers..."Love for
> Sale"...

We'll Always Have Texas

Oh those ladies of the Air Force band. Sometimes you can't take
them anywhere.

We were on the road - again - this time to the nether regions of the
former Republic of Texas where lizards and weasels rule and the
travelers facilities were few and far between and the liquid appetite
of the traveling AFB West stage band remained as robust and
remorseless as ever in its history.

One of the players stumbled along the top of the beer coolers which
were lined up along the entire length of the bus aisle and requested
of the Major that he order a pit stop to allow the troopers to relieve
their agony.

In time the request evolved to whining which soon became pleading
and ultimately perched on the peak of full-throated begging.

At last the Major submitted and asked the driver to pull on to the
shoulder of the highway. The evacuation could not have been swifter
if the bus had been on fire. Even the Major and the bus driver joined
the trough line against the side of the bus.

Moments like these invariably annoyed the ladies of the squadron
who felt the sting of rejection of any consideration of their personal

requirements - or even an acknowledgment that the ladies actually existed. Now the time had come to make a point of order.

The two aboard raced for the front of the bus. One jumped in the driver's seat as the other slammed shut the door and yelled "Hit it!"

They didn't drive the bus very far but, then again, they didn't have to.

The conga line of young, healthy males stood exposed 12 feet from the highway; displayed in all their natural splendor like some demented Roman fountain from the dark days of Caligula.

Unable to switch horses in mid-stream there was nothing left to do but wave to passing families and grandmas with our free hand.

Posted by Tom P.

4 comments:

Chris said...

> Tom, you know you have the skeleton of a good book here... lesser writers have made money at this.

Fred said...

> Tom, you can tell Chris what it is you do now at any time. By the way, that WAS the reason for starting this. Chris, remember R**** from Master Sound? He has a publisher that is/might be interested in stuff like this. I thought this would be a place to get the juices flowing. I didn't expect all this cool stuff though!!!

Tom P. said...

> Chris, thanks for the compliment. I want to be part of the group that preserves these moments and people for history. These days I'm a hired gun for the film industry: screenplays, treatments, business plans, budgets, etc. Damned if I know who Fred wants to play him in the TBOTB movie: Brad Pitt?

Tom P. said . . . (cont.)

> Orson Bean? Who the Hell knows. Personally I think he should play The Major

Chris said...

> Only if I can be the Chief that looks at him with a disgusted face as he steams his trousers while wearing them...

Pay Back

The incident from "We'll Always Have Texas" had a devastating impact on the AFB West pranksters who sullenly believed that they had been slammed by a prank that would be impossible to top.

It was a bitter pill for a crew who regarded their level of pranksterism to be among the best in the business.

During the course of a soul-searching after-action assessment it was decided that only a return to basics and a determined embrace of fundamentals would allow them a chance to right the ship and regain their footing as true masters of the art.

Consequently, the chief strategists decided to reach back into the Prankster Handbook to execute a simple three-step play that had worked for eons:

Step One: Break into a lady's suitcase.

Step Two: Remove all the contents.

Step Three: Form a line.

As the driver who exposed our pranksters to the universe, Jackie was chosen as the target. Larry was the first to greet her as the bus cruised toward our hotel on the first day of a tour.

"Hi Jackie. Do you want to see what I got in Vietnam?"

"Sure, Larry. What did you get in Vietnam?"

Larry reached into the front of his pants and pulled out one of Jackie's bras.

"I got me this real Vietnamese brassiere. Dave, show Jackie what you got in Vietnam."

"I got me these red, Vietcong panties," said Dave as he pulled from his pants an item from Jackie's underwear drawer.

She held out her hand and accepted this item and the many more to follow: combs, tampons, hair dryer, pantyhose, on and on and on enough for everyone and multiple rounds at that.

Dave showed up for a third time and Larry said to him:

"Dave, show Jackie what else you got in Vietnam. You got something really cool."

Dave stood aside and presented George who had pulled one of Jackie's blouses over his enormous body. He was wearing her wig, make-up and about every piece of jewelry she had brought along.

"I got me this real French whore."

"Oooh La-La."

Posted by Tom P.

Moon Over Aviano

The AFB Overseas was in Italy in 1981 or so. We were staying off base, Porta Noni, I think, but had a gig that night at Aviano AFB, just up the road. As was normal in Italy, gigs often started later, 9:00 or 10:00, due to the cultural afternoon naps. So as our Bluebird was nearing the base it was just after dusk.

The bus was not in particularly good health so it was kind of slowly lumbering down the narrow street leading to the back gate. There was a little red Fiat with a Nebraska Corn Huskers flag flying from the antenna, so obviously a US GI, behind us who did not like the impediment we posed him so he was honking his horn and flashing his headlights while tailgating us.

This ticked off one of our guys, so he walked to the back of the bus, dropped his pants, opened the emergency exit and boldly mooned the little Fiat. Unfortunately the Fiat chose just about that time to dangerously pass us with his horn blazing. So the effect may have been lost, but the effort was awarded with much applause, laughter and shouts of "Wobbly, Wobbly, Wobbly!"

A few minutes later we pulled up to the front of the Officers Club to unload. Right next to the bus sat the parking spot reserved for the Base Commander. In that parking spot sat a little red Fiat with a Nebraska Corn Huskers flag on it's antenna. Good thing we were in a generic, motor-pool bus rather than one emblazoned with the band logo.

One final note... As we were leaving the O-Club, about 2:00 AM, the star from earlier calmly looked up and said, "Hey, look, a full moon" and indeed at that moment in the clear night sky above Aviano AFB the man-in-the-moon was bright and full and seemed to have a devilish smirk on his face.

Posted by Fred

Work Ethic

The big topic on the AFB West bus was our light summer work schedule and how we could make our twenty-hour work week look like the military minimum of forty hours.

"Can't we include our travel time?"

"Government says that isn't work."

"But if we spend half the day on the bus it's still a blown day."

"Still isn't work."

"You think so? If you're the only honest guy in a crooked poker game, trying to win money is work."

"But nobody's honest in our poker games."

"That's beside the point."

"Let's rehearse from six to nine. Then we can play golf every day."

"A.M.?

"Yeah."

"I'm not getting up an hour before the Basics (Trainees).

"What about it, Major? We're thinking six to nine."

"You must think I'm a Magic Major. There's no way you degenerates can make a six a.m. Rehearsal."

He had a point.

Posted by Tom P.

10-4 Good Buddy

Breaking from tradition I will be posting a second post for today and it will be short - at least by my standards.

I had the good fortune of spending much truck cab time with some truly exceptional people. One of them was nicknamed "The Pope" because he loved to Pontificate and we loved to listen to him. Throw in that he was a really nice guy, a FANTASTIC musician, and the only trained Truck Driver I ever knew made those trips quite enjoyable.

One day The Pope was behind the wheel of our Ryder rental truck loaded with like a zillion pounds, and rated for like 2,000, on a surface street when a 4-wheeler got his attention and shouted something about "our box being about to fall off the axle." The Pope said, "Thanks fella," which is kinda like "Dude" coming from a Jersey boy in the 80's, and gave him a salute. The four-wheeler drove on.

I glanced at the mirror outside my navigator's window and indeed, I could see nothing of the box. FREAKED! The Pope looked up and a bit to his left, did something to the gears and goosed it, stopping just before he smashed in to the car sitting in front of us. Then he smiled.

I glanced back at the mirror, and there was all the familiar yellow. Un-freaked. He then pulled us into a Southland Corporation establishment and quickly called the 800 number from a pay-phone (remember them?) on the back of the rental agreement and setup a swap-out of trucks, including the Ryder people bringing a crew to transfer the load.Me being the ranking member of our detail, I should have at least taken care of the phone call part. But I had no clue. Fortunately, having worked for many of my subordinates before I was well aware of how to let these geniuses that worked for me make me look good by saving the day. We not only didn't have to unload-reload the truck, we made the gig on time.

I don't think I ever thanked The Pope for that until now but then again he wouldn't have expected that, he was just doing his gig. I did attempt to put him up for Airman of the quarter after that happened but I found out that our CMSgt had already started the paperwork on that - like I said, he was not just a good truck driver. I don't know if he ever got that decoration, but he should have. I hope he and his lady will join us regularly here.

GORT!

Posted by Fred

Getting Your Rachmaninov . . .

When I entered the Air Force in October of 1981, I had just graduated from college in June 1981 with a Bachelor's Degree in Music Education (what a waste of precious time!.... get an Applied Degree people!), and married Ken in September 1981, my fellow musician and partner in military crime. Playing music for a living on Uncle Sam's dime is such an easy, breezy, sinful pleasure it should be a crime! We arrived at the Air Force Band East after six weeks of basic training at San Antonio, TX - no!, there are no coed dorms at basic training - and the AFB East was in the Virgin Islands when we arrived. I had no idea of what an incredible journey we had before us.

Having auditioned in the spring of 1981 and qualified as a keyboardist or a vocalist in the Band career field, I was a little apprehensive when hired to be a keyboardist, which was the only slot available for me at the time. I managed to fool everybody for a couple of years that I was a proficient player..... and then came the arrival of a certain recruit by the name of Tim D***.

Tim was a piano savant, a "name that classical tune" wizard, a keyboardist extraordinaire, an improvisational force to be reckoned with... not to mention one of the most humble, compassionate, loving human beings that I have ever known.

Upon Tim's arrival, I had achieved the rank of Sergeant and moved up to a featured vocalist position. Because of my rank and previous keyboardist AFSC I was assigned as Tim's supervisor. I was assigned to teach him, musically, all that he would need to know in order to move him through the various levels of Air Force Specialty Code requirements for a keyboardist. This is one of those moments in life when you KNOW that God has a sense of humor. There is no way on God's green earth that I could teach Tim anything about playing the piano! He couldn't teach me anything about playing either because I had reached my mechanical pinnacle in the realm of technique on the piano ("chops" for those of you in the jazz realm), long before I joined the Air Force. But Tim taught me so much about compassion, about humility, about looking out for the needs of others, and about pure joy, laughter and a love of music.

I could branch off into so many specific stories of experiences that we had together, but I will save those for another time...

I'll get back to the main point of the post, "Getting your Rachmaninov"...

I guess sometime between 6 and 12 months upon Tim's arrival, he had his "7 level" testing, necessary for moving him to his next rank eligibility.

Our commander at the time was sure that he could "stump the candidate" with the line-up of testing that he had scheduled.

He first placed an exercise before Tim that would display his "chops" proficiency. This exercise required that the candidate play 1,3,6,5,4,5,4,3, beginning on the note "C" two octaves below middle "C", and continue, ascending at a tempo of at least 120 until he had played all 12 keys in one octave. Tim did so with perfection without ever looking at the page... ad nauseam... ascending octaves until told... okay that's good enough...

The commander then announced that Tim was requested to sight read the "Prelude in C# Minor" by Rachmaninov. Tim "sight-read" the music BEFORE the commander even placed the music on the piano music stand.

He was then asked to perform "Rhapsody in Blue" by Gershwin, his prepared piece with the band. He later performed this piece on tour. It is still one of my all-time favorite performances experienced with the Band...

What a musician... what a human being... I will always remember Tim as a musical force to be reckoned with. I hope that he will always be admired for being an example of what every human being and musician should aspire to be...

Posted by Stephanie

3 comments:

Stephanie said...

> Let me add as a post-script that Tim never believed that he
> was extraordinary. He always pointed out the extraordinary
> things he observed to be in others. He performed every note
> of "Rhapsody in Blue" without manuscript and was one of
> the most accomplished improvisationalists that I've ever
> heard. To those who can relate remember the "Indian
> Summer" piano solo - he took us to Mars and back! What a
> beautiful ride! I truly miss him and hope that his life is very
> prosperous. Love you Tim!

Chris said...

> Was that the gig in Jackson Square? Just about died laughing
> at the Chief's face...

Stephanie said...

> Hey Chris, if you're talking about "Indian Summer", I'm
> referring to Timmy's performance on the Master Sound
> recording session. Get out your copy of the recording and
> check out the time signature...WTF!!??

The Bar Ditch

It was another troubling high-wind day for the AFB West bus driver
and we were drifting all over the highway. One of the native Texan
players was concerned.

"If he's not careful we're going to end up in the bar ditch."

That was news to us.

"What's a bar ditch?"

Inexplicably, our Texan remained silent on the matter. He just
smiled.

"No, really, we want to know. What's a bar ditch?"

Not a word. Just the silly smile. We couldn't figure it out until one of the guys floated a hypothesis:

"Oh, I get it. He's found the one thing in the world he knows about that no one else does - and he's not giving it up."

Posted by Tom P.

Appreciation Day

The same AFB West bus driver was often subjected to brutally long work days transporting us gang of idiots across the endless desert prairies. After one savage 11-hour day of wrestling the big GMC Challenger coach through high-wind conditions the driver pulled into our hotel parking lot and slumped over the wheel, spent and exhausted.

Two bandsmen wanted to honor his yeoman effort and had this exchange while exiting past the driver's seat:

"What does your father do for a living?"

"Nothing. He's a bus driver."

Posted by Tom P.

2 comments:

Fred said...

> We could be cruel. Amazing how much time we spent on buses, hence the name for the Blog. This brought to mind two other bus stories. I will have to jot notes for posts for next week.

Stephanie said...

> Hey Fred... I hope one of your bus stories will be the journey
> to the nuclear power plant (Tenn.).

A Civil Rite

It was breakfast time in another coffee shop in another Texas town
on another road trip for the AFB West stage band.

Two road roommates, a Caucasian player, Carl, and his African-
American roommate, Al, were up early and are sitting quietly at a
table. Carl reads a newspaper while Al stares pensively out the
window. Having grown up in the area it was known to Al that this
establishment had been segregated not many years before and it still
seemed to be a little unsettling for him to be sitting among the
morning regulars.

A perky teenage waitress arrived with two menus.

"Hi. I'm Betsy. I'll be your server today."

Carl lowered the paper and took a menu.

"Don't worry, ma'am, the Negro's with me."

Betsy froze. Her eyes widened. Conversation in the room ceased.

Carl continued his thought.

"We just need one menu. This one never learned to read. Oh and if
you want him to eat in the kitchen I'll understand."

Betsy looked at Al who continued to stare out the window. She
looked again at Carl.

"Are you for real?"

Carl handed her the menu.

"Hell, yes. I'll have the French toast."

Al said quietly, "Just coffee for me. Thank you."

Carl returned to reading his paper. Al stared out the window. Betsy backed slowly away from what we can only hope were not the first two customers of her career.

After some time had passed and Betsy was safely out of range Al said softly to Carl:

"You know, someday you're going to go too far . . . and I'm going to bust out laughing."

Carl was horrified. "Don't do that. It'll ruin the whole bit."

Your correspondent has no record if Betsy returned with the French toast and coffee for the laughing maniacs at table six or if she walked straight out the kitchen door and never looked back.

Posted by Tom P.

Skin Tight

In the years immediately following the Vietnam War, new Air Force surgeons sadly found themselves in need of additional reconstructive surgery practice and put out the call for volunteer patients to get in a little workout before tending to those injured in battle.

The Major opted in for a particular procedure to remove the heavy bags under his eyes. No one could quarrel with his reasonable decision. He was, after all, a fairly young man and a little nip/tuck wouldn't have killed him. It was, as they say, a classic win-win about which the AFB West stage band could not help from commenting on. As our readers know by now, it was the nature of the beast.

With the medical work completed and the orange cones secured, the Major arrived to join us on a road trip wearing dark glasses. We said nothing. He wore them throughout the long bus ride. We said nothing.

After checking into the hotel about a dozen guys walked over to the local variety store - which is what we called them in those days. It must have seemed strange to the staff to see a long line of customers holding nothing in their hands and all standing silently as they wore colorful plastic kiddie sunglasses with the price tags hanging off them.

The next morning only the Major and the bus driver sat on the bus at the appointed departure time. Our Major is no fool:

"When they're all late together it means that something's up. Give them a honk."

The bus horn was our cue and the troop of uniformed bandsman ambled out toward the bus wearing yellow and pink and green and electric-blue plastic child sunglasses - except for George, who didn't have a pair and so his head was wrapped in toilet paper and he was led by hand to the bus.

We were polite and all gave the Major a hearty "Good Morning, sir," as we stepped aboard. From toilet-paper head our commander got a smart salute and a muffled "Glr min, flr."

Larry was so pleased with the look that he said to the Major "We're going to wear them on the job."

"No."

Really, sir?"

"Yes, really," the Major said.

"You mean we can't wear them on the job?"

"That's correct."

Larry turned to the band. "Sorry men, we have to take them off."

We did so and the Major saw that his bandsmen had surrounded their eyes with band-aids and drawn-on scars.

Posted by Tom P.

1 comment:

Fred said...

> I had heard most of that but not the last paragraph. Lol. And the version I heard was not as well told!

To Your Health

I've played with musicians who drank a little. Sometimes on the morning bus ride they didn't feel so good.

"My stomach feels like my throat's been cut."

"My body's all upside down too."

"In what way?"

"My nose runs and my feet smell."

Then there were the defense mechanisms:

"Hey, wake up."

"I'm not asleep. If I open my eyes too fast I lose too much blood."

Sometimes they would recognize when the sauce was taking a toll on their bodies. One bandsman tried to fight back by taking handfuls of morning vitamins but of course this called for comment.

"Are those your Scotch vitamins?"

"Nah, they're his Vodka pills."

But the fellow had other tools in his toolkit:

"Gimme some of those menthol cigarettes."

"I can't give you cigarettes, you're part of the Establishment."

"True but I can hurt your career."

Oh, okay, here, take them. I didn't know you smoked menthols."

"I don't. I just need to rub them in my eyes."

Posted by Tom P.

2 comments:

Fred said...

> This is a perfect synopsis of the early part of my AF Band experience. I could have heard those words being spoken by a number of different guys on a dozen different buses, it's just timeless and true to the day!
>
> I wonder what life on the road is like today with those who carry on since we all left? Perhaps I should try to get one (some) of them to join us here?

Chris said...

> Well, no smoking for starters...and I doubt that with the new 35-10 requirements they would be able to carry as much beer as we did without having to seriously work out, which, of course, cuts into the beer time.

Fred's War Story #2

After the overwhelming success of story number one, I will switch gears and go for a bit more humor with story number two.

Athens, Greece – 1980/81 This was with the AFB Overseas stage band. We were checking into the NCO Club Hotel and were all milling around in the lobby with it's sparkling clean solid marble floor. One of the guys, Dave, simply did a free-form pratfall, a-la Dick Van Dyke, and landed flat on his butt. Unscathed by the fall, Dave, picked himself up off the floor and calmly proclaimed, "Minor gravity storm."

Posted by Fred

Tough Guys

One of the Michaels was having a discussion with the Major just offstage at a high-school auditorium. As we transported equipment past them we gave the two a wide berth because it was evidently a deep discussion. Even though Mike was smoking he had his hand on his chin and was nodding thoughtfully.

When the Major indicated that their business was concluded Mike said:

"Okay, sir, I better set up now."

Then he took the lit cigarette out of his mouth and stamped it out on the back of his hand.

The Major stood in slack-jawed amazement as his Oklahoma-tough trombone player walked around a curtain to get his instrument.

He didn't see Mike take the plastic hand out from the end of his long shirt sleeve and put it back on a big pile of actor props.

Posted by Tom P.

The Memorial Shoe

I wish I could use names here, but in the interest of national security I will simply write this in the first person and refer to the only other character as my roommate.

This was one of my first TDY's (That's Road Trip in AF-eese and stands for Temporary Duty Assignment) with the AFB Overseas stage band. We were headed to England and would be staying on Base, I don't remember which one. My roommate showed up late, which I understand was normal for him, so all the equipment and luggage was already on the truck. But, that was okay because all he had with him was a Gym Bag, his trumpet and his round hat rain cover which is a kind of a shower cap for the formal round military hat. Roommate had stuffed his with something, though not the something it was designed to be stuffed with.

By design, the rain cover was supposed to carry the light weight plastic raincoat we were issued in Basic but my roommate had his raincoat on, which was okay, covering the uniform of the day which was Combo 2, long sleeve light blue shirt with tie, and round hat. In this case wearing his raincoat was more than just a convenience, for if you wear it, you don't have to pack it, and it also covered the fact that the shirt he had on underneath had the wrong stripes on it. As I understood it, my roommate had bounced back and forth between the rank of Airman First Class and Sergeant more than a few times. While he was a very good trumpet player, he was not the model troop. He should have been sporting two strips while at the moment that shirt had three. So he schlepped his stuff on to the bus and off we headed to the Flight Line, wheels up within the hour.

By the way, there is very little musical content to this story, this is mostly just a GI tale. So if you were looking for some sort of musical enlightenment here you can stop reading now.

We arrived at our billets room to find it as spartan and clean as expected. Most military billets are spartan, but in England they were a bit more spartan, though exceptionally clean. Roomy plopped his trumpet on the bed, dumped the contents of his gym bag on the floor and unfurled the contents of his hat cover across the desk in the corner. It was his large Combo 1 jacket which had been crumpled into about the size of a cabbage and showed all the wrinkles that might be associated with such a packing job.

My eyes must have been the size of hubcaps. Roomy just said, "Calm down kid. I'll show you a few tricks this week." Yes, this was supposed to be a week-long trip with six performances. That's when I noticed the rest of what he had packed. There on the floor were all his mutes, his trumpet stand, two pairs of socks, one ZZ-Top t-shirt, a pair of beat-up blue jeans, a pair of even more beat up Earth Shoes, a single short sleeve light blue AF shirt – also wrinkled as hell and a large cool looking flask kind of thing of some sort of Cologne. That was it. I think my eyes got wider.

Then he said, "I need to run to the Base Liquor Store and grab a tooth brush. Can I get you something?" While I thought, "You should stop at the BX and get a lot of other stuff" all I said was, "No thanks. I'm OK." So he split.

I unpacked and hung up my uniforms. Hey, I have to tell you I was never an Air Force poster boy; I was often spoken to about the appearance of my uniforms and/or hair, but I had never seen anything like what Roomy had going on. Then again, I had never seen the tricks he was about to show me. Moments later Roomy returned with a big brown bag and two little ones. As he was setting the big one down on the desk he said, "I got us some breakfast and I got you a toothbrush too." Breakfast turned out to be a half-gallon bottle of good British Gin. The toothbrushes were pint bottles of cheap American Vodka. I guess that was trick number one.

We then headed out to the Combined Services Club (NCO and Officer combined, which was not unusual on a US area on an Royal Air Force Base) for some chow and a few beers. In those days I was still a cheap date so a few was just a few for me, not for Roomy.

As we got back to the billets, Roomy was starting the pinball walk, you know, wall to wall sometimes bouncing, but he made it at least to the gang showers/restrooms and ducked inside. I figured he did so to puke or something so I went with him. Nope, he bypassed the stalls and urinals and made a bee-line for the showers. I ran to catch up with him, thinking it was even worse than I had anticipated. He pushed me away and said, "I'm OK. Watch and learn."

He then preceded to crank every shower to full hot water, grabbed my hand and lead me, while leaning a bit on me, to our room. Once inside he grabbed a handful of wire coat hangers, his Combo 1 blouse, Combo 2 and Combo 4 shirts, his only pair of GI pants, his tie and said to me, "Lose the shirt and let's go do some laundry." It was like 2:00 AM, but I was intrigued. So, I took off my nice warm flannel shirt, leaving only my proper white AF-issue tee shirt and followed him down the hall.

Our destination was the shower room, which was at this point was more like a steam room on steroids. My eyes were now small, but my brows were up. He methodically took a few coat hangers and hung his jacket on a shower head. He repeated the process until each of his uniform items that had been crammed into the inner pocket of his jacket were steaming the wrinkles out of them as we sat on the edge of a row of sinks.

At some point, Roomy became satisfied with the progress of the festivities and told me to follow him. I did and we ended up in the farthest stall at the back or the bathroom area, which was just as sauna-ized as the shower room at this point.

When I recounted that part to a friend a few months later all he could say was, "Oh, man you didn't?!?" All I could say was, "No, but I would have" which caused that friend to jump away from me and split. I didn't find out what that friend was talking about for a long time – we eventually made up.

No, Roomy and I did not engage in any sort of bus station restroom sexual activates. Roomy pulled out that cool flask, which I guess had been tucked in the back of his jeans covered by his tee shirt, cool trick number three, all the time. He removed and lifted the rigged top and out, on a chain, came two of those little 35mm plastic film containers. He said, "It's OK. In this kind of steam, nobody can smell nothin' not even this nasty perfume, I use that for the dogs." He was right, I could smell nothing.

In container number one was a couple of balls that looked like they were made of tar. The second had a tiny pipe and some little wooden matches. I was about to partake in something that I probably would have regretted when somebody shouted, "What the f*** is going on?!?" flipping on all the lights.

Roomy expertly, and very quickly, repacked his flask, dropped it into the commode and bent over it making puking sounds. With the help of his right index finger he soon had some coverage for his flask and no longer had to fake the sounds.

At that point I performed the best bit of improvisation of my life. All I can actually remember was leaving the stall and going around the corner and confronting this guy wearing dog-tags and holding a towel and a Dopp kit. I have no idea what I said, must have been something about my buddy puking his guts out. Roomy obliged with more sound effects. I said I would take care of it or something like that. Whatever it was it worked.

Four or five flushes (to wash off his flask) and a few minutes later we returned to the room with some perfect looking uniforms and his flask and contents intact. We decided to celebrate our close call by opening up "Breakfast" a little early and got pretty sloshed.

In one of those, "Only drunks can do this kind of stuff" moves, Roomy reached down and took off his left shoe and handed it to me. I had no idea what to do with that funky thing. He then said, "I want you to have something of mine to remember me by." I didn't know at that time but he had orders to return to the states so this would be our only trip together. I proudly accepted his gift and passed out on the floor.

Coda: Because I now owned Roomy's left shoe, he stuck his right shoe in the drawer of the desk and wore only his Corfams while in Civvies for the rest of the trip. He also proved that "Breakfast" was indeed breakfast for him. Me, I had COFFEE and a bagel.

Later, that shoe was used as a symbol of everything the AF Band system hated about the young troops of the time. If somebody really messed up, or did something completely crazy or even blew an unbelievable solo (things that the lifers couldn't deal with) you were made the keeper of the D** L*** Memorial Shoe. The last time I remember seeing it, it was being passed to Wobbly, he had it in his possession about as often as Lance Armstrong wore a yellow shirt.

Stinger: A year or so after the Roomy trip I found myself back at that same RAF base. In the billeting office you could get those little bottles of booze, like on the airplanes. Below that display case they had a Lost and Found area. Through the glass I could see Roomy's right shoe. I almost claimed it, but then I thought better. It looked like it had been enshrined in a museum there. While they would never have understood how significant that shoe was, I did!

Posted by Fred

Iron Man

It may be hard for some of you who are not associated with the AFB East to believe that such a leader existed among our ranks, or that such a person could achieve a commissioned rank of any kind, or that such an incident as the one to be explained below could occur, but it did...

The AFB East was touring in Florida one year in the mid 80's. All had proceeded as routine. The Band had traveled to the concert site, unloaded all of the equipment and set up the stage and sound equipment. A sound check commenced and all of the appropriate levels were tweaked. Everything was set and ready to go to perform the concert. All that was left to prepare was to change into uniform.

So the males and females retired to their respective dressing rooms to don their mess dress uniforms for the gig.

Let me preface this next segment by saying that I was not present for the main event of this post but there is no way that any of my male counterparts in the Band who did witness this event could have made this up.... yes, they are talented, really talented, every one of them a great musician and every other one a pretty damn good comedian, but no one is this good at fabricating a story this bizarre.

As the guys were in the dressing room, they heard shouts of , "OO, OO, OH OO That's HOT, OOH, OOH! Our Chief Master Sergeant looked up to behold our one and only AFB East Commissioned Officer and Band Commander and Conductor steam ironing his uniform AFTER having fully dressed himself in it.

After completing his task, "Iron Man" looked at the Chief and said, "Would you like to borrow my steamer, Chief?"

The Chief replied, "No sir, I usually iron mine BEFORE I put it on."

Posted by Stephanie

2 comments:

Fred said...

> Airman, Steph, you get 100 gazobee points and are promoted to "even-awesomer" BTZ. Dismissed!

Stephanie said...

> Thank you, sir! I am honored to have the opportunity to serve!

2nd MOVEMENT:

THE SHOW

On the Parade Ground

Damn you, Fred Robinson, sign me up for your stupid blog. Try this one:

The Air Force Officer Training School graduation ceremony is a largely solemn affair soaked with rigid military bearing and swamped with the grim, warrior visages of officer-candidates, command staff and visiting dignitaries.

It was the task of the AFB West to guild the proceedings with the requisite majesterial music to support the grand martial emotions at play.

To begin the event, a hand signal to the band drum major, typically the unit's ranking Sergeant, would ignite a bellowed command designed to gain the musician's attention:

BAND!!!

Without fail, this command would alert us that within two or three seconds an order to come to attention would follow. It would also signal the hundreds of gathered officer-candidates, Generals, Colonels, VIPS and guests that the dignified, pride-swollen affair was about to begin.

On the day in question the band's imperious Chief Master Sergeant detected the awaited signal. He lifted his five-foot long, million-ton command mace and issued the time-honored shout in a great booming baritone that swept across the brutal, sun-baked plain. No witness to or participant in the event could evade the call that the ceremony was about to engage:

BAND!!!

Suddenly from deep within the bowels of the percussion section a veteran rube responded with an equally deep, booming and undeniably compelling roar:

WHAT!!!?

600 people collapsed in laughter.

Posted by Tom P.

Today's Top Ten List

This post is more like trolling for comments than a real post. I actually started out to write another Vegas story when I started thinking about all the places Vegas reminded me of. So, then I started thinking about what went on in those places and this became an obsession. So, here is my first take on some of the best gigs that I was ever involved in. Oh, in no particular order:

Neunkirchen Beer Tent; Neunkirchen, Germany – Why? Happy people, beer, more happy people, more beer, Schwenkbraten, more happy people, BEER. I know we played it at least twice.

The Fairfield Air Show; some place in England – Why? The Vulcan. It was the coolest looking jet I ever saw. Oh, I remember nothing about the gig itself.

The Pensacola Jazz Festival, 1985; Pensacola, Florida – Why? Before we played there was a set which featured Buddy De Franco, a renowned Be-bop Clarinet player, but not necessarily a favorite of mine (the instrument or the player). What made that set cool, and the whole festival so memorable to me, was that two dudes, Nick Brignola and Pacito De Rivera, just walked on stage during a tune with Pain Sticks in hand and the three of them had a major cutting contest. Pacito won, by the way. I had never heard of Pacito at that time. I had heard of Nick, but never heard him play. Kind of odd that I would fall in love with them as Clarinet players first.

The Jacksonville Jazz Festival, 1985?; Jacksonville, Florida – Why? Well, for starters the AFB East opened for the Duke Ellington band, under the direction of Mercer. Then there was the Dirty Dozen Jazz Band, the Jazztet (with Art, and Benny and Curtis). To top things off, I got to meet the legendary Air Force Arranger, CMSgt Cecile T. (Tom) Pomeroy backstage after the gig. He just happened to be in town.

The Hollywood Jazz Festival, 1986; Hollywood, Florida – Why? I met Nick, see "That Other Bari Player" posted on 6/10/2010.

The Mobile Jazz Festival, 1984; Mobile, Alabama – Why? We got to work with and drink with Rob McConnell - there will be posts on that later.

Sembach Dinning In, 1979; Sembach AS, Germany – Why? The Lady In The Red Dress! There normally is a Lady In The Red Dress, but this one was the most Lady In The Red Dress of all the Ladies In The Red Dresses I ever saw!!!

Mainz Kastel Fasching Ball, 1980; Mainz Kastel, Germany – Why? The costume contest was won by The Pied Piper of Hamelin and his mice. The mice were gorgeous, nearly naked - just a g-string women with painted on whiskers and tails attached to their g-strings - thereby justifying that piece of clothing to me.

Christmas Caroling, 1981; B-40, Kaiserslautern, Germany area – Why? Well, it was kind of an official gig but not really. We would wonder from post to post play here and there, but Wobbly, one of our trumpet players, demanded that we stop and play for this one lady who was at her normal post on the northern side of B-40. (The amazing blonde with the green Mercedes – remember her?) We played my funky, Gill Evens like, chart on O Tannenbaum and she actually cried. So the real answer to that age-old question is not "Don't pay her" it turns out that a jazzy version of a traditional German Christmas Carol works just fine. Made my holiday season!

The Mortimer Levitt Memorial Pavilion for the Performing Arts, September 9th, 1998, 8:00 PM EST; Westport, Connecticut – Why? Well, it was my last gig. It was in honor of my Dad for all the bands he ran for the kids over the years. I thought I might be the guy with the longest trip, flying in from LA to attend, but I got beat. Tom Conroy, trumpet from the second generation band, flew in all the way from Australia. And, it was the only time I ever got to play with my long time Sax teacher, Bob, and my beloved Jr. High Band Director, Jack. What a way to go out.

I think that's ten?!? I am sure there will be more.

Did I get you thinking? Tell us about yours!!!

Posted by Fred

A Senior Moment

Hill AFB, UT, 198?, for an "Order of the Sword." That particular military tradition is what is perceived as being the highest honor that can be bestowed on an officer by the enlisted people. Kind of like being made an honorary enlisted person. I always felt it was more like making Bill Gates an honorary mail clerk. Anyway...

We just had a small, six-piece, band so the commander loaded us up for the trip with all our senior NCOs so we could flash some stripes or whatever. That meant that one of our Senior Master Sergeants, who had nothing to do but walk around and try to look good in his mess dress was on the gig. With nothing to do, officially, that dude took it upon himself to tip a few well before the gig started.

I few minutes before the ceremony was to start we filed through the kitchen of the NCO Club on our way to our places. As we were exiting the kitchen our SMSgt had a near collision with this elegantly dressed civilian woman. As she stepped around him she politely said, "Excuse me" not sarcastically, but earnestly.

The reply she got may have surprised me more than it did her. In rather slurred speech, the SMSgt said, "What's a matta lady? Did you fart?" at a volume level that quite a few people could hear.

I cowered off to my spot behind the sound board as the lights were dimming and the lady and the SMSgt hurried to theirs. Saved by the bell, I guess.

Minutes later, the lady of the day was introduced to the audience as the wife of the honoree, some retiring General. Oops! Strangely enough, that SMSgt got orders Overseas just a few weeks later. Go figure?!?

Posted by Fred

Let's Start This Set With a Break

The AFB Overseas was at a German Beer Tent gig which I ALWAYS loved playing them – well except when it was really cold. I don't remember where this one was but it was on a really high stage, like 6 feet above the crowd. This was one of my first gigs with that band so it must have been in 1979 or 1980. I remember playing Alto on that gig, so Tom P. may not have been there to corroborate this tale.

During the break after the first set a bunch of the guys gathered around a vendor who was selling Pickled Eggs. They were rather exotic looking, it even looked like beet juice had been used because the eggs, and the fingers of the diners, were a rich purple. I stuck with the free beer provided by the sponsors.

Back on the stand and about half way through the first tune I hear somebody from the trumpet section quietly say, "Anybody got an M16? Phew..." At first I thought he was talking about the rifle, then I found out why he added the "Phew" and realized that he was talking about the gas mask. As we prepared ourselves for the "balls-to-the-wall" ending of our opener more sphincters loosened up and things got nasty on stage.

The last note, normally held by the piano playing band leader until the horns turned blue in the face, was cut off more like a stinger to a march. He quickly grabbed the mike and said, "Ladies and gentlemen, we are experiencing some technical difficulties and will need to take a short break."

The band piled off the stand as fast as we could. Our rather comical lead alto player almost tumbled head first down the steep ladder-like stairs but one of the large trombone players - who I always assumed to be one of the major contributors in that gas attack - grabbed him by the collar. We filed quickly to the parking lot where it was lightly raining but had FRESH air.

The band instinctively divided into two groups, those with purple fingers and those without. Amid all the coughing and laughter I remember our fearless leader demand, "OK boys, get it out of your systems" which only made things worse... Pfft, ploof, piff, cough, laugh, chortle, choke...

OK, so I always loved playing Beer Tents except when it was cold and when they served pickled eggs. One final note, at the next rehearsal, our leader showed up in full NBC (Nuclear, Biological, and Chemical) gear. That rehearsal also started with a break!

Posted by Fred

1 comment:

Tom P. said...

> Missed that job. If it was 1980 then maybe the jet stream dropped some residual gig molecules on me in Northern Arizona.

Sometimes It Doesn't Hurt To Play
An ODD Instrument

One afternoon in St. Thomas, Virgin Islands, 1994, while doing the cruise ship thing, I met an old buddy; Steve – can't remember his last name, good trumpet player though, at one of the dock bars in the area normally only visited by the crew members. Steve mentioned that their Baritone saxophone (bari) player quit the day before. He mentioned that Ben Vereen was going to be on his ship that week, shows on Thursday and Friday, and that they really needed a Bari player for his book. Steve and I had played Ben's book together on RCCL, he was right. GOOD Bari book! He then asked if I would be interested.

I said, "Sure but how do you make that happen?" He looked up, ordered me two beers, paid for them and scurried off to his ship to get the ball rolling. Before I could finish the second beer, a Kalik from the Bahamas – good stuff, he was back and handed me a freshly made Carnival name tag that said, FRANK Robinson, Musician. He told me to go put my tux on, grab the horns I needed and meet my Music Director (MD) at the exit gate; they would take care of the rest.

It took me about 20 minutes to get to the gate, but Pete was standing there and he walked me through the gate, circumventing normal Customs. Steve and his Music Director met me at the bottom and we repeated the Customs circumvention entering the Carnival ship.

Once on the Carnival ship, Steve took me to his cabin. He had been the odd man out in the band and had a single, though there were two bunks. The cabins were much nicer that the RCCL crew cabins I had been in so we became bunk mates for the week. Steve gave me a tee shirt, a pair of shorts and some flip-flops so I could get out of my Tux. We then preceded to the Ship shops with the Cruise Director's Ship Credit Card to get me the stuff I needed for the week. A pair of tan cotton boat paints, 2 pair of socks, two tee shirts and a pair of cheep canvas deck shoes and a carton of smokes. Total? $600.00 + but we just charged it on the CD's card. Back to the room for some beers.

That night I didn't have to play. I think the MD needed some time to make something up to explain who I was to everybody so I got blasted in the Crew Bar, for about $6.00 ($0.35 for a half-liter Becks).

The next day, Steve brought me the Bari book for that night's show. I looked it over and found some Bass Clarinet and Piccolo doubles. So we dug up some manuscript paper and I quickly scribbled out some replacements with a crappy green felt-tip, for Bari and Sopronio Recorder. A pretty simple show, and I did OK, and the MD didn't seem to mind my substitute doubles.

The next morning was the rehearsal for Ben's show. He stepped in front of the band and said "I see a couple of familiar faces" pointing to Steve and followed with, "It's always nice to have a lead trumpet player who is not sight reading." Then he looked at me and asked if I had done his show. I said, "Yeah, on RCCL a while ago. I was the guy with no Bass Clarinet." He smiled and walked over to the piano, opened his briefcase and retrieved the replacement Bass Clarinet to Bari parts that I had carefully copied in good ink on good paper and left in his books from before.

Then he turned to the MD and said, "With the top and the bottom covered, I don't need to waste your time with a rehearsal. This rehearsal is over as far as I am concerned. You guys can split." The drummer stuck around and talked through a few things but the rest of us all went back and crashed for a while.

The rest of the week went smoothly, washing things out in the sink and drying them with a hair dryer - things do not dry in a cabin 6 decks below the waterline without some help - and enjoying playing some new music, not to mention getting another crack at Ben's show.

Next Tuesday came and we reversed the clandestine exchanges. As I was about to walk up the ramp to the RCCL ship the MD handed me a pay envelope, shook my hand and said thanks. When I got inside Pete also handed me a pay envelope and said thanks.

It turned out that both MD's had gotten brownie points for handling the situation and pocketed $100.00 from each of the Bari player's pay envelopes. But, getting two envelopes, I ended up with $150.00 more than I normally would have made and had a fantastic time!

Posted by Fred

Mi Bateria es su Bateria

The Protocol Trio from the AFB Overseas had a reception at the Commanding General's house one night. The bass player and I had gotten there in the middle of the afternoon to setup. This was another drum gig for me. We had just finished the setup when the General and his aide came over and said hello. That General LOVED the band and treated us like family. I know that to be true because I drank beer and played softball with his son and daughter regularly, so I actually did know the family.

The aide, also the base protocol officer, chimed in, "Glad I caught you, you're the drummer, right?" I said, "Yes Sir" - cringing at perhaps having misrepresented myself. He said, "Good, when we introduce the guest of honor we are going to need a nice long loud drum roll." I freaked, and respectfully said, "Major, I am not a rudimentary drummer, I can hardly play cocktail music." Then the major got tiffed, though not totally ape-shit, as he stood there with his boss, the Commander and Chief of the whole damn Command. At that point he started calling me 'Airman' rather than Staff Sergeant, which is never a good sign.

The general quickly interrupted and asked me if the drum he was pointing at was "His Drum" or "My Drum?" It took me a second but I figured out what he was asking and finally said, "Your drum, Sir." Then he told me to go get it and bring it to him. He took it from me and looked it over for a second then pitched it across the floor as if he was about to bowl a 300 game. He then turned to the Major and said, "There's your drum roll. Fred, how about a cymbal crash instead?" I had to stifle a laugh and almost choked as I said "Yes Sir, I think I can handle that."

The Major stormed off without being dismissed and I respectfully waited until being told to go, still holding back the laughter with tears starting to well up in my eyes. The General said, "You can go now. I hope you didn't really like that drum. Let me know if I need to talk to your Supply Sergeant." What a cool guy! Oh, by the way, the drum was fine though I never did find the drum key that was attached when he let it go.

Posted by Fred

1 comment:

Tom P. said...

Damn fine word-stringing, Airman.

Train Wrecks

Most audience members don't particularly notice when a musician makes a mistake on stage. But sometimes the infraction is so egregious that it is folly to pretend that some kind of serious musical malpractice has not just taken place. One saxophonist's attempt to recreate a well-known solo went so far off the rails that our front man pointed the heavy bottom of a mic stand at him and pumped the adjustable top-part furiously as if spraying the player with DDT. As our liasion to the crowd he felt compelled to address the issue:

"Sorry about that. Our alto player was stricken with 'Sudden Saxophobia' but he'll be all right."

The same could not be said for our trumpet section. A featured player's attempt to capture a high note proved a disastrous exercise devoid of any responsible or meaningful foundation to base a defense. A microphone is not a subtle tool and our Master of Ceremonies shared his assessment with the world:

"Where'd you get that 'G' - at a free clinic?"

Posted by Tom P.

1 comment:

Fred said...

> I have more than once been accused of committing "Harlem Nocturnal Emissions" but never had "Sudden Saxophobia."

Here's Looking Achoo Kid

The AFB Overseas was in England in the early 1980's. We were in the middle of Count Basie's "Shinny Stockings" and were just about to get to the solo immortalized by Thad Jones. I would like to think I as on Bari that night, but I was more than likely on Tenor.

So we get to the two bar, break, and SILENCE. One WHOLE BAR of silence followed by an Achoo, expertly executed on "the and of one" to "two." I know those are the correct words for that but I have never seen it written down - looks odd. The impish grin and the lack of slobber on the mike were proof that this was the break he had intended to play.

The equally as famous Bari "Bah-doop" that was supposed to follow on "the and of four", to "one," did not. There was a pause that could not have been translated into musical notation, and finally. . . "Bahdoop" and the band kicked in perfectly. Somehow we made it to the end of the tune, although there were a lot of pliffs, and ploofs in the first few bars from the sax section, before busting into laughter.

What I wouldn't give for a recording of that!

Posted by Fred

Right Back At'ya

My only musical memory of working an air show comes from England.

On a break, our drummer was approached by one of the pilots of the elite British flying team, the Red Arrows, similar to the American Thunderbirds or Blue Angels. The Captain strutted over and said, "Mind if I sit in? I play a bit of the drums."

Without missing a beat, our TSgt replied, "I tell you what, Sir, I'll let you play my drums if you'll let me fly your jet."

The Captain cracked up and the Red Arrows ran a tab for the band that night at the Club.

Posted by Fred

FWS #6: Name That Tune?

In 1990 or so I got to live a dream and play my Bari with the Ringling Brothers, Barnum & Bailey Circus! Jerry (trumpet) and Roger (trombone) were the other two local Macon, GA players.

There was a short 20 minute rehearsal for almost 90 minutes of music. That show had a bunch of recorded material for the Chinese Acrobats so we got a break. The following year there was more like

2 hours of music. So, needless to say we, the locals, were sight reading a LOT OF STUFF.

Somehow we made it through the two Saturday shows even though I was literally bleeding and ruined a tux shirt with the blood. During the first Sunday show, the tune - if you could call it that, more like a frantic collection of semi-musical sounds with highly slapstick styled percussion accompaniment - that preceded the Chinese Acrobats came and went once again.

Roger, who was just to my right, sat there just as dazed as I was. After a few deep breaths, he softly said "Shit, that's The Mexican Hat Dance." I looked at my book, while dobbing blood from my chops, and saw the title: "Fast Shtick #3" and a tempo marking of MM = WOW.

I would have laughed at Roger for not knowing the name of a tune we had now performed three times. But then I realized that if he had not said what he said, I would not have known what it was.

By the time I finished up my 14th performance, in Albany, GA a couple of weeks later, I was only making about 80% of the notes, but at least I knew the names of all of the tunes. Somehow, I considered that a triumph. Oh, I did get invited back the following year. Go figure?!?

Posted by Fred

An Actual War Story

In 1992 the AFB East was tasked with playing ceremonies for the troops returning from Iraq. Most of them were pleasantly scheduled in the mid afternoon and had local, Macon, TV coverage and swarms of family and friends to greet the troops. After three or four of those I had become rather complacent and was complaining to myself about how we, the USAF, could make a photo-op out of something like this.

Then one day a list was posted for a night ceremony. Odd orchestration, which I think was based more on who were night people than understanding what a band needs to cover SATB type orchestration. Oddly enough, I was not asked to play. For some reason all I had to do was stand in front of rank one, row one and salute when appropriate. I think there is a name for that chair but I am embarrassed to say I don't remember it.

So it's like 2:00 AM and the C 141 arrives. Nobody is there to greet anybody, except a few folks from flight ops. The ladder rolls up and the door opens, five or six people get off in rumpled flight suits. The band played something but we were still being held at attention.

Then, from behind the tail of the 141 came a cargo roller with a box. Yeah, about that size. Then another, then another until the number of boxes to arrive far outnumbered those who had walked down the ladder beforehand.

I would like to think that I did not cry while standing at attention in my cammys there on the tarmac that night. But, I would not be embarrassed to find out I did. I know I did for a considerable amount of time in the parking lot before I finally drove home that night.

I think I posted something like this somewhere recently. With Memorial Day only 52 minutes away here in California, it is somehow appropriate. But that post would have been more abridged.

That night I stopped being just that guy in an AF band and became an Airman in the United States Air Force. At noon tomorrow I will stand looking east and a bit north, approximating the location of Arlington, Virginia, and offer a salute as I have for the past 18 years.

Posted by Fred

1 comment:

Chris said...

> I remember the night gigs there, Fred...as I lived on base then, I got all of them. I, too, look to the northeast...

Swab and Debonair

(Bill C. originally posted this as a comment to one of my earlier posts. It deserved to be a post of its own.)

Back at North Texas State in the '70's, Fred and I arranged and performed in several student-produced cabaret shows. One such show was staged in the "Rock Bottom Lounge" of the then-new student center with an excellent 9-piece band.

The show, too, was excellent, with many high-stepping Broadway and jazz bits but the director choose to end the show with a very slow and pretty waltz, "Seesaw", from the Broadway show of the same name. While the cast members mimed, in slow motion, children at play, Fred was called upon to play the sweet melody on sopranino recorder, and the effect was very touching.

One show, after the tinkling piano introduction, Fred stepped to the fore with his recorder, placed it gingerly to his lips and out came, "Wthp...fwrtt...swhpt..."

Fred's expression was shocked and confused, then he pulled the sopranino apart to discover the drying swab still blocking the instrument.

With that self-disgusted look that only those who know Fred can picture, he threw the bits and pieces of the recorder to the floor and crept back to his seat on the bandstand.

The band completely cracked up; the bass player, John Adams, was laughing so hard, tears were literally streaming down his face as he kept playing.

I imagine Fred has never since blown through a woodwind instrument without checking for any similar embarrassing impediment. - Bill C.

Only one correction I can offer, I threw the swab to the floor (and never considered retrieving it) but kept the recorder. In fact, it is sitting about two feet from me right now. It's about the only axe I play anymore, other than the alto recorder sitting right next to it.

Thank you, Bill C.

Posted by Fred for Bill C.

"Pass" in Review

While I was in the AFB East we often played for parades, including pass-in-reviews. Sometime in the mid-eighties the band was in formation for a Change of Command ceremony. The band was called to attention, awaiting the signal for the downbeat of the first ruffle and flourish. An Air Force official took his position at the podium, as the lead trumpet player, who was a dedicated body builder that consumed large quantities of amino acids, protein and other muscle building components, decided to discharge a high pitched emission (think of allowing air to slowly escape from a balloon!). God only knows how the band was able to keep it's composure, but only a slight wave of whisper-level snickers were audible. After a few seconds, someone in the squad next to the band whispered, "Hell, I wish I had known it was okay to do that. I would have let one fly long time ago!" Another guy whispered, "I thought someone was already playin' their trumpet!"

Posted by Stephanie

Best Post So Far

"Pass" in Review Leave it for a true "Lady" to post something like that. Thank you Stephanie. I am sure that Nate would be humiliated by that, but he would have laughed too.

I have something like this from Germany to post later. But, I think I should let the air clear a little before I do.

Comments Ladies and Gentlemen, to Stephanie's post?

Posted by Fred

7 comments:

Stephanie said...

> Thanks Fred! I couldn't let Tom P. overshadow our motley crew at the AFB East with his parade story, now could I?

Tom P. said...

> Now Stephanie, we both know that the twisted Robinson is setting us up for a race to the bottom. Even now he is petting his cat while waiting for further debaucheries to unload. We are roadies on the path to Hell.

Fred said...

> This is an interesting combination. Steph, meet Tom. Tom and I were stationed together in the AFB Overseas for about a year before I got to AFB East. He was/is an excellent alto player and Hank's little brother - that will be a later post. Steph and I and her adorable husband, Ken – OK, also a really fine saxophone player too - were stationed together in Georgia where Steph played pretty good keys and SANG HER ASS OFF every time she stepped on stage. Oh, and she somehow also found a way to put up with all the shit from the guys.

> Tom, I think you left before my chart on "Light My Fire" so you may never have seen me abuse the people in the band with my writing. On the other hand, Steph was the brunt of MOST of it. Starting with a George M. Cohan medley (simply called "Cohan") through "Modern Broadway" through "The N. Y. Medley" - thanks for finding that, Steph, you brought that on yourself - to "Yada, yada, yada" I wrote stuff for her that would have gotten me kicked out of NTSU, even though my arranging teacher loved me like a son.

> You guys were my pallet. For every clap (not curable with penicillin) a chart of mine ever got, you should have gotten a zillion.

Fred said... (cont.)

> Steph, is it OK to mention you being with us at that club on
> Orange Blossom Trail, in Orlando in a future post? Lol.

Stephanie said...

> To Tom, I say, "Hey, bring it on!" I've always loved a good
> duel! Hit me with your best shot!
>
> To Fred, Orange Blossom Trail - of course it's okay... just
> refresh my memory... what club? Sounds like at least another
> great one-line punchline in the making!

Tom P. said...

> It could be that I have an unnatural advantage in this forum.
> The people I served with in the AFB West were largely killer
> road musicians who were evading the Vietnam-War draft by
> volunteering for the Air Force band. These were
> swashbucklers who drank Southern Comfort with their
> morning coffee and whose natural uniform was the standard-
> issue straitjacket. Perhaps, in time, I can devise ways to craft
> their exploits in a manner that won't be too horrifying to
> gentle 21st-century souls nor will cause the black helicopters
> of the FCC to descend on FJR Drive with C-4 and Napalm.
> We will see how it all unfolds.

Fred said...

> Hum, I forget about those Black Choppers. I think I need a
> more complete and aggressive archiving strategy. But, who
> do I know that would not be suspect? Maybe I will have to
> open an account in the Cayman Islands to store the XML
> files?
>
> These stories must be preserved, much like the well pickled
> livers of the people Tom mentioned above.

Tom P. said...

> I'd have French Benedictine monks store vellum copies in the
> catacombs of an Alsatian castle . . . Doh! Too late now. Sorry.

A Gem From An Old Sax Section Mate Of Mine

OK, today I am passing along a story from an old AF band buddy,
Tom P. Tom and I were stationed together at AFB Overseas, but this
did not happen there. According to Tom, it happened at an AFB West
big band concert in the mid-seventies. Enjoy.

On an outdoor Air Force stage band job, near the end of a tune, one
of the trombone players rose from his chair and walked backwards
off stage and out of view while playing the final notes of the piece.

As the audience politely applauds, the bone player calmly returns
and proceeds to pull out the next chart. The irked band commander
approaches the wayward brass player and demands "What was that
about?"

Our hero innocently looks up and says "I'm sorry, sir, the music told
me to fade out."

Posted by Fred for Tom P.

1 comment:

Bill C. said...

> After Louis Armstrong left Chicago (actually, chased out by
> "The Mob"), one of the bands he gigged with was Fletcher
> Henderson's, known for it's sophisticated and complex
> arrangements. Now, Louis could read music very well, but on
> a quiet section of one tune, Louis kept blasting through
> loudly. When Henderson pointed out the dynamic marking
> was "pp", Louis replied, "I thought that meant 'pound
> plenty'!" Of course, the band cracked up.

Short War Story From Rick

Back in late 82 or early 83 the AFB East was doing an arrangement of some Spike Jones material which included hijinks like gargling and gunshots. As I was doing quite a bit of shooting at the time I volunteered to do the shots.

OK, lets forget the fact that I was carrying an unauthorized firearm onto a military base. We were performing at the Officers Club at Patrick AFB in Florida and the Spike Jones chart was on the list. The whole band couldn't fit on the small excuse for a stage so only the percussion section was up there. For whatever reason I never noticed the low dropped ceiling over the stage, you could just about touch it while standing on the floor. When the time came I held the gun over my head and pulled the trigger. I had a major "Oh Shit" moment when small, powdery pieces the ceiling tile came floating down all around me. Even though it was a blank, and a light load at that, it still blew a hole above my head since the barrel was up against the tile. I worried myself silly till we pulled off the base several days later. Thought I was going to jail or loose the few stripes I had. Nothing was ever said.

Posted by Rick

3 comments:

Fred said...

> Oh yeah, the ice is broken. He's got a million of 'em folks. I should know, I was there for about five-hundred-twenty-two thousand of them! He'll be at TBOTB all week so drop back in to see Rick! "Gentlemen!"

Stephanie said...

> I think we should erase this post immediately!
>
> Homeland security is surely alerted by now!
>
> Terrorist! Terrorist! AHHHHHHHHHHHHH!

Chris said...

> I remember...I was doing the gargling. You damn near blew
> out my eardrums!

> You remember mixing the loads up for the same chart at W.R.
> Civic Center? Outdoor load indoors...MAN!

How Do You Follow That?

I would guess you could have a Blog with nothing but peeing off the
bus stories and never run out of material, but thanks for Tom for
breaking the ice. Here is one from my past.

The AFB Overseas had just done a Fasching parade. The band's
participation had started at O-Dark-Thirty with a steaming cup full
of hearty pea soup spiked with some sort of Schnapps supplied by
the sponsor. Considering the temperature, that was a welcome
aperitif. In case you have never seen one of these parades, they are
as much a reason to promote public drinking as anything else.

Bottles of wine were trust in our faces as we marched and if we had
to stand still for any length of time you may have been able to down
a BBK or two before trudging farther into the crowd. Needless to
say, bladder maintenance was of the utmost importance. Fortunately,
for parades such as this, the normal stringent military policies for
maintaining our formation were set aside. If you had to go, you
could drop out of formation, find a Gasthaus or whatever, relieve
yourself and catch back up down the street. Not that I remember ever
being formally briefed on that, it just kind of happened that way.

After the parade the band had to wait for the Commander for a
while. Seems he had wandered away into the crowd at some point
and not been seen for quite some time. Once we were reunited with
our fearless leader we piled into the Bluebird and headed for home.

As in Tom's post one of the guys went forward in the bus and
requested a potty break. He was turned down once or twice but
finally his request was granted. As soon as the bus came to a stop the

requester was out the door and quickly assumed the position. Fortunately, in Germany this activity was not considered obscene. You would commonly see an Oma or two relieving herself on the side of the Autobahn while out for a drive, so those that needed to do the same, both male and female, did.

After a few minutes everybody was back on the bus except for the one who had started it all, he was still at it. So a couple others got off, did their business and got back on. The requester? Still at it. At that point somebody started chanting his name, the whole band soon joined in. Soon our star returned to a standing ovation, wiped his nose with his sleeve and said, "Gosh fellas."

He then did a command performance of "Swing Low" and followed that up with an encore of the "...And it's deep too." joke.

Posted by Fred

3 comments:

Tom P. said...

> Bluebird? Did the Crown Coach die on your watch?

Chris said...

> That commander wouldn't have been a former leader of the S. Sergeants, would he? I seem to remember him regularly getting lost, losing uniform parts, etc...

Fred said...

> Yeah, and I understand he will be at the reunion. We better assign Jimmy to keep an eye on him. Lol.

The Rockets Red Glare,
The Bombs Bursting in Air . . .

A short one for the 4th.

When I first got to AFB East in 1982 there was no big traditional Independence Day concert by the band. That was soon to change. The new Commander, a bright young Major was a fine musician. I don't throw those words around lightly, especially when talking about Officers. He was also about as patriotic as they come and decided that we were going to do a show at the HS football stadium complete with cannons - big-ass howitzers actually - going off during the "1812 Overture" finale. "Yeah, right, I'll believe it when I see it" was stated by more than one senior NCO at that meeting though not to the Major's face. Then all of a sudden, one of the Ops guys got behind the idea and suggested, "How about paratroopers to start things off?" It was set in stone.

Our PA gear was meager at that time, so on that first year we played to only one side of the stadium. Lighting was not that big an issue because the show was scheduled to end right at sunset, so the city could do the fireworks show. The rest of the logistics were also pretty simple except for the big guns. We finally got them in, without totally ruining the stadium track and grass, and they settled in behind the home end zone.

So as the band took the stage the paratroopers were in the air and it all started to come together. First chute opens, the crowd really liked it. Then another, then another. I don't remember how many there were but I do remember one of the guys landed somewhere in the base housing area not far away. The rest made decent landings in the stadium.

The concert commenced and was going quite smoothly when our Ops guy got a little frantic about calling the howitzer shots, so I helped him mark up his score a bit and he calmed down enough to do his gig. He was to call "FIRE" through the cool Motorola walkietalkie he had to the Gunnery Commander, about two seconds before we wanted a boom. He did amazingly well. I later found out how hard that job was when I got to do it at later concerts.

So there it was, Quaker Oats flying all over the place, people going crazy, the band almost ducking as each volley was made. I was having a blast from my seat at the sound board. Then, the fireworks went off right on time. What a finale! Good idea Major!!!

As we started to tear down, somebody noticed a problem. Oops... not knowing ANYTHING about any type of firearm, let alone artillery, I could not tell you if it was the wadding used in the blank shells or if it was simply the percussion of the air escaping the guns, but somehow we had blown a bunch of holes in the BRAND NEW scoreboard. Like I said, OOOPS.

I don't know who worked what out with whom, but we continued to do those concerts for as long as I was stationed there. I understand they still do something like that now. But, there is nothing like your first kiss, especially when it is a 150 caliber one!

Posted by Fred

You Gotta Love Them

Near the end of a four-hour dance band job at an officers club in England one gin-soaked colonel tried to compliment us by saying:

"You guys sound just like real musicians."

Posted by Tom P.

1 comment:

Fred said

> Yeah, and how many times did you get asked "What's your day-job?" or "Do you fly jets?"

> Then try working for AFB East for 10 years and get people to understand we were active duty.

> You're right, "Gotta Love 'em!"

Give That Tiger Two Stars!

It was a typical Dining In/Out kinda gig. The AFB East combo is cranking out jazz standards (Fly Me to the Moon, Take the A Train, All of Me), pop favorites (Come In From the Rain, When I Give My Love To You) and a few originals. Everything is moving along as planned with Senior Airman Bill D. at the keys, along with all of the normal crew. Then, break time! Major General James McAdoo, commander of the Air Force Reserve is in attendance at said gathering. He approaches the bandstand to commend the performance of the combo.

As the general is shaking hands with the bandsmen, he gets to Senior Airman Dryden who politely and naively shouts, "How're you doing, Tiger?" The General looks at Bill with a countenance of total bewilderment, having no idea of how to respond to this greeting, he simply smiles and shakes his hand and moves on to the next musician.... Ken, saxophonist with the combo looks at Bill afterward and says, "That's General Tiger to you, Airman!" explaining to Billy exactly who he has just de-ranked!

Being the man of integrity and grace that he is/was (I don't know if Gen. McAdoo is still among us today or not), sensed that Bill had the utmost respect for him, although Bill may not have had the greatest grasp of protocol and etiquette.

McAdoo (a widower for many years, but finding a new love to share his remaining years with) later invited Bill and I to perform the music at his wedding at some renowned historical site? in Macon, GA.

What a refreshing memory to know a man with such great power that could temper that power with a keen sense of humor and sensitivity to the personality and intent of his subordinates! We all should strive to demonstrate his level of grace and humility in our lives. Gen. McAdoo is/was a true leader - one that had genuine respect for the team effort and all of those who make that effort a success....

Posted by Stephanie

2 comments:

Fred said...

> OK, I did this backwards. I commented on your comments before commenting on your post. Maybe that is good, because I know now not to mention paragraph spacing. Lol
>
> I must have been on sound for this one, because I do remember most of it. McAdoo WAS cool. My list of officers I truly respected would be pretty short, if I ever put one together, but he would definitely be on it if I did.
>
> This post has brought back memories of two more stories I need to post. Note to self; self, make notes...

Stephanie said...

> I love it when I start a fire! Can't wait to see what this spark started!

Read the Sign

It was shaping up to be a good week for Rico. Earlier he had won a spaghetti-eating contest in San Antonio. Later he was scheduled to be a featured singer during an AFB West concert at his high school alma mater.

The trumpet section prepared signs to accompany Larry's front man patter.

"This next guy is so handsome that if he doesn't turn you on, you don't have a switch."

"Crock"

"His name is Rico ******, a graduate of this school. He started out by taking bugle lessons at 25 cents an hour from a local trumpet player."

"True"

"Then he worked his way up to become the best trumpet player in MacArthur history."

"Lie"

"As some of you know, last month at the Grand Hotel downtown Rico entered a spaghetti-eating contest and set a new world's record. But he was so full of . . ."

"Bull"

". . . spaghetti that he was nearly hospitalized."

"Laugh"

"But here he is to sing for you today. Let's have a big hand for Rico ******."

"Applause"

Posted by Tom P.

Mission Accomplished!

I will in no way give you any more information about the central characters of this post other that their initials, R. and K. (K. being Mrs. R.). But, this IS a true story.

It was my second trip to Mardi Gras with the AFB East band. Dig this deal... I was in the Jazz Band so I all had was like two park gigs and got to be in New Orleans for 10 days with a LOT of time off. Sound fair? On the other hand, the Dixieland unit from the band was expected to work it's ass off and had a bunch of Float gigs so I decided to grab my clarinet and tag along on at least one to help ease my guilt about not working.

It turned out that I was useful. There were some problems with the sound setup, and funky little things that Rick had passed on to me over the years came in handy, though I am not sure if we ever did fix the problem with the ground to the generator. The float was just a motor-pool flatbed truck with simple decorations and a 2x4 railing most of the way around, nothing fancy. As we were pulling out I went over to the NCOIC (band leader) and offered my services to help stretch out the tunes so the guys wouldn't bust their chops quite as quickly (those were LONG parades, lots of playing) and he accepted (not knowing how bad a Dixie Clarinet player I was, yet).

The uniform of the day was Flight Suits (yeah, like real Air Force pilots wear) but with all insignia removed (Name Tag, Squadron Emblem, etc.) therefore officially making the flight suit civilian clothing, which came in handy because K. was not a GI. Being Mardi Gras, the band implemented a rather loose set of protocols that basically amounted to don't get hurt and make it back alive. Unlike the dilemma posed in my Fasching Parade post, this float came complete with a porta-potty, sweet.

As we got closer to The French Quarter those of us who were not "officially" on duty had gotten a sheet or two into the wind by graciously accepting the beer and wine offered to them by the throngs while the Dixieland guys only partook enough to keep the folks in the crowds from getting insulted by turned down drinks. That's a fine line to walk, by the way. They did a good job. Once in The Quarter, all bets were off. It was just as important at that point to toss beads and party as it was to attempt to stay stoic or play anything precisely, so a real jam broke out on the flat-bed. That was when I noticed that R. and K. were missing. I asked the guys but nobody knew where they were. R. was seasoned, so I wasn't worried just a little concerned.

At some point I took over on drums for a tune so the drummer could relieve himself. I did OK, I think I was just keeping time on "Saints" or something. No drum features for this cat, even when he was the official drummer in whatever band was unlucky enough to have me. A few minutes later the drummer returned and we did a mid-tune transfer, where he kind of took the sticks from me as he walked around the kit playing and slid in as I slid off, pretty slick as I recall.

Before I got away he said, "Found 'em. Check out the latrine." I could "go" at that point so off to the Green Tower I went.

As I reached for the door I must not have let the "Found 'em" part sink in, all I remembered was the "Check out the latrine" part otherwise I may have knocked rather than just flinging the door open, which is what I did. There inside were R. & K. entwined like something from the Kama Sutra, advanced version, making out like a couple of 16 year-olds, though still in their now rumpled flight suites. I don't know what possessed me to blurt out, "Can I get you two a room?" but I did. R. substantially out ranked me and some of those of his station would not have taken kindly to that kind of ribbing from a subordinate. Fortunately he did and simply said, "Already got one!" and he slammed the door shut. I cracked up.

A short time later, when I was beginning to NEED a latrine I noticed that somebody had stuck a sign assembled from some manuscript paper, sharpie and duct tape that said "OFF LIMITS!" on the door, so I assumed that everybody knew what was up at that point. Again I cracked up. Fortunately, before things became critical, two or three of us were considering going off the back of the float at that time, R. & K. exited their little bungalow and made sort of a Prom King and Queen entrance. We draped them with beads and bowed to them, then quickly made use of the facilities, two or three at a time.

Once it was all over I evaluated the situation as I was breaking down my clarinet: Nobody got hurt and we all made it back alive. Mission Accomplished!

Posted by Fred

3 comments:

Chris said...

> Fred, I remember the gig, as I was getting the crap shocked out of me every time I got close to the mic while plugged up to the banjo... you remember balancing on the tongue of the trailer, rewiring the power line from the generator? That was the first year I had a pickup on the banjo, so if I was playing

Chris said... (cont.)

> and touched the mic with a lip, it kinda stung! The spread
> metal floor on the float didn't help, as we had put cardboard
> down to try to insulate me, but the rain had wet the
> cardboard, making it a dandy conductor.

Fred said...

> Thank you sir! That was a fun trip even with all that. Then
> again I didn't have to do the vocals on mike... lol Perhaps you
> feel differently?

Chris said...

> Mardi Gras was ALWAYS a fun trip, even if I did work my
> ass off!

Putting A Spin On It

Back to the studio for this one. Once again in my favorite studio in
the world with the AFB East. It was a Concert Band recording, about
the third I was involved with and so I was rather seasoned and very
chummy with the Studio Family at that point. Our Commander was
new to the scene, though he had performed as a player in recording
projects he had never been involved in a Producer's role. Oh, I was
co-producing.

The material for that session was heavy on vocals, we had a fine
crop of what we called The AFB East Singers, made of a couple of
actual Vocalists and some horn players that sang well. I did my best
to make their lives miserable by writing some impossible voicings,
took odd turns and rewrote lyrics and threw key change after key
change at them, but they took it in stride and showed up well
prepared for what was to be a grueling session, at least laying the
vocal tracks.

The first two and a half days we did the band parts. That went rather smoothly. While the tape was rolling, the Commander was in the room and our master engineer (M.E.) and I were in the booth. We got about seventy minutes of stuff in the can in a very reasonable amount of time. Then came the vocal tracks.

As we started with the first one, full six part choir stuff, the Commander was not pleased with what he could hear conducting in cans (headphones, Fostex T-20's as I recall), so he insisted that he work from the booth and conduct through the glass. I can remember seeing M.E.'s eyes roll to the back of his head as he said something like, "Oh, brother. Stall him for a minute, I'll be right back" and he split the booth. A few minutes later the Commander was all setup with a spot behind the board with a stand and his scores waiting for M.E. to return. When he did, he had a strange looking piece of equipment that looked like the guts of an old amp or something and a few cables in his hand.

As he came through the door, he brought the lights up to full, from there more normal Bar Light setting used while tape is rolling, and stated, "I've got something here that will help even more." Somebody asked what it was and he said something like, "It's an Ambiance-er, we call it 'The Spinner'" he then looked at me with a look I had only seen him used at The Gold Club or Tattletales. He proceeded to stick cables here and there before returning to the button side of the board where he pulled out a roll of masking tape. As he was labeling the new channel on the SSL (those channels were not connected to anything) he asked that the Commander to move his setup over to the right so he could have access to the new toy M.E. had just setup. The Commander was impressed and happily schlepped his own stuff over to where he could see the new track name: "SPIN" written in nice bold sharpie.

M.E. went on to explain that when you push the fader up it will increase the Room Ambience, pulling it down would decrease it and he demonstrated. I don't think I had to go first. I think it was our Chief who jumped in and said something like, "Oh, yeah, I can hear it. That's cool" even though nothing changed no matter what you did with that slider. The Commander was happy, M.E. was happy, the Chief and I had to excuse ourselves to the back parking lot for a smoke so we would not burst out laughing.

What M.E. had done was not only give the Commander a feeling of power, and a very important job, he had also moved him directly under the one independently variable light in the booth, so that he could be seen while the rest of the booth looked black to the singers in the room. Cool.

Take Two... NAILED IT!!! For real, there was no dissent from any of the AFB East folks at all. But, fortunately, the M.E. said, "Let's just do one more for a safety. And 'Cappy' try this one without conducting. They can follow the previously recorded tracks and that way you can adjust the Spinner as we go." He bought it. It worked just fine, the lack of conducting, and we got another full take on the same tune. By the way, the safety was the track that we ended up using. It must have been the way the Commander massaged things with the Spinner. The lighting was returned to normal and the recording was completed before the Friday deadline.

The M. E. gave us the scoop on the Spinner over drinks at Harry's later. It turns out he had been doing that for years to puffed-up producers on his commercial projects. He did not intend to imply our Commander was puffed-up, he was just trying to keep a rookie out of trouble by putting a new spin on his role.

Posted by Fred

Twos

In musical forms that utilize improvisation it is not uncommon for soloists to trade solos back and forth. Most commonly a full chorus, less frequently 8 Bars (Eights), quite frequently 4 Bars (Fours) and not very frequently 2 Bars (Twos). The reason for the infrequent us of Twos is due to the fact that it's hard to make a full statement in 2 Bars. Just as the thought starts to come out, the other cat starts up...
Here, I will use the term "Twos" to mean, very short musical memories.

Remote Radar Installation somewhere in Northeastern Italy, early
'80's. If anybody remembers the name of that place, please let me
know. This place was far enough north and up in the Alps that it had
a rather German feel to it. In fact, the gig I remember was a classic
German Beer Tent, though it was on an American Outpost, in Italy.

We are up on another one of those nose-bleed stages, at least eight
feet high, doing a not-so-heavy-into-Glenn-Miller set. The crowd
was delightful, little kids, young lovers, Moms & Dads and party-
hearty octogenarians all together enjoying the fine August afternoon
as only the Europeans can. During one of the sets we did a tune
called "Turn Yourself Around." It featured our world class trombone
soloist, Stan. My wife was along on that trip and was very good with
our modest SLR and she took three pictures of the band and one
audience member during that tune. The shot was medium wide but
you could clearly see Stan up in front of the band blowing and a
little boy, perhaps 5, right in front of the PA speakers with his eyes
closed, arms straight out twirling around. The reason I know that he
wasn't just jumping or whatever is that the sequence of shots clearly
showed his rotation. Amazing, the power of music.

Fast forward a few years... For a short time at AFB East I had the
distinct privilege of running the Jazz Band. On one of those tours, to
the east coast of Florida, my family was along so I guess it was
summer time or Susie would have been working her pre-school
teacher gig.

My daughters were real young at that point. I don't remember
exactly, but like maybe 4 and 6. They had become good buddy's with
one of the singers in the band, Kathy, who Susie and I also
considered a close friend. Somewhere along the way Kathy had
taught the girls "Rhythm In My Nursery Rhymes" a tune that is not
normally considered a serious Jazz tune, but Kathy brought it to me
a few months earlier and I did a kind of serious Basie style thing on
it and we did it a lot, people liked the cute hooks.

So, one day on that tour we had a Mall gig. Those gigs seldom drew
more than a few that would stick for more than a few tunes before
toddling off to do their shopping so we took them rather lightly.
When it got to be time for Kathy to do "Rhythm..." she looked at me

and went ahead and invited my girls up on stage to sing with her without waiting for any kind of approval. I was a bit surprised, but the band was all smiling. So once they got up on stage, I kicked off the tune, Kathy crouched down to share the mike and the all started singing. Well, OK it took my younger daughter a few bars to get what was going on but she eventually kicked it in and they did pretty good.

All I could think about was that little boy back in Italy turning himself around. I was that little boy that day, thanks to those little girls - all three of them. Amazing, the power of music.

Posted by Fred

Pay No Attention To That Man (Woman) Behind The Curtain!

In like late August of 1989 The AFB East Brain Trust held our annual Christmas Concert planning meeting. "Yes, Virginia, Santa Claus does need to plan ahead." Somehow I came out of that meeting with an OK to go ahead with a really wacky chart on "The 12 Days of Christmas" (to be known as 12D for brevity), thanks boss. The hook was to get the two local Warner Robins, GA High Schools involved by providing students to perform the parts of the "Drummers Drumming" the "Swans a Swimming", "Lords a Leaping" etc.

So I stared drafting the chart and I got in contact with the Band Directors and the heads of the Drama Departments to set stuff up. Things didn't go very smoothly. I have never been good at politics, so I had a hard time understanding that these folks were bickering over stuff that had been going on between the two schools for years. All I wanted to do was to DO A CHRISTMAS CONCERT! Excuse my shouting. By mid September the chart was scrapped. Instead we stuck in a few other published things in the program and continued to shoot for December 10th in Macon.

Late October and I had finished all my stuff and was still trying to get over not getting to do 12D. So, The Lady Behind the Curtain said, over dinner one night, "Then why not come up with another chart? I'll help you." That was all it took. When this lady said "I'll help you" shit got done, and it does to this day. I walked into the Commander's office the next morning, wearing civvies and looking like crap, having stayed up late to put together the sketch, with a new 12D proposal.

I pitched hard, though I was mostly tossing junk, and before long I found out I was preaching to the choir; turns out I had him at "I got a new idea for a 12D chart." He asked me if I could do it. I said that I could. So he told me to go "Make It So."

By the time The Lady Behind the Curtain got home that day the house was a wreck. I had papers and crap spread all over the kitchen table and the living room floor was covered in lead sheets. So, as she stood there just to the right of the Hamilton, looking down on me she said something like, "I guess you got a new idea?" I think I responded with something like, "A few."

So I started spouting. I ranted about things like "We need this prop." Her reply, "I can do that" or "That prop." Her reply, "I can find that" and eventually she gave the me the real scoop. She joined me on thefloor, took my face in her hands and said something like, "What you need is me, your children around you, dinner, a beer and a good night's sleep though not necessarily in that order. Let Santa's workshop start tomorrow."

She was right. What else was new? Figuring the kids into the equation turned out to be a stroke of genius. The girls were about 7 and 5 at that point, perfect little giggly bundles of Christmas excitement. They helped make that project one of the best entertainment experiences I ever had.

I will skip a rundown of the production, but here is what we had when the chart went into rehearsals.

For the first eleven verses the part of the Partridge In A Pear Tree was played by a large potted Banana Plant, almost four feet tall, sporting a large Pink Flamingo yard ornament. She procured the plant from a friend and took joy at purchasing the Flamingo at a local hardware store. The hook was, "A Flamingo in a Coconut Tree" along with a disclaimer that we were working on getting a Partridge.

Two Turtle Doves; were hand-made Dove Christmas Tree ornaments.

Three French Hens? How about Rubber Chickens, yup, her idea.

Four Calling Birds; four telephone handsets complete with curly cords with store bought bird ornaments attached, a collaboration.

Five Golden Rings; we missed Hoola-Hoop season so had to settle for large Needlepoint Frames spray painted gold, she found those at Hancock's.

Six Geese a Laying; a huge stuffed Mother Goose figure, being a Preschool teacher allowed her access to such things, with real chicken eggs that she "Blew" - you know, you take a pin and poke tiny holes in both ends and gently blow the insides out leaving you with the shells intact – Mom's can do that kind of stuff. She did this for each performance so that I could crush them on my forehead during the shows.

Seven Swans a Swimming; a cute pink tutu that I could wear doing bad ballet moves to the tune of Swan Lake; she made the tutu.

Eight Maids a Milking; a handmade gingham bonnet and an old metal bucket. She added that I should go behind the conductor, a Commander with a GOOD sense of humor, and do milking motions using the tails of his Mess Dress.

Nine Ladies Dancing; she collected nine, not so used any more Barbie dolls so that I could flail them around to the music of "The Hustle."

Ten Lords a Leaping; a paper crown which resembled the one from that margarine commercial from the 70's, I have no idea where she found that.

Eleven Pipers Piping; this one was a gimmie. We already had a miniature set of dysfunctional Bag Pipes around the house, though I don't remember where they came from. That and the fact that the band at Robins actually had a Pipe Band was all we needed. I faked the playing while one of the pipers played live on a back stage mike. Oh, they changed the pipe tune every night so it was always a surprise to me.

Twelve Drummers Drumming; handmade paper dolls. These were huge, made from full size sheets of that card-stock type musical manuscript paper (Alpheus M-102, for the copyists out there). Then she hand painted meticulous detail each of them so that they could clearly be seen for what they were even from the balcony.

But wait, there's more...

On the final verse, we would finally find our Partridge, and the Pear Tree. She drew, cut out and painted this twelve foot tall Pear Tree from this heavy cardboard stick used to make theatrical flats. It was joined with a hinge in the middle and had a back leg so it could be freestanding on stage. In the center of this two-dimensional masterpiece hung a three-dimensional gem. A handmade and hand painted papier-mâché partridge about twice the size of a football. She used that metallic model paint so when it was hit by the spot, it really shined nice.

Top that all off with a red flannel shirt that she adorned with wonderful little appliqués like a Santa peering out of a pocket, candy canes here and there along with ornaments and lights, with a BIG Rudolph face on the back. The best costume I ever got to wear – that shirt is in the closet right behind me now - or is it in Texas?

All this for? Three performances, yup, that's it, and I doubt the chart has ever been used again. But, then again, without the props, the chart was a dog.

Coda: The premier performance of 12D was in Macon Georgia. It came off OK, but not having a recording of that night I cannot be sure. At least I have no disaster memories, so it couldn't have been that bad.

Shows two and three I have on tape, audio and video (and now on digital), so those memories are annually brought back. The second show, in Warner Robins clicked. The mugging/ad-libbing of the characters (Emcee, Commander, Featured Vocalist and myself) really worked and the crowd was eating it up.

While I was prepping to make the Milk Run (Eight Maids a Milking) I slipped on the large plastic bag we used to cover the Flamingo in a Coconut Tree with and sprained my left ankle but we finished up OK.

For the final show, also in Warner Robins, I was on crutches (though adorned with a nice red Christmas bow) and on Quarters. That meant I had orders, actual lawful Air Force orders to "STAY OFF THE ANKLE FOR THREE DAYS" in writing, in my medical records, from the actual Flight Surgeon Colonel who happened to be on duty when I went to have the ankle checked out. But, like they say, the show must go on...

Because of my limited mobility I enlisted the services of the only person in the world who could have done it, the Lady Behind The Curtain, only now she had to appear on stage. She threw together a wonderful Christmassy outfit, and being diminutive in stature really did look like Santa's Helper. I don't remember running things down with here before the show. I think all she asked was, "What do you want me to do?" To which I probably said, "I Dunno, just help me out." To which I am sure she would have said, "I can do that." And she did. In fact, it came off so well that it actually looked like I faked the ankle thing. That was one of the best moments I ever had on stage.

Aside: After the concert was over, the afore mention Flight Surgeon made a trip back stage to have a word with me. He had been in the front row of that show, in the VIP seats, but I never saw him. I thought I was in for a world of shit, but instead he shook my hand, said; "Good Show" and "I guess you can disregard the Quarters Orders. Oh, I guess you already have." Cool guy.

Unfortunately, at the end of 12D I allowed something to happen that has embarrassed me for years. I allowed her to get off the stage that night with no acknowledgment (remember, I have the video). I never even pointed to her while we were taking our bows. Nothing. I didn't do it in Macon or show number two either. I don't know if it makes things any better or not, but:

Thank you Susie!

Posted by Fred

1 comment:

Fred said...

> A friend commented to me, in a phone call not through the Blog Comment feature, that the second to the last paragraph looked to him like I was trying to say that my blunder of not acknowledging MY Band-wife, now Ex-Band-Wife, was a factor in the EX part happening.

> I had nothing like that in mind when I posted. While I guess it could have, I just can't see her taking it that way. She did, and still does, know me better than any person on this earth. I think she understood how significant I thought she was in pulling 12D off-and about every other project I was involved in for almost 15 years.

> What I was trying to say there is I just blew the perfect opportunity to allow her to share the spotlight, which she truly deserved. I know posting that thank you on this Blog is not like plastering it on the front page of the Times, but the Warner Robins Civic Center is not like Carnegie Hall either. While that post could easily have ended without the last two paragraphs I just thought a somewhat public acknowledgment was finally appropriate.

Fred said... (cont.)

> By the way, we are still very close. She is still my best friend, and I adore her current husband. It's just she and I seem to make much better Ex's than Currents, I guess.

Share The Wealth

After a screamingly excellent show band auditorium job Larry, our singer/front man, accepted the cheers of a wild, appreciative crowd.

"Thank you. Thank you very much."

He gestured behind him and continued to shout over the ovation of a packed audience that didn't want to leave.

"I couldn't have done it without a great background!"

The band sat a little straighter and readied to wave an acknowledgment to our fans.

"Let's have a big hand for those curtains."

Posted by Tom P.

1 comment:

Fred said...

> Everybody's a comedian! Lol.

Larry's Last Job

Eventually Larry, our front man-singer-trumpet player, decided that his first tour with the Air Force Band West would be his last.

His final job fronting the band occurred at the river amphitheater in downtown San Antonio. It is a lovely spot below street level where the audience and performers are separated by a narrow stretch of the San Antonio River.

On this day the crowd was criminally small but audience numbers were immaterial to us so Larry and the band proceeded with our usual enthusiasm.

"Hi. My name is Larry. This is Diane. There's the Major. That's the band. You're the audience. Oh, hi, we're the Air Force Band West. If you have any requests - keep them to yourself - this is our show; we'll do it any way we want."

And we were off.

About midway through the show one of those packed, flat-bottomed tour boats drifted through our set. Larry dragged his microphone to the edge of the stage.

"It's Rent-A-Crowd. You're late."

Near the end of the show a family of six, which was nearly half our audience, got up to leave. Larry called them on it.

"Hey, where are you going? Sit down. We're not done yet."

The patriarch of the little enterprise shouted his apologies across the river and explained that they had to meet someone at a nearby bar.

"Okay. We'll meet you there in about five minutes."

Job completed. Bus packed up. Larry, not the sentimental sort, addressed the band.

"Guys, there's one thing I've always wanted to do and I know I'll never get another chance. I'd like you all to follow me."

What could we say? Of course we would follow him. The Grand Air Force of the Republic trooped down the sidewalk behind its leader and followed him into a pharmacy. Deep down one of the aisles Larry stopped and called one of the veteran players to his side.

Larry gestured to the multitude of mouthwashes on display and said:

"Pick one, Dave. I'm buying."

Posted by Tom P.

April 27th 1979

I have alluded to this story in at least one other post. I had hoped that I would get some input from some of the other people who were there to help me with the sketchy parts, but that didn't happen. Then I realized that this had made the national news. Perhaps there would be some stuff on the internet. Just Google that date and the city name of San Antonio, TX and you will get lots of hits. Here is my recollection of about ten minutes of that day.

The band bus pulled up and we all had our instruments in hand, having run a short rehearsal in the parking lot prior to our departure. We were to told to disembark and form up just outside the bus and we would be marched into our position in the parade by our Drum Major. So we piled off the bus.

As I was getting off I noticed people crouched behind cars and anything they could, some were running away from the area. I had no idea what was up. I fell in line in the second row as was normal for me on tenor sax, right behind the trombones.

Before we could dress the formation I remember hearing over a bull horn or something, "...Blah, blah, blah TEXAS RANGER, blah, blah, blah..." we all froze. Our commander ran to the front of the band. Something that I had only seen in movies or TV shows before came hurtling over the band and bounced in the street and skidded, spewing smoke, towards a Winnebago type thing about twenty yards in front of us. The commander gave the order, "BAND!" we came to attention.

Seconds later there was another announcement over the bull horn and while it was going on, more Tear Gas Canisters were tossed (shot?) towards the mobile home. Our commander once again gave the order, "BAND!" after a short pause he added, "SPLIT!" Therefore having officially created the new command "BAND SPLIT."

I don't mean to trivialize this event but I was amazed. The Commander used the most straightforward language that he knew all of us would understand and acted like a true Commanding Officer under fire, literally and I was there to experience it. Anyway...

All of us ran towards the bus. As we did one of the canisters was bouncing into one of the open equipment bays under the bus. One of our Tuba players was near the lead and he held his rather large instrument up like it was a Piccolo in his left hand and reached into the bay with his right hand, grabbed the smoking canister, dropped it and kicked it a good thirty yards down the road. I did not know until my NBC training a year or so later that those canisters are very hot when discharging. We were discouraged to even consider touching them.

We piled on the bus along with some unrelated civilians and some family members who were along for the celebration turned nightmare. The Commander shouted, "Shirt, headcount?!?" The reply was something like, "Good, Captain." The Commander then shouted, "Driver, get this thing in the air!" and we headed away from the parade site.

On the ride back to the base I noticed that one of our Band Wives was covered in blood. Her husband, one of our trumpet players, was calm so I assumed it was not hers. I don't remember anything else until much later that night.

Back at our little rental house on "Kon-Tiki" I remember sitting with my new bride when I finally lost it. She held me and just let me go at the same time.

We did do the parade that was scheduled for April 28th, 1979. I don't remember there being one word spoken between bandsmen that day. I had assumed I had just lived through the most emotional thing I would ever experience. But I was wrong. Setting aside the birth of both of my daughters, which is inappropriate for this Blog, there is another story to come.

Posted by Fred

2 comments:

Chris said...

> Did this commander, by chance, play trombone in a previous
> career?

Fred said...

> That would be correct.

A Forgotten Gig

Chris' recent comments on a gig in Gulf Shores, AL, sometime in the
mid 80's reminded me of a gig in Germany, years earlier, that I had
not thought of for a long time. Here goes.

This was one of the last gigs I did in Germany before shipping to
AFB East. I remember that because I had already turned in all my
horns, and my beloved drum kit, so when I was asked to sub on Bari
(I have no idea where Barb, our real Bari player was) that night I had
to dig up horns, oh and a Mess Dress. It was some sort of Dinning In
at some Army base. That's all I remember about the logistics. Almost
everything else I remember about that gig had to do with the
audience, well three members of the audience to be exact.

On like the second tune, normally a nice down dance thing, these
three young women who must have been sisters, dressed in almost
matching gowns, though the colors were; red, white and blue
respectively, that if you added up the material used for all three
gowns you would have had enough to clad one person discreetly. In
the case of these young ladies, the lack of material was a very
positive thing.

Guys started missing entrances left and right as soon as the wave of, "Oh, shit, did you see them babes" rippled through the band. I remember thinking to myself that if we had more of the Old School guys that were in the band when I first got there, we would have not even made it through the first set. But somehow, we did.

We were called to the kitchen by the leader, even though there was a tab for the band at the bar, for a pow-wow after the first set. There we were all appropriately reamed for our unprofessional behavior and informed the Article 15's would fly if that continued. Not knowing if I should laugh or frown, I think I just stood there hoping there would be enough time after the lecture to grab a beer and a smoke. That's when the tension was broken.

One of the younger troops spoke up; "Well, I don't know how it is with the Piano, but it's hard to play the Trombone with a major woody!" The whole band lost it, even the leader, I got my beer and smoke.

The second set was better, but not perfect. The third set was good musically, because the trio of babes was not present. I remember that specifically because that was all we could talk about at the break.

Then the finale was to come.

We opened the fourth set with something up, not a normal dance number, and only a handful of adventurous dancers took the floor. Fortunately, three of them were the Red, White and Blue Babes! For some reason the band did NOT loose it. Then one by one, those who had them started slipping on those mirrored GI type sunglasses. I never wished I had owned a pair until that night. Soon we resembled the Secret Service Dance Band but continued to play pretty well. Well, until we got to "String Of Pearls."

As most of you know, "String Of Pearls" kind of winds down near the end and there a few turnarounds that have piano fills in them. Well, thanks to the proximity of the babe in the blue dress to the piano player, none of those fills were played. In fact, the piano player/leader, completely stopped playing and simply admired the scenery for the rest of the tune. The lead Alto player had to cut it off.

Not missing a beat, our fearless leader in his mirrored sunglasses grabbed a mike, regained his composure and immediately asked for a round of applause for the dancers. He added that there was nothing more gratifying to a dance band then seeing a floor full of dancers enjoying themselves.

The trombone player who had lightened the mood earlier, then punctuated the evening by shouting: "We know what you mean, boss!"

Posted by Fred

2 comments:

Stephanie said...

> This post gives new meaning to "dress blues", "Devil with A Blue Dress On", "Hurray for the Red, White, and Blue" and "I Wear My Sunglasses at Night". ;)

Stephanie said...

> Oh! And I forgot one - "Lady In Red."

Flight Of The Sugar Plum Fairy

After completing Air Force basic training in San Antonio, TX at Lackland AFB, I made my way to the AFB East in Nov of 1981. The Band was in the Virgin Islands on TDY, so all was quiet for another week before the Band's return.

Shortly, thereafter, the Band began practicing music for the Band's Christmas concerts. I had auditioned for a vocal or keyboard slot in the Air Force Band career field, and had qualified for either duty. There was an opening for a keyboard player and a saxophone player at AFB East - the choice of station for both myself and my husband the sax player - so that's where we ended up after basic training.

My gig as a keyboardist would meet it's first challenge - being assigned my first solo concert band performance playing the "Dance of the Sugar Plum Fairy" - I used the celesta setting on the Band's YAMAHA synthesizer to simulate the 19th century instrument. Learning the part was nerve-racking! I had not had much experience at the time with synthesizers.

Rehearsals were complete and we were on stage for the first performance of "The Nutcracker Suite", of which "Dance of the Sugar Plum Fairy" was part.

Our illustrious commander at the time, came to the microphone to introduce the aforementioned movement that I was to solo on, and my hands were sweating, my forehead was sweating, and I was sure I would pass out before eight bars had passed. Our commander/conductor gave a little background on the celesta, including it's Parisian inventor, Mustel, who invented it in 1886, and that Tchaikovsky was the first major composer to use the instrument in a work - citing that Tchaikovsky flew over to Paris to obtain the instrument for use in the premier performance of "The Nutcracker" Suite in St. Petersburg in 1892.

Hmmmmm.... let me get this straight... the first successful airplane flight was achieved in 1903......... celesta invented in 1886........ "Nutcracker" premier performance in 1892.

Needless to say, it took eons and eons for our commander/conductor to live down this faux pas. This group of musicians of the AFB East never let a good faux pas go to waste.

The bright spot for me was that after this hilarious yarn was knitted for me at the concert, I was totally at ease for my performances of the "Dance"... Thanks so much to Col. K, one of my all-time favorite AF musicians, for being human .... and hilarious!!!!

Posted by Stephanie

2 comments:

Fred said...

> This was about six months or so before I got to AFB East, but it was legendary by the time I got there. I had the pleasure of working with Col. K. both in AFB East and AFB Overseas.

> I second your feeling for the Commander, Musician, and Human Being. One of a kind, and my friend!

Chris said...

> One of the most gentlemanly people I ever met!

3rd MOVEMENT:

AFTER THE SHOW

The Crown Prince

Occasionally band members were permitted to drive their personal vehicles during a road tour; particularly if family members lived near our destination. Houston was just such a case.

When the AFB West stage band found themselves inexplicably assigned to one of the premier hotels in Texas we found ourselves perplexed but resolute:

"Let's give them something to remember us by."

"Okay, what do you want to do?"

"Well, since we have our vehicles and a new movie camera let's . . "

A few afternoons later, after the band had finished performing for the day, a van pulled to a stop in front of the hotel. Larry got out of the driver's seat and began to set up a camera while Charley, dressed in a sport coat and tie, juggled a microphone while consulting a notepad.

In drips and drabs, band members began to approach from multiple directions to act as onlookers in order to draw a crowd. Eventually a fairly large number of innocent civilians gathered to witness the arrival of whatever celebrity or dignitary this news crew had been assigned to cover.

Then a big new Buick pulled slowly into the parking lot. Its headlights flashed on and off; from high beam to low beam. Band members dressed in sport coats and ties and sun glasses trotted alongside the vehicle.

When the car stopped in front of the main entrance Billy Bob alighted from the front passenger seat and opened the rear door. Ike got out. The dark-skinned bass player was dressed in flowing black robes and a huge pink turban.

As Larry ran the camera, Charley stuck a microphone in Ike's face.

"Prince Abnormal, welcome to America."

Billy Bob translated as Ike riffed in a strange, fictional language.

"The Prince say he is very happy to be in your beautiful country."

Charley pressed on. "Prince Abnormal, some have said that you know the meaning of life."

Billy Bob translated again. "The Prince say that the secret of life is petroleum, kid."

The moving party then crashed through the lobby doors in a maelstrom: news crew, Prince and his entourage, security agents, onlookers all gathered around a lobby couch where the interview continued.

Then a strange phenomenon developed. As our false security agents prowled the lobby they began to notice the room filling with large men wearing suits and sun glasses and communication devices. A woman was overheard barking into a lobby phone.

"I want to know what's going on and I want to know now!"

The heat in the room rose to a temperature that even interviewer Charley noticed.

"Well, Prince, thanks for your time. It's time to conclude the interview."

The AFB West stage band personnel walked nonchalantly to the main doors and then broke into a dead run, scattering in all directions.

The next day the Major pumped his Pentagon connections and discovered that the Premier of Russia was staying at the hotel while making a secret trip to the U.S.

The joint had been brimming with U.S. Secret Service agents.

Posted by Tom P.

Caribbean Joys

Anyone else remember "Captain Weekes' Seafood and Discount Liquors? The AFB East home away from home during the weeks surrounding Memorial Day from late 70s to 1984... the gravel floor slanted toward the street, of course; the amazing collection of ...stuff... hanging from the ceiling; dim lighting; HUGE Pina Coladas; cheap food; and a staff that lost count of the drinks ordered after a couple dozen.

More drunken foolishness there than anywhere else during the trips. Captain Weekes wouldn't open the liquor store part of the establishment until the morning we were due to leave, then he would give truly amazing prices on liquor and tobacco products... I think he was a smuggler, really.

The Caravelle Hotel on St. Croix, where every year some fool would jump into the pool from the balcony room overlooking it... the bar with the hole in the counter, into which at least one drunk would slip per year... burning out multiple blenders... hurricane party with Dixieland band.

Anyone else have VI stories? I'll post a major one from the last trip on Friday.

Posted by Chris

4 comments:

Fred said...

> Oh yeah! Marty and the whole in the bar. I think that may have been what made him give up drinking. Lol

Chris said...

> Could be... the funniest thing Marty did was forge a bar bill and sign a previous commander's name to it... we mailed him the bar tab the year after he left us and went to Scott... he may have paid it!

Chris said...

> I should have added "Fred Robinson playing the ride chorus from 'St. Thomas' on the sopranino recorder on a gig in Fredricksted" to the memories.

Sgt Flattop said...

> I remember promoting Capt Weekes to Major and pinning the Gold Oak Leaves to his T-shirt!

> BTW, all that "stuff" hanging from the ceiling in nets was just piled around on the gravel floor around the supporting pillars the first year I got down to St Croix in 78. By the next year that stuff had been moved to the top sides of the netting strung across the ceiling where it remained until the place burned down.

> I also remember the Island Alarm Clock which was the Virgin Island Seaplane Service's first flight of the day from Christianstead Harbor at 08:00. Just TRY to sleep late!

> And how many people did not notice that the "metal barriers" planted in concrete at the corners of the intersections of Christianstead were actually old cannons buried muzzles down?

Caribbean Joys, Pt. 2 – Late Night Larceny

For anyone who participated in the "Every Day's a Holiday" series of tours of the Caribbean with the AFB East back in the 70's and early 80's, the memories of "Captain Weekes'" still are strong. But many wonder, whatever happened to that wonderful establishment of cheap food, booze, and entertainment?

In November of 1984, the AFB East made what was to be its last trip to the VI. As the rear of the C-130 opened to allow the 80+ degree air into what was a very cold aircraft (8 hours in air-conditioned discomfort), one of our advance crew greeted the us with the statement, "Captain Weekes' burned down!" Needless to say, those of us who were veterans of this particular tour venue were crushed... not even the prospect of warm weather and free-flowing pina coladas could lift the black mood.

As luck would have it, that whole tour was seemingly cursed; between the afore-mentioned tragedy, and an inconvenient hurricane that caused three days worth of performances to be canceled - in some cases because the venue was no longer standing. Nothing seemed to go right. The only thing that remained constant was the hotel bar at the Caravelle and the frequent jam sessions that occurred after gigs.

One of these was a band "hurricane" party that started as a Dixieland band jam in the bar, and ended up as refuge when the storm hit and the lights went out. Fortunately, the bartender didn't actually need electricity to mix drinks, so with the help of a few strategically placed flashlight, the partying continued well into the wee hours. Only with the dawn did we realize just how bad the night had been.

The following two or three days were grim, as the entire island of St. Croix had been pretty well beaten up. Some of us helped out, as best we could, the merchants and citizens we had come to know over the years as they attempted to dig out and rearrange what the storm had FUBARed.

As the day approached that would end the tour, I was approached by a very good friend - everyone's favorite flat-topped senior NCO with an interesting proposal; liberation of the sign over the ruined building that had once housed "Captain Weekes' Seafood Restaurant and Discount Liquors." He figured that since the good Captain and his lady had returned to their native Martinique and since the island was in a shambles, that no one would miss the sign.

At the appointed hour he and I, appropriately dressed in all black, stealthily approached the ruined building, having parked a panel van a block or so away. The doorway to the old restaurant was covered with an iron grate, padlocked with a heavy chain. But the sign was still on the wall above the portal; a bit charred, but intact! After watching to make certain that no traffic was nearby, we ran across the street and up the grate, where the sign came away with us after only a couple of tugs to free it from the burned-out building. Success!

Giggling like a couple of idiots, we carried the sign to the panel van, scooted back to the hotel, unloaded the sign into my room which was on the ground floor, and retired for the night, as we were to load at o-dark-thirty the next morning.

In the morning, we were the first to meet the National Guard truck to load luggage, so we could put the sign on the bottom of the load, so as not to arouse the local citizenry - just in case. At the plane we hurried the load of our prize and so brought home the icon of so many trips.

When last seen, the sign was hanging in the same senior NCO's office back at AFB East. When he retired, the sign mysteriously disappeared... perhaps it still hangs in a place of honor.

To this day, I am still called "Commando H[*****]" by this friend, and partner-in-crime. I wouldn't have it any other way!

Posted by Chris

5 comments:

Fred said...

> I have been leaning towards more anonymity for those I have been writing about - after getting a couple of e-mails - and considering this was an actual heist I thought it particularly appropriate. Oh, and I have had personal experience with SMSgt Flattop expressing his concerns about Internet Security/Anonymity. So, having done his name, I thought it only appropriate to do yours too.

Chris said...

> Not at all... had I not been laughing as I wrote it, I would probably have done the same. Thanks, dude!

Stephanie said...

> As the late great Bob Hope would say,"Thanks for the memories"....

> Ah yes, "Capt. Weekes.... The PLACE to be for the ultimate lobster dinner and pina coladas, plus many other exotic Caribbean delights.... all served in a rustic setting of dirt floors and walls that are indescribable! It's still amazing that the Band toured there year after year, consuming edibles from said establishment without one report of chronic food poisoning... Ah yes, life is good! and so are the memories....

Sgt Flattop said...

> Well, I HAD to comment on THIS war story!

> All of it is completely, 100% true. Commando H***** has related most of the story, but he may not know that Capt Weekes' Great Wooden Coat Of Arms now resides in a secure location somewhere in AFB East and will be making an semi-public appearance on 18 Sept. 2010.

Fred said...

> Wow...

Caribbean Joys, Pt. 3 – the True Fuel of the Band

The exploits of the band trips to the Virgin Islands are legendary, if only to the participants; the question that kept popping into my mind, even after four trips, was "How do some of these people do this day in and day out?"

As with all of the "Every Day's a Holiday" trips, Demon Rum played a major part in the diet of most bandsmen during the rigorous schedule of the concerts and parades surrounding the Veteran's Day holiday. There was the never-still blender in the bar at the Hotel Caravelle, our base of operations; the never-ending variety of sponsored meals, parties, and cookouts, all with their obligatory bar, complete with absent-minded bartender, who could not remember that a jigger is only1.5, NOT 3 ounces of rum.

But, by far, the largest single contribution to the deterioration of so many livers and brain cells was the annual trip to Buck Island. This day-long outing to a beautiful wilderness area, surrounded by a top-notch underwater national wildlife preserve, complete with snorkeling tours, would usually begin at 0800 at the docks on St. Croix. The whole group, some 40 strong, would embark on a catamaran sailer large enough to hold all, plus crew, plus necessities (booze). The able crew made a semi-famous rum punch that, as the day wore on, could eventually buckle the knees of an ox... I think they just kept pouring rum into the keg, rather than the other ingredients! Most of us were sober when the boat departed, but hurried to remedy that poor condition as soon as humanly possible, with the helpful crew's assistance, of course. One of our number, though, usually arrived at the pier thoroughly toasted, as he was deathly afraid of the water, but refused to miss the party. This little guy, drummer in one of the rock bands, couldn't swim a lick, but after a healthy dose of liquid courage, staggered to the docks and boarded the cat for the island. There he would reinforce his courage level steadily as the cruise proceeded, until it came time to disembark at our destination. Here was presented the first major problem of his condition - the cat was anchored some 15 yards offshore because of the rocks, and we had to wade or swim ashore, depending on personal preference or physical size. Our hero was gifted with neither preference for the water, nor size to do anything about it. Never ones to abandon comrades, our hearty lads came up with a simple solution - carry the hapless hero ashore on shoulders. Alas, by this point, our hero was too far in his cups to sit upright of his own volition, so we convinced him to lie as stiff as he could, and we carried him ashore like a 95 pound surfboard, a foot above the water's surface, until he could touch dry land, there to stagger off to the tables where the feast was set up for lunch.

On the trip back, the transfer was much more simple, as our hero was toes-up, passed out, limp as a dishrag. I threw him over my shoulder and carried him like a sack of potatoes back to the boat. He blissfully slept all the way home, where he and the other casualties were helped from the craft, and guided back to the hotel.

After seeing this the first time, I realized that I was in the company of professionals, and never doubted my comrades' ability again!

Posted by Chris

4 comments:

Fred said...

> I concur 100% with the distinguished gentleman from Georgia on this. But, if I may add (of course I can, this is MY Blog).

> Chris was not kidding about the size of the protagonist of his post. 95 pounds and easily transportable as a shoulder loaf, for someone as formidable as Chris, truly describes the drummer's almost "elfin" physique (sorry, I couldn't resist). The only thing left out about the guy was that he was a KICK ASS drummer, when sober.

> Chris was also truthful in his characterization of the way the fantastic local rum (hey, I am a beer drinker, and I loved it) was freely distributed. But, I think he may have forgotten that the islands not only had there own "Time" (concerts started when they started not necessarily when the program said they would) but they also had their own system of measure. For example, the pint glass I procured from Green Dolphin Street, a local St. Croix club that regularly featured Jimmy Hamilton, holds almost 2.5 bottles of beer - or close to 30 ounces – trust me, I still use that glass - while a US pint is supposed to be 16 ounces and the Sterling Pint is supposed to be 20 ounces. So, I assume the proper jigger size in the islands would be 3 ounces, or more.

> Come to think of it, I can't remember any of the bartenders there using jiggers. Then again I actually can't remember much that involved a bartender there. Burp.

Chris said...

> I stand corrected, sir! Honestly, I don't think I ever saw a
> jigger, or even a pony, used there, either. if you said, "Two
> fingers" of liquor, chances were better than even that the
> bartender would measure from the top, rather than the side
> with his fingers... I do remember the Pints; I figured them for
> an Imperial pint until I had a real Imperial in Bull Feeney's in
> Portland, ME. Green Dolphin's were closer to a liter.

Fred said...

> Those were the good old days, but fortunately, these are the
> good old days too! I need to post something recent next.

Tom P. said...

> My gig at the Ford-Carter Hotel runs a couple of more weeks
> but I look forward to your postcards from the 21st-century.

Consequences

Oh where would this Blog be without the gift of alcohol.

Chinese Proverb (Thought to be from The Lost I Ching).

There was once an incident on the beer-soaked AFB West bus that
was so twisted and beyond the carrying capacity of even the hard
and bitter wiring of readers of TBOTB that there is nothing more to
add other than that the lieutenant:

Banned Alcohol From The Bus.

It was a noble effort on the part of the young lion and as can be
imagined the troops of the AFB West stage band arrived the next
week at our South Texas hotel sober and bewildered.

"Now what do we do?"

Rather than surrender to the normal reflex that would have involved invading a local gin mill it was decided that we should not pass up the opportunity to explore this new state of being.

"Why don't we go over to that field and have a football game?"

"Okay, how do you want to work it?"

"Let's have Blacks and Mexicans versus Whites in a full-tackle game."

"That sounds like a good idea."

Sure. What could possibly go wrong.

I nearly missed the opening kick-off because I was stuffing hotel towels under my tee-shirt to simulate the shoulder pads that I hoped would shorten my stay in Intensive Care. But I did catch most of the pre-game Knute-Rockne pep talk:

"Men, what you are about to witness here is a perfect example of the Law of Unintended Consequences. Back when we could drink on the bus we would stagger to our rooms and pass out. Now, after we get through killing each other in this football game the lieutenant is going to wish he had a full bar on the bus."

Eventually the game ended and the aftermath looked like the denouement of the Battle of Bunker Hill. All we needed was a little boy with a drum.

As predicted by the wise man, all it took was two sprained ankles, a wrenched back and a wrecked knee to open up the beer taps aboard Challenger One.

Posted by Tom P.

1 comment:

Fred said...

Oh the pains the Enlisted folks would go through to keep our Officers in line.

Feel the Love

No matter the affection and respect you can't get along all the time. During an argument one bandsman said what he really felt:

"I can stand people who are stupid. I can stand people who are ugly. I can stand people who are fat and I can stand people who are white. But I can't stand all four wrapped in one."

Posted by Tom P.

Poolside

After another tough day in the salt mines playing two forty-minute shows on the road it was time for R&R at the motel pool.

Tim did well taking off his shoes and socks at pool edge but ran into trouble from the peanut gallery as he rolled up his pants legs:

"That's no way to take off your pants. You have to start at the top."

One of the trombone players walked by carrying a glass of straight Scotch and the pool rats gave him an earful also.

"If the real Mel was here he'd be in the water."

Mel never broke stride as he held up his glass and said:

"I never drink the chaser first."

Posted by Tom P.

1 comment:

Fred said...

Sometimes no comment is the best comment. Lol.

The Happy Wanderer

The AFB Overseas had a gig in Stuttgart, Germany in September of 1981 to celebrate the U. S. Air Force's anniversary. It was at the Stuttgart Opera House, one of the finest acoustic halls I ever played. We were splitting sets with another band, though I don't remember if they were German or American, for that gig. The way the rotation ended up was that the other band was on stage for the finale, the playing of Happy Birthday, so that our guys and gals could snake through the caverns beneath this 200 year old building so that we could enter through the back of the hall to play a Dixie Land version which ended together with all the players on stage.

Very cool, except where was sax player Walter?

The logistics of the deal was that we were led to a pair of tunnels; one back stage left and the other back stage right. We were told to take the tunnel all the way to the end and it would open into the lobby, where we could make our entrance through the same doors the audience used. I don't know about the tunnel I was not in, but the instructions worked for me in mine.

We did not miss the sax player until we were packing up and getting ready to go back to the hotel. It was determined that because we were staying only a few blocks away we would blow off searching for him and just expect him to find his own way home. Well, I should have not implied me into that we. I was not in any sort of management position at that time in my career, though I had fronted a few maneuvers and pranks.

So we got back to the hotel, changed, grabbed our "Groovies," term used to describe the currency of whatever country you were in at the moment, or for example there were German Groovies, Italian Groovies, French Groovies, etc., and headed out on the town. Oh, still no Walter.

Stuttgart was not a real US GI town so you did have to know a little German to get around. But about half the band spoke pretty good German and the rest of us had gotten to the point that we could order beer, find the bathroom and ask for directions to the train station though we normally would not have understood the answer to the last one. It was easy for me. I was in love with a dish called Jaeger Schnitzel and preferred Pilsner. Oh, and putting your knees together and pointing to your crotch looking distressed normally got you directed to the bathroom.

We were a few beers into the after eating part of the night when somebody at our table, which was right in front of the big window to the street, pointed and said, "Here comes the Happy Wanderer." And, sure enough, there was Walter in full uniform, clarinet in hand walking up the street towards our hotel. Somebody got up as if to go get him, but was quickly pulled back into their seat. Instead, we simply sat there and sang, "Val-deri, Val-dera, Val-deri, Val-deraha-ha-ha-ha-ha..." until we were asked to leave. Hey, they were nice about it though. As I was leaving I still had about a half of a beer left. The waitress handed it to me and gestured that I take it and get out. I still have that mug!

Posted by Fred

That Other Bari Player

Back in 1986 or maybe 1987, the AFB East got booked at the Hollywood Jazz Festival. I was tempted to put a bunch of blank lines so you would have to pause before reading, Hollywood, FL, not CA, but I am trying to keep this post short. It was indeed the Florida one.

Also on the bill for that festival was Nick Brignola. I had never heard of Nick until the year before when we got to catch him, along with Pacito De Rivera and Buddy De Franco at the Pensacola Jazz Festival. I immediately became a major fan and eventually a disciple!

I was on sound that trip, and Tim was covering the Bari book. Tim was not a shy fellow. So, when he ran into Nick in the back of the band-shell staging area, he struck up a conversation with him. For some reason Tim mentioned that we had a Bari player from Upstate NY too (Nick was from Troy, I was born in Schenectady, though I moved away when I was 5). I guess Tim must have pointed me out to him through the crowd at that time.

A short time later, I was in that back stage area and saw Nick like 10 yards away. I would never have dreamed of going over and talking to him. In fact it scared me feces-less when we made eye contact and he gestured for me to come over. I froze and just made some silly face but could not move. So, Nick walked right over to me and said, "I understand you're the other Bari player from Upstate" and reached out and shook my hand. All I could say was, "Yeah, I guess so." Then he said, "I gotta split. I hope I can catch your set later. Oh, and why don't you join us at that bar over there around 10:00" pointing to this place just down the street. "Foster's band (The Basie band) is gonna play and some of us are gonna jam. Wanna come?" My nervous system had shut down to the point that all I could say was, "Sure." He said, "See you there."

I got a few of the other guys to go, so I might have somebody to catch me if I fainted, and we got there just as the band was starting. We grabbed a table or two and I finally calmed down. Well, mostly because I was having my first beer, and I didn't see Nick anywhere. A few minutes later here comes Nick carrying a tenor gig bag. And he walked right over, pulled up a chair, said, "Hi Fred" and started introducing himself to the others. He was just a normal guy (well, a normal guy who just happened to be one of the 10 best Bari players ever born, in my humble opinion). He even had complements for everybody there, he had obviously dug our set, and the band DID play well that night.

He hung, we drank, he jammed, he hung, we drank. Awesome evening. As he was splitting, he pulled out a business card and scribbled something on the back, handed it to me and said, "Hell, tell your Chief I'd like to do a gig with you guys some time" and walked quietly into the night. We did get to work with Nick the following year. More posts on that layer.

Coda: I didn't read what Nick had written on the back of his card until the next day. I flipped it over and there he had clearly written "Dyslexics Untie!" My roommate ask what that was, so I handed it to him and he cracked up, clearly and loudly pronouncing the correct words correctly as he read it. Needless to say, I seldom get spelling based jokes right away. But, once I heard it, I cracked up to. Then it was time to reuntie with Nick back at the festival.

Posted by Fred

2 comments:

Stephanie said...

> Wow Fred! What a memory! I wish I had been at the performance! Or was I?......

Fred said...

> No, You were not at the Basie gig, if that's what you meant. The reason I remember that was because Nick asked where you were. lol

Peer Review

I like to think that after 35 years this sign is still taped to a wall in the AFB West Band Hall:

> These light switches are dedicated to Larry P***.
> He hasn't worked in months either.

Posted by Tom P.

1 comment:

Fred said...

> Tom, that sign was still there when I left to join you with AFB Overseas in 1979.

A Foreign Affair

Who doesn't love it when your moderator talks French? (FWS #7)

The AFB Overseas marching band had just completed a parade through the streets of Mulhouse, France. Circumstances forced our return bus ride to follow the parade route where large and enthusiastic crowds continued to cheer us as we rode a raggedy Crown Coach toward our home base. The band's wacky bassoonist, who had probably been advised to play cymbals or triangle or some damn thing, decided that it was a good and appropriate time to force open a window and deliver an address to the nation:

People of France!

We are here to collect the war debt.

Pay or Die.

Posted by Tom P.

Bassoon Redux

The diplomat-bassoonist from "A Foreign Affair" surfaced for a second memorable call on the sovereign soil of another Euro-Pal a few months later. While navigating a tight corner on a Belgium military installation our driver required assistance and shouted to the back of the bus to ask if there was anything behind us. Luckily bassoon-boy was in a perfect position to help:

"No. Go ahead. It's only a Belgian jeep."

Miffed that the line failed to get a chuckle our guy turned to see a wall of stoney faces staring at him - plus one other face - that of the Belgian base commander who was sitting next to our major in the front row.

Posted by Tom P.

FWS #8 & 8a:
Deux for the Price of Un

After reading, and thoroughly enjoying Tom's "Bassoon Redux" I paused for a while to contemplate bassoon-boy's soon to be cult status. Then my mind drifted a bit to the left where I smirked about the similarity of the words Redux and Rodox. While most of you probably did not have to Google Redux, my guess is that a lesser number would be familiar with Rodox.

Rodox was a Danish porn magazine from the 70's, which I was surprised to find out, only moments ago, is still in business. So other than being two syllable words that start with an "R" and end in an "X" Rodox is also the Color Climax Corporation's magazine that specializes in Retro-porn, hence the correlation to "bringing back."

One evening in Germany, maybe 1981, while my wife was off gallivanting in Italy with one of her girlfriends from work, I paid a visit to my favorite Full Featured Adult Bookstores in K-town. Having a rather conspicuous vehicle I chose to park in the back lot rather than in front of the store. The rear entrance led to a very narrow hallway that connected the main magazine area to the private viewing booths which featured both 8 mm film loops and live dancing girls.

I followed that hallway to the magazine area, where Rodox was proudly displayed, and browsed until Jacob - yes, I went in often enough that I knew the guy behind the counter by his first name said "Buy or fly my friend." Having only US currency on me (and Jacob's exchange rate was not very good) I decided to head on out. As I was entering the hallway someone was exiting a booth and heading in my direction. After a few steps I recognized him and it soon became evident that he recognized he me. As we squeezed past each other I said "'Evenin' Captain." He replied "Good Evening Sergeant." Nothing more was ever said and we continued on our separate ways.

It didn't occur to me until I was about half way home that running into your Deputy Commander in an adult book store could be a career enhancing event. Within a few weeks I was nominated for the NCO of the quarter and put up for a Below the Zone Promotion.

Numéro deux:

I don't know the details, but this is too similar to pass up.

Some of the guys, and gals, from the AFB East were hanging out in an adult bar somewhere in Florida one night. Why I was not there, I don't know. During their stay another bandsman, well I should say the uber-bandsman – the commander, walked in and took a table not all that close to the stage and started sipping on his beer.

Like I said, I don't have the details but as I understand it there was eventually a moment of acknowledgment, like a wave or something, between the commander and his subordinates. I think I remember hearing that he stayed even after the guys and gals all split.

To make this a bit more fun, that commander had a reputation of being a Teetotaler and a God Squad type.

Qui est le prochain?

Posted by Fred

4 comments:

Stephanie said...

>Help me out Fred, was this Commander "Iron Man," prior to him or post?

Fred said...

>A former French Horn player that you knew...

Stephanie said...

>Okay, I remember now.....

KF said...

>He was just making sure everyone behaved themselves!

The Party

Once upon a time...

There were these young men who were stationed at Strategic Air Command (SAC) headquarters near Omaha, Nebraska. For young men from all over the United States there wasn't a lot to do in Nebraska, but during one particular summer there was even less than usual to do.

It so happened that a General picked up the phone one June day and ordered a world wide "alert". For five days bombers orbited at key locations around the globe, and tankers flew missions night and day to keep them fueled and airborne. When it was all over the powers that were called it a huge success, and there was much mutual admiration among the upper echelons as they congratulated themselves on their preparedness for the prophesied "War" to come.

As the handshaking and ritual grimacing started to wear off, however, the realization started to sink in that SAC had spent its entire budget for the fiscal year, and no further funds were to be had until October. It seems no one had thought of that.

The rest of that summer was a skimpy one at SAC. when a form, or piece of equipment was out of supply, no replacement was to be had for five months. The motor pool had barely enough fuel for day to day needs, and all activities were curtailed severely. For the young men in the SAC band the upshot of all this was that all gigs out of town were canceled until the new fiscal year, in October.

With lots of free time, and not much to do, entertainment had to be improvised. Fortunately the base liquor store was a short walk from the barracks, and beer was very affordable. As with most good parties, this one wasn't planned, but started spontaneously, and just sort of happened...

On this particular Sunday morning, after arising late and contemplating the limited options available on a Sunday in Nebraska, these particular young men decided that beer and music were the thing for today's agenda. So, while a couple of them made the short walk to the liquor store, the others brought a stereo system out onto the front porch of the building, and got Led Zeppelin playing for all to hear. Each room had a mini fridge, so one of these was brought out to the porch to ameliorate the tedious walking to the beer and back.

At this point it might be appropriate to describe the barracks building in this story. It was built at the turn of the twentieth century as the hospital for Fort Crook, a cavalry post at the time. The basement contained the band hall for the SAC band, and this basement protruded about five feet or so above ground level. The first floor, above the band hall, was a dozen rooms for the band members who lived on base. The rest of the first floor, and all of the second floor was given over to the squadron whose job it was to work in "the hole" and program computers for SAC. Each story had twelve foot ceilings and there was an attic with a sharply pitched roof, with gables. This made the very top of the roof about forty feet high.

The stereo that was brought out onto the front porch was a very good one, with a Crown 300 watt amplifier, and JBL speakers. Nevertheless, it was decided that an improvement was possible. In the band hall, which was only a flight of stairs down, were the large speakers used by the bands on gigs. These speakers, in conjunction with the 300 watt Crown amplifier would enable anyone within several hundred yards to enjoy (or not) the music emanating from the front porch.

Now as it happened the band building was just across the street from the security police headquarters building, and just about 50 yards from the base church. At this base church worshiped the twenty-three generals and one bird colonel who lived across the parade grounds from the band hall. At some point, early in the afternoon, the security police dropped by to ask that the music be turned down, as the churchgoers couldn't hear the choir over the Led Zeppelin and Cream coming from the band building porch. They were very nice about it, and with a smile and a shrug, the music was turned down until the police car was at least 50 feet away.

Two or three more times the police returned to admonish and entreat with the young men to reduce the volume, each time in a less friendly manner. Each time assurances were made and the volume was promptly restored to its previous level, or perhaps a bit more. Additional trips to the liquor store were made during the course of the afternoon, and additions were made to the population on the front porch, as the band hall was on the direct route to the chow hall.

During the course of the day it seems that some property damage was incurred in the form of broken doors, damaged Sheetrock, and most importantly the padlock on the band hall door was torn loose when the door was kicked in to procure the speakers. This last was gratuitous damage, because everyone in the band knew the combination, but impatience combined with alcohol made a more direct entry seem advisable at the time.

The next morning, at some hour best left for cow milking and such Nebraskan activities, one of the young men ventured downstairs for a Coke from the dispenser at the entrance to the band hall. Upon hearing voices at the bottom of the stairs, he paused, and listened before proceeding further. It so happened that the respectable big band, under the auspices of the colonel himself, was getting together for a gig when they found the band hall had been broken into. They promptly called the security police, who promptly took fingerprints from the door and related areas.

The next morning, also at some hour best left to those who enjoy such times, the young men were summarily hauled out of bed and called to the colonel's office.

The colonel was a very nice man, who wanted to pursue his career in quiet obscurity until he could retire to a quiet, obscure life in the suburbs. The last thing he wanted was to get phone calls from generals about the conduct of young men under his purview. This was a catastrophe and he was going to let the fecal matter proceed downhill in the tradition of military organizations from time immemorial.

Now occurred a maneuver seldom rivaled in the annals of military history. The colonel paced to and fro with his hands clasped behind his back and "read the riot act" to the young men for twenty minutes. This was not something he enjoyed doing, but he felt that he had no choice. As unpleasant as it was, there would have to be "consequences."

Then one of the young men, a bit older and more sanguine than the rest, stepped forward and came to attention. He said in a clear and reasonable voice: "Colonel, nobody here had anything to do with what happened last Sunday." The colonel visibly relaxed and said "Well, good, then go on and forget it." It was the answer he had been dying to hear. He called his superiors and said "It wasn't my boys."

Of course this story is a fable, and these things couldn't happen in a modern, well disciplined military unit.

Posted by Jim

5 comments:

Fred said...

> AWESOME, Jim! Welcome aboard. Next time some space between the paragraphs? Lol

Tom P. said...

> Ignore him, Jim, he just works here. Keep 'em coming.

Stephanie said...

> Fred is of course, the ultimate authority, on proper syntax, punctuation, sentence form and other hierarchies of English etiquette... not to mention spelling... take heed, my man lol!

> Just kidding, Fred. Don't go changin' to try and please me.... I love you just the way your are....

Fred said...

> English? This is English? I thought this was Oolia-koo-shabop? My bad. But man, I just need some space. Can you dig it? Oh, and Steph, Jim is a grunt friend just like you and

Fred said... (cont.)

me.

Also the best F@#$%n Bass Trombone player I ever played with! He can take it!!!

Stephanie said...

I can dig it! Look forward to more words of wisdom from Jim!

Fred's War Story #4:
"A True Turkey"

What's with me and food analogies? Appropriate yet again...

The AFB Overseas made a trip to Turkey in 1981 with stops in Ankara and Istanbul. We were sponsored by the Military Government and had one traveling sponsor who was an full Bird Colonel named "Attila" – or maybe we just called him that. Then there was the Lt./Translator who wanted to write an American Slang Dictionary, which our folks graciously helped out with by providing bogus definitions of true slang terms/phrases or by just making stuff up altogether. I bet it was a successful book, knowing the contributors.

Anyway, I think I kept my nose clean in Ankara but when we got to Istanbul . . .

Attila and the Lt. took us to the Topkapi Palace one afternoon. In one of the rooms there was this spectacular wall carving of the Arabic Alphabet, which the Lt. described in lavish detail with such pride it almost made me feel guilty for having fed him a bogus definition for "Road Apples" only minutes before. Perhaps I was clouded by that guilt when this happened, but as soon as he finished his spiel, I raised my hand (hey, I did go to Catholic school and this was an official military formation, of sorts) and respectfully asked "What do your Arabic Numerals look like?"

There was absolute silence. Even those who didn't speak English must have sensed the stupidity that had just gushed from my lips. All eyes were on me for what felt like an eternity, probable a second or two, and then Dave B. did another pratfall and everything was OK.

Well, OK, Dave didn't do another pratfall but I needed something to get me off the hook there.

I was actually so embarrassed that I don't remember the rest of the day, and I had not yet had an EFES (local bear) or a Raki (local White Lightning masquerading as a liquorish liquor), though I am sure I had more than one of each later that day.

Bill C. is now free to post the "Swab" story...

Posted by Fred

Applied Mathematics

It would be unfair to let your moderator choke on his Turkey sandwich alone (FWS #4).

The great saxophonist Paul Desmond sadly never finished his book whose working title was taken from a question posed by an airline flight attendant:

"How many of you are there in a quartet?"

Posted by Tom P.

2 comments:

Fred said...

> When I moved to California my daughters were still young enough so that a visit to Disney Land was appropriate when they first came to visit.

Fred said... (cont.)

> So there was daddy and his girls wondering through the park and we came across the famous strolling saxophone quintet, The Firehouse Five. They were not playing that that moment and I could only see three of them from where I was. So I strolled over and spoke to the Soprano player. I mentioned that I used to play and whatever and asked where the others were (only Soprano, Tenor and Bari present and accounted for). Without any hesitation he said "This is it."

> Her turned his back to me so I could clearly see Firehouse Five in large elaborately embroidered letters on the back of his shirt and untucked it so I could see the addendum he had added, in Sharpie, to the tail: MINUS TWO.

> I hope that guy only did that because I told him I used to play. I would hate to think that was normal Disney protocol.

Stephanie said...

> Seriously Fred, I think I would ask for a partial refund of the cost of my entry ticket.

Rise and Fall of the CD

I was with the AFB Overseas in the late 70's when one of the french horn players was able to procure one of the earliest compact disc players and a small collection of CDs.

None of the band members had ever heard this new technology although most of us had followed its development.

A large number of us gathered in a dorm room that was equipped with top-of-the-line speakers and a magnificent amplifier. The compact disc player was plugged in and a CD was inserted. It may have been the Berlin Philharmonic but I don't remember now. Anyway, we listened with our musician's ears to hear how the future would sound.

The sound was as pristine as advertised. We continued to listen carefully in silence.

Furtively at the outset and then more openly, we began to look at each other. Then the bravest among us said what we were all thinking:

"CDs suck."

We didn't understand at the time that digital technology removes the chordal overtones that give music its depth and body and color and warmth. To us the cold, metallic compact disc sound was joyless and empty.

We filed out of the room and returned to listen to our vinyl records.

Posted by Tom P.

Spy Games

Back in the Cold War days the AFB Overseas took the troop train through occupied East Germany to the free city of West Berlin for a series of concerts.

While walking along a road next to U.S.-controlled Tempelhof Airport some of the players spotted a car with Russian license plates parked next to a military office building. One of the car's occupants was taking photographs. The players were alarmed and notified a nearby Air Force security policeman.

"Yeah, we know," said the cop. "They can't see anything from there so we let them take all the pictures they want. It makes them feel like they're doing something."

Posted by Tom P.

The Field Of Battle

Don't get too excited about some sort of combat situation being discussed here. The "field" here is a small diamond shaped piece of dirt in the middle of a bunch of grass containing four bases, each spaced approximately 60 feet apart .

Tom P. made a couple of observation about things like how we can understand what makes a person join the military and what makes a person become a musician, while combining those two is hard to fathom. He also mentioned things about what happens when you get groups of like musicians, saxophone players, trombone players, trumpet players, etc. together and what they are likely to do (I loved that post). What he left out was the part about GI musicians mostly just being Team Players. Here are a few short stories about AF musicians in uniform working together while never playing a note.

August, 1978, AFB West. I had been in the Air Force for like no time (Been in all day, like it just fine) and for some reason I got invited to join the guys playing softball. There is no way that they could have known that I loved baseball, although had played very little softball before, so I was thrilled. So I showed up at the appointed time with an A-2000 wearing blue jeans and a t-shirt.

The team sucked. We were down like 5 runs in the second inning when Speedy called me from the bench and asked where I played. I told him that I was mostly a catcher but had played some outfield and third base. So, the next inning I went in at third.

For those of you who may not have ever played Slow-pitch Softball, there is NOTHING more embarrassing than striking out, except maybe being called out on strikes. So, that's how I introduced myself to the team. Three pitches, three misses, walk to the bench.

Somebody commented on my way to the bench, that perhaps I should try not to suck so hard the next time. Everybody, even me laughed.

I never had to field a ball in that game and we got killed. But, after the game Speedy asked me if I had fun. I could only say yes. He said

something like, "Good. It's all about the team and having fun."
Ladies and gentleman, that is also the unwritten motto of GI Bands.

July, 1980, right behind the AFB Overseas Band Hall stood the
headquarters for the base liquor store and the Mental Health Clinic
(were they trying to tell us something?). Just to the south of those
three buildings was an overgrown, under-maintained softball field.
One day, my wife and I decided that we wanted to play some ball
she was a much better ball player than I - so we decided to spruce up
the field and invite the guys to play ball on the following Sunday. By
the way, the AFB Overseas was not allowed to play any sports in the
base intramural leagues due to the fear of getting hurt. Fortunately,
this was not a sanctioned AF activity. So we spruced the field the
best we could and invited people, mostly band people but some
others too.

The first Sunday was not a major success, I don't think we had
enough people for two teams. But we had fun. So, we decided to do
it again on the next Sunday. Well, it grew and grew (perhaps in part
because we drank a lot of beer as we played). After a year or so, we
had people who could not even get in the game because there were
just too many people that wanted to play.

Note: The MVP of that experience was a young German guy, Klaus,
who had never even seen a softball until he came out with his sister,
who was dating one of our trumpet players at the time. Just a natural.
I understand he also later became a Polizei Bandsman later. Good
team player.

Fall of 1992, AFB East, Field 1. This was to be my last softball game
I would play in the USAF. It was what we called "Fall Ball" meaning
that not all the serious squadrons fielded teams but we got to play.

In about the third inning of that game I found myself at third base, I
have no idea how I got there. At that point, whoever was batting, hit
a soft pop-up to left field. I don't know what possessed me but I
tagged up and sprinted (slug-like) to the plate. In USAF Softball
there was the unwritten law of: "Go down, go around or give it up"
meaning never consider colliding with an opponent in order to gain a
base. Well the ball got to the catcher before I got to the plate. I

attempted all three of those options. What ended up happening was a safe call and blood squirting from my left knee as I jumped up triumphantly to run to the dugout, collapsing as soon as I hit my left leg.

I got back up before the guys could come get me, which they did try to do, and hobbled over to my teammates who really looked worried.

I have to tell you I had VSI (Variable Separation Incentive) paperwork in at that time so I was kind of a lame-duck dude by then but the guys, even those who I would not have considered close personal friends, who rushed out to see if I was OK didn't see it that way. While I contemplated passing out somebody from the stands shouted, "I bet you a case of Old Mil' - my beer of preference at that time - it takes 20 stitches to close that up." My buddies helped me to the bench. I asked that somebody get me a shit load of napkins from the concession stand and reached into my ball-bag for the roll of duct-tape that I knew was there. A few minutes later I was back out on the field all taped up and wishing for the first time in my life that I was not playing catcher, squatting on a ripped up knee sucks.

When the game was over somebody took me to the Base Hospital (more of a clinic). There I met Airman Barnes, a rather attractive young female one-striper med-tech who was going to take care of me. As she was irrigating my wound, I asked her what she thought about stitches. She said that I was going to need quite a few. I asked if it would be more than 20. She said, "If the Major does it, yeah. I could do it in 15."

To make a long story shorter, I had to sign a form that said it was OK for a Med-tech to stitch me but she did it. Soon I limped out of the room with 15 stitches in my left knee. Moments later I exited the rear of the RAFB Hospital and there was my team. Almost everybody who had played that night was there. When you added in the wives and kids, I would say there must have been like maybe 30 people. I was gassed. Somebody shouted "Did you win the bet?" Fortunately he caught me before I got overwhelmed and all I could say was, "Yup, 15." We all split to drink beer at the Rec-Center as the kids played the pin-pall machines and ate pizza.

Coda: She paid up, I got my case of beer, though I gave it to Airman Barnes. Klaus WAS the correct pick for MVP. And, finally, Speedy was right. I really is all about "Team" and "Having Fun."

Posted by Fred

Limited Time Only

It must have been a slow day at the AFB Overseas three-story dormitory . One of the players put a commercial "For Sale" sign on an outside wall with the phone number to the base commander's office.

We were told that the commander's office fended off calls for weeks from local civilians wanting to buy the property.

Posted by Tom P.

What A Class Act!

While working on the RCCL Ship, the Sovereign of the Seas in 1993 & 1994, I had the pleasure of getting to know the resident Gaucho (Argentinean Cowboy/Cowgirl) group. That was the kind of an act the ships were made for. They sang, danced BIG Flamenco style, River Dance kind of stuff, played with Bolas, the Argentinean Killer Yo-yos, and told jokes in broken English even though none of them had even a slight accent, off stage. They were the only act on the ships that I looked forward to every time they performed.

One day the lead Gaucha (female Gaucho?) found me someplace on the ship and asked me to do two charts for them, one would be a dance number the house band would play as they splintered the stage with their fancy boots. The other for Tenor Guitar, South American flute, three Field Drums and STB vocals.

I was honored. So the Gaucha handed me these well copied lead sheets and I toddled off to the pit with my headphones and some score paper to get to work. I had the charts done the next day and gave them to the head Gaucho after the show that night.

It turned out he knew nothing about the charts, I guess his wife had circumvented the Gaucho Chain Of Command. He wasn't really mad, just that kind of annoyed you can only get at your spouse. So, he said, "We will have to rehearse this one before we can except it" pointing to the one that they had to play on. So, we stuck around until the room cleared out and gathered in the first few rows of seats where the parts were handed out. I talked them through what I had attempted to do and explained a few pieces of notation that they were not familiar with.

Then they all put their parts down in their chairs and went up on stage and NAILED it the first time! They had Sight Memorized 172 bars of music in like 5 minutes! I was so blown away, I gave them the charts for free. They were so pleased at my prices that they had a six-pack of ice cold Becks, the best the crew bar had to offer, delivered to my cabin every night until I finally got off that ship, about two months later. What a Class Act!

Posted by Fred

Horror Show

The film "The Exorcist" was rampaging across America on its first run and tearing jagged holes in the nervous psyches of an unsuspecting public.

We had a player who was known to have one of those delicate nervous constitutions and it was conjectured that he would be a shattered, whimpering shell of a human being after seeing the movie. Naturally it was decided that he should be scared some more.

Breaking into a room of our World War two-era barracks did not present a challenge. Larry had no problem entering Mitch's room and positioning himself behind the refrigerator with his jaw resting on top of the box. He arranged some knick-knacks around his face and waited for the victim.

As expected, Mitch nervously entered the room and paced about a jangled wreck.

Then he saw, floating above the refrigerator, a twisted, evil grin and heard a demonic laugh.

Posted by Tom P.

With Friends Like These

After Mitch from "Horror Show" declawed himself from the ceiling he immediately began to plot his revenge.

He broke into Larry's room where he replaced green mouthwash with green shampoo.

The next day was Larry's assigned day to answer the phones at the band hall office and many would stop by to ask how his breath was that day.

"Shiny and manageable" was the usual reply.

The strange thing was that he began to receive non-stop calls from women asking him about his new shampoo.

He couldn't understand it until one of the band members mentioned that while driving into work he saw the huge electronic sign next to the highway at the megamall repeatedly flashing the band hall phone number along with the message:

"Ask Larry **** about his new shampoo."

Posted by Tom P.

Didn't See That Coming

One night an Air Force guitarist got drunk and fell down a flight of stairs bruising his arm so badly that he couldn't play for a week. His supervisor wrote him up for damaging government property.

Posted by Tom P.

Don't Ask, Don't Puke

The AFB Overseas was on a trip to Athens, Greece (yeah, tough gig...) and were at a reception one night. I was standing there with one of the guys munching on these hors d'oeuvres that kind of looked like strange Pigs-in-a-blanket, he had wolfed down about a dozen and I had about six at that point. Then my buddy grabbed one of our sponsors and asked him, "What is this stuff? It's wonderful!"

The sponsor paused for a second, to gather his translation I suspect, and said, "Marinated Goat spleen wrapped in intestine." My friend puked on the sponsor, I got the rest of those hors d'oeuvres all to myself.

Posted by Fred

2 comments:

Stephanie said...

> This story could have been copied/pasted into the Virgin Islands archives of the AFB East. I think every reception with refreshments provided in the V.I. by locals was accompanied by food simply tagged as "meat", (meaning some part of a goat) simply fill in the blank... as desired!

Sgt. Flattop said...

> Yes, Steph, but the Callaloo and Conch were really tasty!

East Tennessee Tales

Fred will remember this story, as may others.

After a late-night tear-down in some small town in East Tenn., the TROGS setup crew made their weary way back to Kingsport, TN, where we were staying in a small Comfort Inn. Nothing else around except a Waffle House... and musicians being what they are, all hungry. We piled into booths and some on the counter... pretty much taking the place over, but at 0200, nobody cared.

Fred, Sam, me, Dick and someone else were in the booth, contemplating "scattered, smothered, etc.", when the waitress young, local - starts to take orders. Sam ordered something with eggs (or "aigs" in the local vernacular); the sweet young thing taking the order asked him, "How'd ya lahk yer aigs cooked?", stretching the space between "aigs" and "cooked".

Sam answered with the ultimate response...

"That'd be nice," pronouncing the word "nice" in much the same way that the waitress had pronounced "like" - a long, slow, East Tennessee drawl.

After we'd picked ourselves up off the floor, we proceeded to laugh for the next hour or so until the staff looked tired of our foolishness, and we left to start the post-gig games.

I still get the giggles thinking of the look on the waitress' face...

Posted by Chris

2 comments:

Fred said...

> PERFECT! Kind of like with German, I finally learned to "Hear" and could "Speak" a little Southern by the time I moved away, but I never learned to write it, oh, kind of like me and English too then.

Fred said... (cont.)

That is one of my favorites!!!

My only shot at Southern story, because there is nobody else around that could post it.

When Susie and I were processing in to AFB East we had a stop at the clinic to drop of medical records and fill out a few reams of paperwork.

The charming woman behind the counter was in perhaps her 60's and of African American decent. Taking information from Susie, while staring down at the AF Form XYZ she was scribbling on, she said, '"Wah mon ja bone?" Susie said, "Excuse me?" To which the lady once again said, '"Wah mon ja bone?" but this time she was looking directly at Susie.

I don't know if Susie read her lips, or her Texas upbringing finally kicked in, but her eyes lit up and she said, "August." The lady smiled and continued her interrogation.

My assumption was that '"Wah mon ja bone?" was local for "In what month were you born."

Tom P. said...

I knew a conductor who was hired to lead an orchestra in Virginia. Sadly he got hammered at the hotel bar on the night before the first rehearsal and was a hungover mess the next morning. Nonetheless he dragged himself to the nearest coffee shop and in an anguished whisper pleaded for a glass of orange juice. The waitress looked at this poor disheveled soul and said:

"Smile."

The conductor would have strangled her if he'd had the strength. He was helpless to do nothing but submit to this cruel dominatrix. He was desperate and with the last of his

Tom P. said... (cont.)

fading strength he hoisted the corner of his lip into a ridiculous sneer. It was the best he could do.

He had nothing left. The tank was empty. The game was up. The evil hussy continued to stare at him. What more could she demand? She had won. His broken spirit sagged as she opened her mouth to make her final demand:

"Smaaaal or large?"

Louie The Shirt

It was the height of the disco era and tight form-fitting clothes were the order of the day.

The band's chief clothes-horse went so far as to buy a dress shirt that snapped beneath the crotch to give him the sharpest look possible for all the local club action.

Comes the night to take his new shirt for a drive. All begins well. The music is pounding. The booze is flowing and the beautiful people are busy being beautiful people. No one could ask for more.

Eventually the call of nature incited our subject to seek out facilities that the club had provided for and were expressly designed to address that fundamental issue. Positioned squarely before a nondescript, but no less adequate, urinal he lowers his zipper in accordance with standard operating procedures - or order of battle, as it were. Suddenly he thought to himself "Oh, the snap."

Yeah. The snap.

Moments later he is in wrist deep and letting the world know it. "Where are you? Damn it. Come back here. Almost got you." Before long he is bent over and in up to his elbow, cursing up a storm.

"S.O.B. I know you're in there. Damn it to Hell."

Now as it happened this big, old Texan had been privileged to witness this event unfold from its inception and shook his head in wonder.

"Son, if you haven't found it by now maybe you're in the wrong room."

Posted by Tom P.

7 comments:

Fred said...

    It takes balls to post something like that, Tom... lol.

Tom P. said...

    See what happens when you leave town? Can't turn your back for a second.

Stephanie said...

    I'm a little bit hurt by this one, Tom. I'll have you know that I had an extensive bell bottom collection in the 70s, accompanied by some pretty hip looking body shirts complete with, not one... but two snaps!

Fred said...

    @Stephanie: You should not have been hurt, but felt proud. If I may presume, I think Tom may have been commenting on something a guy named Leon (any chance I am right this time?) might have been going through? You, Stephanie, would have done a "Swish, zam, zowie and swoosh" and been in and out in two minutes.

    @Tom: I didn't meet Stephanie until the 80's but she could make a Combo-4 look fantastic. So, I can only imagine what she would have looked like in one of "them" bodysuits. If I

Fred said... (cont.)

> didn't love her husband as much as her, I might just go on about that.

> I think this is what a Blog is supposed to be.

Tom P. said...

> I feel like a coma patient with the relatives talking over the beeps and ventilator compressor.

> Leon was completely innocent in that caper as the title would suggest.

> I thought the tale was told with great love and affection. Maybe something was lost in the syntax.

Fred said...

> 10-4 on the title. My "attention-to-detail" circuits have not come back online since last weekend.

> Reading something and reading into something often produce different results. The love was there.

> It still tickles me to think that there was a "big, old Texan" handy with such a good punch line!

Tom P. said...

> I'm not good enough to make this stuff up.

One For The Road

In 1981 a small combo from the AFB Overseas made a short trip to Camp New Amsterdam, The Netherlands, for some sort of dinner/dance thing. Due to less than perfect personnel management and an unfortunate drug bust I was appointed to be the drummer in that band. Needless to say, I was more of a chair filler than a driving rhythm machine.

That trip was to conclude just a few days before my good friend and amazing Trombone player was about to ship back to the States. I remember nothing about the performance, but I remember that after the gig we; the Trombone player, the Tenor player and I, were sitting around drinking. The Trombone player did not normally consume alcoholic beverages, due to strong religious beliefs. After about a six half-liter Carlsbad's I piped up and told my soon to be departing buddy what a shame I thought it was that I might never see him again and we had never gotten drunk together.

I was quite surprised when he replied by saying, "It's not like I can't drink." Me, "What do you mean?" He, "Well for example, if my life was threatened and I had to drink a bunch of beer to survive, I could do it." I think it was the Tenor player who then piped in with, "Then all we have to do is threaten your life and you will drink with us?" He, "Depending on how serious I find the threat, yes."

Without a word we jumped him and quietly informed him that if he didn't start drinking... He interrupted our threats by saying, "Hand me a cold one!" I know that it had been years since he had tipped a few, but he held his own that night.

Fortunately, I did run into him again. We were stationed together in AFB East for a while, just before I got out. I never offered him another beer and we never discussed that night in Holland. The only reference that I can recall was in Savannah, GA, at this cool little Pub. A bunch of us were there for customary post-gig libations. He sat quietly sipping a Sprite while the bartender placed a jumbo Killian's draft right in front of me. He looked longingly at that beer then looked me straight in the eye and gave me one of his patented grins. I don't know for sure, but I think he had good memories of that night in Camp New Amsterdam too.

Posted by Fred

2 comments:

Tom P. said...

> Hard to say if it was a "patented-grin-good-memory" or the
> cat was hoping you would pull a knife. We may never know.

Chris said...

> At least it wasn't a Big Gulp and a long bus ride, eh, Fred?

Night Sounds

Lack of sufficient housing at AFB Overseas in Germany necessitated
that band members be allowed to live "on the economy" the military
parlance for renting civilian homes and apartments.

Things generally worked out well especially if servicemen honored
the German's fierce determination to maintain "quiet hours" after
about 10 p. m. They could not be more serious about this. Trust me.

One night Ricky stumbled home to his German apartment in a
terribly drunk state but not so drunk that he could forget that it was
not unusual for the quiet rules to be enforced by a squad of German
policemen or Polizei if necessary.

Still he wanted to listen to music at his preferred volume so he
secured headphones to his ears, fired up his sounds and laid down on
the floor.

All was bliss but eventually our hero began to wonder why the floor
was shaking so violently.

Oh, he was wearing his headphones all right but he had neglected to
plug them into the amplifier and the volume on his stereo was
cranked to a level that would pulverize a soccer stadium.

Instantly sober he shut down the equipment and sat down in a corner
to wait for the Polizei to throw a net over him and haul him away to
some unknown fate.

They never showed up but I think, to this day, he is waiting for a knock at the door.

Posted by Tom P.

A Heart of Gold?

There are a zillion stories out there about tough "Working Girls" with a heart of gold. Well, here's another one.

This was my first trip to Mardi Gras with the AFB East. Yes, the same deal, I was in the Jazz Band so I had a bunch of time off. One night I was alone in the quarter, I am not sure why. Once and a while I just liked to get away on my own so as to not to have to deal with the "I dunno, what do you wanna do" dilemmas my friends and I often got into. Maybe that was it that night. Whatever it was I thought for a while I had made a bad mistake.

I had just bopped out of a very disappointing Gentleman's Club and was lighting up a smoke on Bourbon St, man, that still feels good to write. A very attractive, though way too made up woman of Afro-American extraction walked up to me and asked if she could get a smoke. Being the '80 and I could get a carton of smokes for about $3.00 on base, passing out smokes came natural to me. So I held out the pack and she withdrew one and asked for a light. She huddled close and I flicked my Bic for her. She drew in, exhaled and then flicked MY Bic for ME; she grabbed me expertly in the crotch and ran her other hand all over me. I don't remember exactly what went on, it took me a moment to react, but in that moment she had what she needed and apologized saying something about my wedding band. She then pranced down the street. I made a sigh of relief and wondered the other way heading for that famous Hurricane place, though all I wanted was a beer, oh and to have been there. When I got there I bellied up to the bar and reached into my right front pocket to grab my cash and order a beer when... empty! I reached into my right rear pocket, same thing. I checked my shirt pocket and still had half a pack of smokes and about six bucks, I must have stuck that there from change from the other place or it would have been in my right front pocket too. So, yeah, my wallet, ID,

Drivers License, and all my serious cash was gone. I split.

I had no idea what to do but I was hungry. I spied a cheap Chinese take-out place and wandered over. I could afford a spring roll and a soda. So that's what I got, along with Hot mustard. I stood there eating and here came my pick-pocket. A million things went through my mind, mostly like I know I am going to be a pussy and run away, when she came right up to me again. She was apologizing as she approached just as she had when she had departed a short time before.

She reached into her fake fur jacket and pulled out my wallet and some cash. She handed me my stuff and said, "Sorry, I didn't know you were a GI. I was an Air Force Brat myself." I had no idea what to say. Then she added, "I hope you don't mind. I extracted a finder's fee" as she held up a ten. I still had no idea what to say but I think I smiled. She then took that ten and ordered herself a beer at that same little stand and asked me if I wanted one too. I told her sure so she change the order to two. She handed me my beer and we chatted for just a few minutes, where she attempted to school me on proper preparation for the French Quarter during Mardi Gras and then drifted off to this guy, just up the street who was lighting up a cigarette. I could hear he say, "Hey, can I get one of those from you, buddy?"

Coda: Once I got back to my room I checked out all my stuff. Indeed, only a ten was missing. Odd, she spent half of that on me... I never again carried more than drinking money into The Quarter and I always carried my GI ID and Drivers License in a buttoned pocket of my shirt form that day on; still do.

Posted by Fred

3 comments:

Stephanie said...

> I'm thinking there might be a Donna Summer's "She works hard for the money" song sequel waiting to be written based on this.

Fred said...

As long as she doesn't re-record "Last Dance." Lol.

Stephanie said...

I hear ya!

You Can't Tell A Book By Its Cover

1980, London, England. This was one of my first trips to the UK with the AFB Overseas. I know that because the drummer on that trip was not with us long. It must have been early in the day, pre-gig time, or perhaps an off day (we did try to schedule those as often as Uncle Sam would allow when going to such a hip town), I am sure it was daylight.

There may have been more of us bit all I remember was three of us standing at a corner waiting for the light to change. I was still a bit confused as to which direction to look first so I was being particularly cautious. It was then that a well-dressed man walked up. He was reminiscent of John Steed from The Avengers. He had the whole ensemble; sharp patent leather shoes, well fitted black suit, a matching umbrella and the bowler hat. The only obvious differences he had with Mr. Steed was that he was younger and of African descent.

In my row of three bandsmen were a rather large trombone player, myself, medium sized, and a more diminutive drummer. The taller were pure honkey, but the short one was of African descent. When the drummer noticed our new sidewalk mate, he said, in a perfectly friendly American way; "Hey, brother, what's happening?"

The gentleman raised the tip of his bumbershoot and pointed it at the drummer, though not in a threatening manner - more as an Italian would use his index finger to orchestrate a dialog, and said, "Sir. I am not your brother. And what is happening is of no business of yours" all in a very thick, though high-brow, British accent.

We lost it...

Posted by Fred

Just Trying To Get Your Attention

I had the AMAZING good fortune to have worked for some of the finest bosses in the world while I was in the AF, both officer and enlisted. Strangely enough, with my general disdain for those of the officer type, I find the numbers to be about equal, with a slight advantage on the Enlisted side. This story is about an officer I had the pleasure to serve with two and a half times, twice on station, once on a TDY. He treated me like a son and was an excellent musician and administrator.

Morning of the day I was supposed to test for a promotion to Technical Sergeant. I look over at my alarm clock and saw: 8:30. The two hour test started at 0800. I was screwed! I took extra time getting ready, making sure that I was as 35-10 as I could be because I was about to seek forgiveness from my biggest fan who was also a hard-knocks guy. About an hour later I showed up at the Major's office.

"Fred, what are you doing here?" the Major said in his best Southeastern Texas accent, "Aren't you supposed to be in testing?" I felt like shit but this was a man I could not lie to. "Yes, Sir." There was a long pause. "I overslept, Sir."

"Come in and please stand at attention." That's actually a direct quote because he could have said a million other things that would have been much worse but that's what he said, including the "please." I stood at attention in front of his desk as he left the room.

By the way, now that I am thinking about it, I may have attempted to post this story as a Comment to some other post. If I did I apologize, but this is probably much more thought out and accurate, so please read on...

In my heart/mind I remember standing in front of that desk for "40 days and 40 nights" but it was probably more like twenty minutes. When the Major returned he handed me a "Pink Slip" (the good kind, remember those "while you were out" note pads?) which was in Sue's, the perfect secretary, handwriting. I looked back, straight ahead before I could read it and awaited my sentence.

"Did I get your attention, Fred?" "Yes Sir, you did." "Dismissed." I did a Basic Training type exit, which if I had the courage to turn around and look at his reaction I would be sure made him chuckle. I made a bee-line for my truck. There I read the "Pink-slip." I had been rescheduled to test the following week.

I could have been refused promotion for a cycle or gotten an L-O-R (Letter For The Record), or an Article-15 (serious shit) for what I had done or maybe even a Dishonorable Discharge. Instead, my mentor gave me a second chance. Yes, he got my attention.

I made the next test date on time. No, I didn't get promoted that time around but at least I had a gig. With a young daughter and a "bun in the oven" that was important. Thanks, Major. See you in September...

Posted by Fred

2 comments:

Chris said...

> That particular major could even give you an Article 15 and have you thanking him, he was so much a gentleman! JoAnn (my wife) tells me that when his son broke an ankle all the nurses on shift were fighting each other to go in and fluff pillows or ask if anyone needed anything because the major unfailingly got to his feet if a female entered the room - JoAnn also says that he was "a mite easy on the eyes, too!"

Fred said...

> Gentleman and "easy on the eyes" I guess I left those things out. Lol. Did I ever post the story of how I met him?

Chris said...

Not that I remember...

Plan Overboard?

This was a TDY to Atlanta with the AFB East but I do not remember the gig. It probably was not a recording session or a normal jazz gig because we were staying in an actually nice hotel. To a GI, a "nice" hotel was a place that got half of a star. All others were simply called "dumps." I would like to think I was NOT the instigator of this prank but I probably was. In fact I couldn't tell you who all was involved except for one other prankster and the person the prank was played on. So as not to embarrass them, I will call the prankee "Beloved Friend" and the second prankster "Prankster #2."

Prankster #1 and Prankster #2 thumbed through the local yellow pages looking for an "Escort Agency" that looked seedy enough to provide other services, which proved not to be that difficult. For those of you who never spent much time in Atlanta you might think of it as a pristine, conservative over-grown town, as I did before 1982, rather than the modern, open-minded city I discovered later. In my opinion, Atlanta had the best "Gentleman's Clubs" (we just called them Strip Joints in those days) anywhere in the world.

Believe me, having done research in New York, Amsterdam, Berlin, Munich, San Francisco, Miami, Los Angeles, Dallas, Houston, and a number of other smaller places (I took my appreciation of the Art of the Female Figure very seriously) I know what I am saying there. So when the second Escort Service we called asked if we would be requiring any additional services, we figured we had found our place. I think we ended up ordering "The Girl Next Door" package and gave them Beloved Friend's room number.

I don't remember covering which responsibilities but we did have one person in the lobby and one upstairs in the room across the hall from Beloved Friend's room, just in case.

A short while later a "Girl Next Door Type" showed up at the hotel accompanied by a rather large gentleman who fit the bill of bodyguard/bouncer/pimp quite nicely. Here I get more fuzzy, though not intentionally. What I do remember was what we had anticipated, a major yet hilarious scene, did not transpire. Instead, our Beloved Friend and his new "acquaintance" had what he described later as "A lot of fun." Oh, yeah, he actually sought us out later to tell us about this cool thing that happened to him. I guess we were both disappointed, no big laughs, and pleased for him at the same time. He was not known for being a ladies' man and perhaps that was just what the Dr. should have ordered.

As it turned out, on subsequent TDYs, and even personal trips that our Beloved Friend scheduled in addition, he kept up that relationship (as professional as it may have been) for some time. He was never shy about sharing his experiences, though never in graphic detail, but as a gentleman might tell you about walking hand in hand with his girlfriend in the park. I also remember that we even had special tee-shirts made commemorating that event. All and all, I guess we didn't go overboard after all.

Posted by Fred

4 comments:

Chris said...

> Beloved Friend wouldn't be capable of faking anything in any key, would he?

Fred said...

> Oh yeah...

Stephanie said...

> Always missing a uniform item on TDY?

Fred said...

> Oh yeah, again...

Bull's-Eye & F.O.P.

I don't remember the exact time of this events but I think it was closer to 1990 than 1980. I had the pleasure that day to be sharing the cab of one of our GI equipment trucks with one of the guys who normally was with AFB East rock band. He was a hoot and a fine keyboard player, though not a Jazzer. For some reason we were in front of the van carrying the Ops guy and the loading crew, normally they would have left the slower moving equipment truck in the dust, but on that day, crawling up I-95 they were right behind us, I know because I was keeping an eye on them from the mirror from my passenger side seat.

We came across a construction area, you know those orange car cones and all, with equipment about but no people. The driver got an EVIL GRIN on his face. Being the ranking person in the cab, and the detail for that matter, my stomach sunk just a bit as I pondered what that grin combined with my driver's reputation meant. He just said, "Make sure you watch the mirror." Then he did a little swerve and ran over a couple of the car cones. My eyes got wider as I could see one get kicked up from under our truck and skid right under the front of the van, getting stuck, and the other bound a few times before bouncing off the hood of the van and flying harmlessly to the shoulder. He then flashed his lights and pulled over so the van could dislodge its newly acquired ornament.

We popped out of the cab and the van unloaded. The truck driver walked back apologizing all the time and attempted to make it look like it was an accident. The van driver, a seasoned old drummer who had spent time in the rock band was not buying it at all. All he said was, "You piece of SHIT! Nice shot..." Our tall and lanky few-striper cleared the car cone, keeping it as a souvenir, while the rest of us were cracking up. We were back on the road in no time.

After the gig that night, the TROGS got together to do our part to financially support the local beer distributors in my room and listen to the gig tape. I am not sure if that day's truck driver was there but I do know that the van driver was. As was his custom, he entered the room, grabbed somebody else's beer from the cooler and helped himself to one of my smokes; he only smoked O. P.'s. But, that night he paid us back tenfold with the following story.

He told us of a day, also on I-95, but in a rental truck (before AFB East sprung for two trucks of their own) when the van driver was at the truck wheel and the truck driver for the earlier story was riding shotgun. This time there was no construction, just one of those people driving about 35 mph in the left lane on an Interstate.

The obvious thing to do would have been to pass the slug on the right. But, the passenger requested that the driver go out on the left shoulder and slowly start to pass him. I can only imagine that both of them broke into DEVILISH GRINS at that point.

Shotgun then pulled something bright orange, like a small bumper sticker, from his bag, opened the door, remember, moving on an Interstate in broad daylight, leaned out and stepped to the little step-up while holding on to the door with his left hand. He proceeded to reach out and slap his sticker on the upper left-hand corner of the slugs rear window. Then he told the driver to drop back as he pulled himself safely back in to the cab. Somebody shouted, "What did it say?" Our story teller replied, "F-O-P" Then after a short pause, "Florida-Old-Person." We lost it.

Later that night I was hipped to the fact that the F did not stand for Florida. The story teller softened the explanation because we were in mixed company - or "Amongst Mixed Drinks," as that band used to say. Not having experienced the F.O.P event I cannot vouch for its authenticity, but considering what I witnessed with the car cones I can certainly entertain the possibility that it could have. Oh, after that I noticed more than one car with a bright orange F.O.P. sticker while touring in Florida. All of them were either doing well under the speed limit or driving with their blinkers on for miles and miles and . . .

Posted by Fred

2 comments:

Chris said...

> Having gone on the road with RG, and with the other rock
> band of the late 70s and early 80s - Thrust - which had these
> two characters in it, I can attest to the distinct possibility of
> that story being spot on... bottle rockets frequently took the
> place of stickers, given the right provocation... of course, the
> bottle rockets were a favorite of our close, personal
> pyromaniac homebrewer ...also a fine clarinet and electric
> bass player.

Fred said...

> Prankster #2? LOL.

Almost An Hour Late And Yet Early?

In 1986 I got this really cool assignment while with the AFB East.
We were to do a Jazz Band album and I was going to be the
producer. But that's not it. I got to write seven of the eight tunes we
recorded. But, that's not it either. The cool part was that I was going
to get to pick the studio to record it. WOW!

Remember, I was already in love with the studio in Atlanta, and it's
people, but this was a chance for me to be a big shot. Man, I dug in.
This was years before the Internet. So, I picked up ever trade rag I
could find, Billboard, Jazz Times, Downbeat, etc. and even dug up
the stuff I brought back from the REA convention and went to work.

I came up with three candidates, for bidding out an AF contract you
always had to have three bidders, and kept my old friend as the
backup. One was right in Atlanta, the other two were in Nashville.
Oh, did I mention that the studio would have to be in our area... I
checked out the place in Atlanta on my own nickel. I just hopped in
my 1978 VW van and drove up there on my own, though in proper
Combo 1, and did my thing. NOT impressed. Room too small and
the engineer I was introduced to was NOT hip! Cool, a good third
place bid.

A week or so later the concert band had a trip to Gatlinburg, TN. So at the end of that trip I was given the staff car and off I went to Nashville to check out the other two places. I got to my "dump" after sundown, picked up a 12-pack and settled in to watch some of that new-fangled "cable TV" along with a few microwave burritos from the nearest icehouse.

My alarm went off at 0800 and I was up and at it by about 0845. I am not a morning person. Grabbed a shower, climbed into my Combo 1 and headed to find some coffee, leaving my briefcase in the room, or so I thought. I stopped in the lobby of the dump to partake of the free coffee, looked over my directions and fired up the Staff Car and headed out. About ten minutes later I realized I had left my briefcase behind. SHIT! All of my notes were in it. I had no idea who my appointment was with without it. I checked my watch and decided I would rather be late than stupid, totally discounting the possibility of being both at that time.

Back at the dump... PANIC! Where is it?!? Shit... Back to the Staff Car... SHIT! There it was, right behind the passenger's seat where I left it the night before so I wouldn't forget it.

I pulled into the parking lot at about 1040, according to my state-of-the-art $12.00 Timex and felt like shit. Big shot becomes big screw-up. I grabbed my briefcase and was attempting to formulate some story about why I was late as I went through the door. There in the reception area was a big clock that read 0945. Huh?

I walked over to the desk, where the receptionist was sitting with her back to me and asked if the clock was correct. Before she turned around she glanced up and said, "No, I think it's a little fast. I have 9:30." Then she turned around and shouted, "Fred! Is that you?!?"

Jumping to her feet she ran over and hugged me like an old lover. "Shirley!?!" I said. It turned out her hug was well founded.

We jibbered and jabbered and stuff for a moment and then she said, "Ron likes people who are early, maybe we should continue this in bed after you meet with him?" She had a sly grin. I held up my left hand and wiggled my wedding band. She pressed the intercom and told Ron that I was there, no longer a sly grin on her face.

I met with THAT Ron and got a tour of the place. Not impressed. The room was too small and the piano sounded like something from He-haw, which did record all their tracks there. So when he walked me out I thought I had another third place bid in my pocket. I was getting into the staff car when Shirley ran out and said, "Wait! Fred, wait!"

She raced over, slinging this long hippy purse as she ran... "Late lunch. Early dinner? Just some drinks?" she asked. "Yeah. OK." I said. "Where are you staying?" she asked. "The 'dump' at 5th and Grand" I said. "Cool, there is a place right there that will be perfect. Meet you there in ten."

She obviously knew a better way or drove much faster, because I didn't get to the dump for about 30 minutes. When I pulled in she was sitting on the hood of her beat up Chevy Nova having a cigarette looking as if she had no a care in the world. I pulled up next to her even though my room was on the other side of the motel. "Hey, Lady" I said as I got out. "Hey, Mister" she replied. "I have to get out of the monkey suit, give me about 10?" I asked. "Sure. I'll be right here."

I ran to my room, changed, checked my pockets for bucks, not much, and returned to the parking lot. It was about dusk then. When I got to her there was this tidy little pile of cigarette butts on her hood and she was singing something, though I could not tell you what. We exchanged our Hey Mister/Hey Lady greeting again and she planted this big old kiss on my chops.

Allow me to describe this lady to you. Shelly Duvall in Popeye. Enough said. Except for the fact that she was sexy as Hell... I have to admit, I returned the kiss. As we pulled apart she said, "I will not try to attack you again" and smiled.

She was right, there was a place about 100 yards from my dump that was perfect. The BBQ was wonderful and they had cold, really cold beer and a jukebox. Shirley went to the jukebox as I ordered the first round and plugged in what looked to be a whole roll of quarters into the machine and kept plugging what appeared to be the same number, over and over. We converged at a table in the center of the room moments later.

We ate really good BBQ. We talked about everything. We drank drafts and after the tenth time of playing "Still Crazy After All These Years..." somebody went over to the jukebox and kicked it (they don't call them kicker bars for nothin'). A moment later out came "Tennessee Waltz." We danced, though I did really shitty.

We didn't make it to 4 o'clock, as in the song but we did close the place. Shirley picked up the tab. I couldn't refuse because it was more than I had on me and ATMs didn't exist everywhere in those days. We walked back to her car.

At her car she pushed me away and said, "Stay over there or I might break my promise." Then she added, "Be as good a Dad and Husband as you have been a Lover and a Friend to me, please" and she got in her car and just drove away.

The next morning my alarm went off at 0800 again. This time I was up and at it at 0801. I was at my last appointment 20 minutes beforehand. I was blown off... The guy I was supposed to meet with called in sick. All I got was a rate card and an offer to reschedule. Glancing at the rate card I knew I had what I needed, another third place bid.

For those of you who have never driven through Tennessee in the middle of the summer, I should tell you it is one of the most beautiful places on the earth. Having seen the Alps and the Rockies I will place the Blue Ridge Mountains in that category. So, as I am driving home, I spent some time talking to whoever it is up there that made all this possible and complemented that entity for not only having made this place but having allowed me to be there, meet those that I had met, spawned and have fallen in love.

The session went down at MY STUDIO in Atlanta with the real Ron at the board. I have never heard of or from Shirley since.

Posted By Fred

Who's On First & Who's On Third?

We were TDY with the AFB East concert band in West Palm Beach, FL in the early spring of 1987. I know it was early spring because it was Baseball Spring Training time. I know it was 1987 because that was the only year that the new Braves third baseman played for them. It was after a gig and three of us were on search of chow or a drink or both so we were outside our Holiday Inn, right at the bottom of the off ramp from I-95, standing at the corner waiting on the for the light to change so we could cross to where all the stuff was. As the light changed, somebody called to us and said, "Wait up a minute." Thinking it may have been one of the other band members, they had similar outfits on, waist length jackets with ball caps we did not cross and up walked these two RATHER LARGE DUDES.

As they got closer to the street lamp my friends and I were standing under we could see these were not bandsmen. Their jackets were not flight jackets, they were Braves Warm-up Jackets. Their ball caps did not say BAND on them, they had a big red A. Before I could pass out the smaller, Caucasian guy said something like, "You GI's always know where to get a drink late at night. How 'bout it?" His companion, a much larger Afro-American gentleman, just stood there smiling.

With no hesitation one of my friends pointed to the left to The Black Stallion and said something like, "Hey, with outfits like that on, maybe the owner will buy you drinks. That place is a big Braves hangout." Then, the big guy spoke to me. "You're a fan, huh?" "How'd you know? I asked. He said, and I quote: "Your mouth has been hanging open ever since Graig said hello." I shut my mouth. The light changed, and as we were crossing they said thanks and shook hands with all of us. We split up, they to the bar and us to the late night burger place to the right.

Minutes later we were eating, I was mostly staring at my fries, still a bit overwhelmed, when another of the guys came in. He came over to us and asked what was up. One of the guys said something like, "You missed it. I think we just met two actual Braves players." This guy was as big, maybe bigger, ball fan than I so he looked right at me and said, "Who?" I looked up from under the bill of my cap and said, "Nettles and Chambliss." His reply, "F***!" at the top of his voice. As I recall I had twice before been kicked out of a hamburger joint for something like that. So I guess that was a night for a First and a Third.

Chris Chambliss played First Base with the Atlanta Braves from 1980-1986 and remained on as a coach through 1989. Graig Nettles played Third Base for the Atlanta Braves in 1987. They had actually become idols of mine when they played for the Yankees a few years earlier. My mouth was open during most of the time I was typing this...

Posted by Fred

$$((5*2) + ((30*6) / 24))* 0.5=?$$

I know that title makes no sense, so here is the key:

The five times two indicates that we had two people in the AFB East get promoted to TSgt during the same promotion cycle, a rare thing in a squadron of only 60 people.

Thirty times six? Thirty was the number of people we thought would attend the promotions party. Six, was the number of beers we wanted to have on hand for each of the attendees. Oh, and divide that by 24 so you knew how many cases to get.

The times one half, well that's because I only remember firsthand the first half of this story. The second half had to be recounted to me a later.

Hey, it's just a title. Here is the story...

Just before we were to leave on our annual first TDY of the year trip it was announced in a concert band rehearsal that I and my good buddy had both made TSgt. My buddy was to get to put his on before we left for the trip. I would have to wait until we returned. It took us about 30 seconds to decide that he and I would through a Promotion Party on the upcoming TDY, knowing that we had the

Sunday off. Sweet! The advanced crew for that TDY, which included both new TSgt's, was hard at work ordering beer and stuff for the party - instead of checking out this one hall that we had never played before in that area like we were supposed to be doing - long before the bus would arrive. This TDY was always to the same town, we stayed at the same comfortable, though not fancy place and the first gig was always at the Civic Auditorium about 50 yards from our hotel/motel/resort/place we were staying. On that gig number one, I spied some really large heavy-duty trash cans back stage (perfect for icing down a 16 gallon keg) and asked the house guy if we could borrow one for a kegger we were going to throw on Sunday. He said, "Sure, take all you want (there were like ten of them) as long as I'm invited." I invited him. Then he pulled out his keys and took one off his ring and handed it to me. "Here's a spare key so I don't have to show up early on Sunday to let you in to get an ash can" he said. Like I said, we played there a LOT.

Sunday morning. Day off on the road. It was Super Bowl Sunday, we couldn't draw a crowd in FL on Super Bowl Sunday so we just quit tryin'. Day of the PARTY! I grabbed the keys for the van and two younger/stronger Trogs along with my fellow promotee and we headed off to pick up the keg. A few minutes later we pulled in to a deserted parking lot. Seconds later we were standing in front of the sign that said, CLOSED ON SUNDAY. Oops. I think somebody actually said, "Lucy, you got some 'splainin' t' do" but maybe that didn't actually happen.

Back to the van. Back to our place. I banged on a few doors and shouted, "TROG meeting in my room..." as I went. Minutes later there were like 10 people in my room all wanting to know where the keg was. I explained that I had screwed up. Those on the van ride corroborated. Then I said something like, "We need a shit load of beer, some chips and a shit load of ice... We'll settle up when you get back." We did the math and people scattered. I took my fellow promotee across the parking lot to pick up not one but ALL of the big trash cans...

A short time later we did have a SHIT load of beer, more like 20 cases than the 8 or 10 that would have done, enough ice and about three bags of chips. PERFECT!

This is about where I stop being able to accurately remember stuff...

I was later told...

1. By the time we got around to having the congratulations ceremony, that I (we) were already 4 sheets into the wind.

2. A short time later I (we) sat at the edge of the pool puking out guts out singing "Just Friends."

3. He and I slept on the floor of his room because we had puked all over both beds in my room.

4. Only 4 beers were left.

5. The next morning two of those beers were used as "hair of the cat." Nice ending to that equation. Anybody know an equation to figure out brain cell loss?

The Monday gig was at 8:00 PM, so we made it there OK. The place with the keg gave us our deposit back. I returned the key and trash cans, cleaned. My buddy and I are still alive.

Posted by Fred

Housekeeping!

How many of us have heard, "Housekeeping..." and a couple of rude knocks even with the DO NOT DISTURB sigh hung nicely on the door knob? ...I thought so... Well, here's a little something that fixed that for me and my roommate; for at least most of one trip.

When the AFB East band played Homestead, AFB, FL, we often stayed off-base even though we may have been there strictly for on-base gigs. This was due to the fact that they held a lot of conventions there so base billeting often got filled up with convention attendees, not the hired help, the band... Let me tell you, getting bumped out of Temporary Living Quarters (TLQ) at Homestead to a 1/2 star motel (the dump) was an upgrade. Then figure this, the dump was about 50 yards to the back gate of the base. There was a 24-hour Sub shop about 50 yards the other direction. There was also a convenience store in that same center and to top it off a Video Rental place which had a rather large selection of Adult material. After discovering this, the next (and subsequent) time (times) we were booked there, we came prepared.

The members of F. L. I. C. K. (the Federation for the Liberation of Indecent Carnal Knowledge), of which I was a charter member, assembled the gear. Two full blown VHS machines - these were the days before miniaturizing, so these were the big puppies and dubbing decks didn't come along for a few years - enough cables to wire TBS, blank tapes and labeling materials all in an anvil case (you know, those indestructible road cases bands use). So, with our portable Dubbing Studio all loaded up, we descended on the little town of Homestead and the afore mentioned video store.

Dubbing went on 24/7, well, OK we did have some gigs here and there so not really, but we did keep tape rolling as much as we could. Sometimes we would watch, sometimes the dubs would run unattended.

The morning of the second day of the first time we had this system in place the dreaded, "Housekeeping!" rang out at about 9:00 AM. We did have a reasonably early call that day so instead of kicking the lady out we asked for a second to get decent got up and got going. As we were leaving the room in search of coffee, my roommate flipped another tape in the master deck, flipped on the recording deck, flip playback, flip the TV off... off we went.

We got our coffee at the Sub shop so we were back at the room about maybe ten minutes later. We just stood outside sipping coffee because we could see the housekeeping cart in front of our door. Moments later we heard a bunch of Spanish and a few words of English as our chambermaid exited looking all flustered. She stopped and collected herself for a second and in decent English told us that all we would be getting would be towels left at the door. Sweet! That's all we ever wanted anyway...

Back in the room, we found that she had not been disturbed by the piles of beer cans or the Pizza boxes or the overflowing ashtrays.

The TV was now on and one of the "Dirty Debutant" series videos was just reaching its climax - so to speak. We chuckled, sat down on the freshly made beds (the last we would see of that for a week) and enjoyed the last few minutes of Mr. Powers' masterpiece.

A few minutes later, new tapes in the VCR's, there was a knock at our door but this time it was one of the ladies from the band. She asked if she could come in while "Housekeeping" did her room. I flipped the TV off and invited her in. As soon as she came in she looked at the Dubbing Station and said something like, "So, what kind of filth are you stealing now?" and she flipped the TV back on. She continued once the screen warmed up, "Cheerleaders? You guys have no imagination..." We went on to have a normal conversation about our day ahead all the while commenting on the action, or lack thereof, on the video. Talk about equality of the sexes...

Posted by Fred

4 comments:

Chris said...

> Geez, I remember that! We got the stink eye from housekeeping the rest of the trip... how many did we dub, anyway? 15? 20?

Fred said...

> Probably... lol Your top loading Panasonic and my front loading JVC. We kept them warm all week.

Chris said...

> I remember... this was before the adult industry started worrying about copy protect... I seem to remember that the "engineering" crowd increased in size and gender makeup as the week progressed, too...

Fred said...

> Yeah, that actually freaked me a bit (the ladies having no
> problem with it - not that we got more F. L. I. C. K members)
> at first. Then I remember what we used to do to those ladies
> (Hey, you out there... This is... well it is what it is but we only
> treated the ladies in the band with the utmost respect, though
> we never took into account that they were any less TROG-
> like than any guy).

A New Way To Express Oneself

East Coast of Florida, 1986 or so. This was a trio excursion, two of
the others in the AFB East with sound technician chops, and myself.
We must have been all in the same truck or there would have been
more of us. We had spied an "Adult Establishment" on the way to
the gig that night and we decided to stop there on the way back.
Having recently been asked not to park GI vehicles in such
establishment's parking lots we parked the truck just up the street in
a shopping center that was basically all closed up for the evening and
wandered down to "The Mermaid A-Go-Go." (Sounds classy, huh?)
Wonderful DIVE... I am thinking this was our first time there.

The stage in this club was narrow and ran along the wall all the way
from the front window, tastefully blacked out, to the rear, stopping
just before the DJ booth. You had to pass through the DJ booth to get
to the dressing room, which as I recall did NOT bother the DJ. So,
why so much talk about a DJ in a strip joint? That's not supposed to
be the main attraction... Well, this guy was good.

He had a good voice, nice mic technique and some rather intelligent
patter. Each time a new girl went on he would introduce her and
include her age and where she was from. After visiting the Mermaid
a few times we did realize that he was just making all that up, well
except for the Stage Names. He would also work the crowd between
each tune in the girl's three song set, which I found unusual. Finally,
he had an elegant, if that word is appropriate for such an
establishment, way of wrapping up the set for the dancer. It always
started with a robust, "GENTLEMEN!" followed by "Put your hands

together for (fill in the name) and don't forget to tip her, your lovely waitress and your DJ." Well, we were a cheap bunch of dudes we tried to make up for our lack of tipping by enthusiastically applauding, cheering and altogether promoting a party atmosphere which was generally appreciated at this joint, and others like it.

So after about the third dancer, we had the shtick. All he had to say was "Gentlemen" and we would erupt with applause and toss in other rowdy stuff as the scenario dictated. To this day (I hope to substantiate this statement on the 18th of September, 2010, at the AFB East reunion) simply, robustly sounding a; "GENTLEMEN!" in the presence of TROGs should get you rousing applause.

Later that night the DJ introduced a new dancer. In her introduction we not only found out that she was from Scranton, PA and was only 22 (yeah, right) but this was her first night back dancing after a special leave of absence. We, our audio trio, did our best to make sure she got a GOOD welcome back (the least we could do considering we probably never tipped her).

She was a little paunchy and was very well endowed. She took a liking to us right off the bat and said something to us as she started her first dance. A good time was had by all. I don't remember if it was at the start of her second or third tune, but she wandered down so that she was right in front of us, literally just a foot or so away, and told us that she had something special in store for us. As the tune started she placed her hands on her now unclothed breasts and "EXPRESSED" herself in a manner that could only be accomplished by someone who had indeed just gone through a special leave of absence, AKA Maternity Leave.

One of our guys managed to get one of his hands over the top of his beer mug and the other over the pitcher, you should have seen the expression (sorry, I had to milk this one) on his face. So, our consumption of the exchange was limited to what may have dripped here or there as she hosed us down for a few seconds. The place went bonkers!

Between sets she came over and hung out with us, not hustle us. We just sat there a shot the shit. We even talked about her newborn, our kids, kind of like catching up with an old high school buddy.

Just before her next set, we moved away from the stage to make more room for the line of guys with their singles in hand who stormed the stage to tip her. To each of the tippers she offered a little thank you expression. She really made some milk money that night... OK, OK, I'll quit it before I make an udder fool of myself... I wonder if we played that place in Sarasota on that trip?

Posted by Fred

Waxing Poetic-Ish

A few months ago I went through a phase where I transferred a bunch of old cassette tapes to digital. One of the tapes I dug up did not make the cut because the material (my compositions/arrangements) kind of sucked and the session was never completed. But, the story around that recording session is worth mentioning.

This was with the AFB Overseas. Not far from the squadron was the little village of Landstuhl. Landstuhl was a charming little place that had a charming little Adult Establishment down this little back street near the train station. This particular club used to feature "Circuit Dancers" actual professionals with an act, much like I can only imagine State-side Burlesque dancers of the 50's & 60's. One of those dancers became known to the band guys as "The Candle Lady" mostly because of the way she used candles in her act.

The Candle Lady's Finalé consisted of dousing herself with the wax of a extra large candle, which she would light at the beginning of the set and allowed to burn/melt for 10-12 minutes while she did other tricks with lotion and smaller candles. To top even that, she would then peel off the sometimes rather impressive wax sculpture, after a short cooling process, and hand it, or portions of it, to the big tippers. We caught her act often enough that eventually we brought along the wives and/or girlfriends to enjoy the show. Never being a big tipper, I thought of a scheme that I hoped would win me some of one of her wax sculptures.

So, I sat down and composed five pieces of music; "Open Doors," "Motion Lotion," "Second Stage Decent," "Close 1/6th'" and "Two Candles" - my memory is not that good, I have the tape sitting right in front of me. Like I said, they sucked, but I did write them, and we did record most of them.

This was an odd mix of guys from that band that while it did consist of the core party people and also involved our Chief and a MSgt concert band-type who also was in charge of the modest recording studio at the band hall.

So there we were, a bunch of Uncle Sam's kids, with a couple of senior chaperones, using an official US Government facility and equipment to record music for a French National who performed nude in a local German club. While it sounds charmingly international, we could have gotten in big trouble for that. But we did it anyway.

We managed to get all of the rhythm tracks recorded. We would have gone later and perhaps finished up the project when the Chief said that we better shut down for the night so we did not draw attention to the squadron being used in such a manner. We all agreed and got out of there before it was too late.

The next morning I was called in to the Commander's office. Not like an official "Report" but this Old Man was not beloved by the enlisted members of the band and no particular fan of mine so I was a bit concerned. Once inside, the Colonel handed me the bass parts that had been left behind the night before and asked me what that was all about. My copy work was not something I could deny so I told him it was a little experiment we were doing to try to learn how to use the recording studio. He took that well and then asked if the title that included "Candles" in it had anything to do with that stripper all the boys were talking about these days. Ooops.

Busted, at least figuratively... this Colonel was, like I said, was not beloved and had more of a reputation of being a... Well, let's just say that he ended his staff meetings with a prayer, long after Uncle Sam had said that was a no-no. I didn't know what to say. That's when I found out I was okay because he addressed me by my name, not my rank for the first time I could remember, and asked - not ordered me to answer him. So I told him, yes, she was part of my inspiration. Then he asked how the tape turned out. I told him that we never got it finished. He politely suggested that we find some other studio for that. I agreed with him. That was that.

As I left his office the Chief was sitting in the "Hot" chair outside the door. He just looked at me with a quizzical expression. All I said was, "It's cool." He smiled.

About lunch time I ran into the MSgt who ran the tape on the session, remember, he was a concert band dude and I was a jazz dude, so we didn't see that much of each other, and he handed me two cassette tapes and said, "I had to wipe the master."

Coda: I don't remember what was left to record, I have no scores any more but the last time that session band met officially was at a charming little Adult Establishment in Landstuhl, down this little back street near the train station. The bass player, who had blown our cover by leaving his parts behind, was being given a world class ration of shit by all as we enjoyed the warm glow of the candlelight from the stage.

Posted by Fred

A Fond Adieu

Oh, the blog is not going away ... Read the story, it's a short one.

This comes from an old friend via a Facebook comment. I have not seen this particular old friend since the mid '80's but I do remember him being sharp and basically honest so I can attest to the probable accuracy of his story. But, before I get to his story, a short thing on how I met this guy...

In the Air Force, when you PCS'ed (Permanent Change of Station went to a new base) each person got a "sponsor." Now that I think of it, sponsors may have only been for people going over-seas. I will check that out next week when I am at AFB East with the dudes... Anyway, this guy was my sponsor in the summer of 1979. He picked me up, right on time at Frankfurt and we hopped in his car for the short trip down the Autobahn to K-town.

The trip got extended just a bit when we pulled over so he could buy me my first real German beer. What a wonderful gesture. I was not even a real beer drinker until that moment but I just thought it was cool. We stopped again a little later for a second beer because we had gotten to a different region and the local beer was a bit different. By the time we got to K-town, I had my first FRIEND in Germany. OK, here is an "anonymized" version of his story:

I Remember a certain tuba player standing outside his Social Actions class, 5 days before he separated. He was so mad about the class he wore a KKK outfit and was leaning on the buildings' sign with a large wooden cross, and he asked the black captain in charge as he approached..... "gotta match?" His name was R****! The captain laughed his ass off!!

Just another example of "The finest deterrent force the world has ever assembled" - what the recruiter told me I was joining in 1978 boy, was I gullible. I think I may have known that R****, but I know I would have liked to meet that captain! Thanks, S**** for that!

Posted by Fred

Furniture Clearance – Everything Must Go!

It was a beautiful Saturday afternoon in Tampa, Florida. The AFB East was on tour.

Lodging - Days Inn, downtown Tampa. Suites, the usual residence of the upper NCO ranks, were on the 8th floor and had an outside balcony, complete with an accessible ledge.

A certain master sergeant who loved to order a chicken sandwich at BBQ restaurants (probably did this just to p-off the southern born-and-raised members of the Band) had a suite as described above, along with several other senior players in this story.

The Band had time off, just enough to view some College Football, and the aforementioned "chicken sandwich" master sergeant had left his room to visit his wife's parents, who lived in the area, but said he would return soon to watch the Notre Dame/USC game with his fellow Bandsmen.

The Senior NCO buddies were in a certain other master sergeant's room to watch the game.

This Senior NCO (from here forward to be referred to as "KAFLD," thought, "Hmmmm...., I wonder if "master sergeant chicken sandwich"..... left his windows open to get some fresh air?"

KAFLD looked at a co-conspirator.... (Our AFRES Band "King of Micro-Logistics Management" - Oh, Can't Ya Figure it Out? -"If It Ain't Broke, Don't Fix It" Himself - Or---Better Yet--If It's Broke, "We'll Convince Them, It's Not ...Because It's In Everyone's Best Interest To Believe, It's Not Broke... And You Know We.... the MIGHTY 581st!!!.... And ONLY WE.... The MASTERS Of All Things Musically Magical....... Can Fix It...... The Show Must Go On........ etc..... etc..... etc.... Any Questions Class?....) and said, "Should we go for it?......." CC said, "Yeah, man, Let's do it!!."

KAFLD opened the sliding glass door to the balcony, crossed over the ledge, and counted down the room numbers to "MSgt chicken sandwich's room. Sure enough, his windows were open.

KAFLD opened the screen door and went inside. Other co-conspirators were waiting outside the room, in the hallway, to help with the heist.

They took everything..... I mean everything..... clothes, pictures off the wall, bedding, the TV, toiletries, phone and chairs, etc.... and placed them in a nearby co-conspirators' room.

"Master sergeant chicken sandwich" came back from the wife's parents' visit to watch the game with everyone, and had yet to go back to his room. Then, during a game break, he went to his room.

Everyone acted as expected...... "What happened?? Really??

"Master sergeant chicken sandwich" came back and asked, "Where is all MY STUFF!?" All co-conspirators put on their "game face" and said, " Hey, you must have somehow gone in the wrong room!"

Being the experienced master sergeant that he was, he challenged the "house", "All right, I know you guys have my stuff!"

All co-conspirators defended their honor and assured him that he was losing it.

He went back to his room again, scoped it, and then left to confront the hotel service desk with his situation.

The co-conspirators quickly climbed back over the ledge, and repeated all steps in reverse, putting everything, perfectly back in it's place, and then returned to KAFLD's room to resume watching the football game.

"Master sergeant chicken sandwich" came back directly to KAFLD's room, immediately after visiting the hotel service desk, asking about his "stuff," threatening that hotel security was coming, and that you A--Holes better "come clean" or else heads are gonna roll! YADDA, YADDA, YADDA . . .

He was once again told "You must be losing your mind." We've been watching the game all afternoon. Come on, the game's on. Leave us alone!"

"SMSgt chicken sandwich" went to his room, after raving to hotel management that his room had been stripped clean, and found that everything in his room was just as he had originally left it.

KAFLD, to this day, thinks that "SMSgt chicken sandwich" still doesn't know what happened...

Posted by Stephanie

2 comments:

Fred said...

> I cannot believe I missed this when it was posted. Fantastic!!!
> So, did "chicken sandwich" get promoted during that
> incident?

Stephanie said...

> Nope, simply a typo on my part. I messed up in referring to
> "MSgt chicken sandwich" as "SMgt chicken sandwich."
>
> I believe that "SMSgt KAFLD" was the only senior master
> sergeant involved in our saga. Ken says he believes that
> chicken sandwich was a master when he retired.
>
> My bad!

A Not So Stony Ending

First let me say that there will be little or no humor in this post.
Second, I had to call in the Marines to clear up some foggy points in
my twenty-plus year old recollections of this. With that said, I will
do my best to recount this story from my perspective for you.

Mid 1980's, east coast of Florida, near Cape Canaveral and Patrick
AFB. I have not done this before but allow me to cast this story
foryou. The star of this story was a wonderful female vocalist from
the area around the home base for the AFB East, therefore a favorite
-but she could have been from Boston and her fans would have liked
her just as much. There will be two co-stars; our star's boyfriend and
our star's normal female co-star on stage. The supporting case would
be made up of the senior staff of the band. I don't remember who
made what decisions but they did the right things so they should get
the credit.

Just before report time for the bus ride to the gig, where we were to
do a medley of mine ("Streisand, A Woman And Her Music") which
featured our star and female co-star, there was a commotion in the
parking lot outside out motel. "Somebody get the Chief and some-

body call an ambulance!" Please notice the order of that statement. I don't remember who shouted that but I do remember that it was in proper order. All I remember about the next few minutes was people running all around and then our star coming out of her room, helped by her boyfriend, with a wet towel covering her face eyes, to be more specific. I freaked.

I don't remember if I was actually our star's supervisor at that time although I know I covered that gig at some point, but I did know that I was her friend and even more closely bound to her by the fact that I was her arranger. I'm sorry, there is no way to explain that bond.

If you could have found a way to give me those 60 people, a good agent and a bus, we would all be still be playing music and making a comfortable living. This was a family, much like I can only imagine a combat unit becomes. Sorry, back to the story...

Someone shouted something like, "Screw the ambulance. Fred? Do you have the Staff Car keys?" "Get those two to the Patrick clinic NOW!" I didn't even reply I just checked my pockets for the keys and the three of us kind of waddled (hard to walk somebody who cannot see when they are not used to it) together to the K-car wagon. Our star properly seated in the back, the boyfriend said, "Give me the keys" in a very authoritative voice although I out ranked him by a couple of stripes. I just looked at him for a second and he continued, "You drive like an old woman (I still do). You navigate." We were off, down I-95.

On the trip our story was solidified. Boyfriend was to be fiance and I was to be supervisor. We also agreed that this might be a time to let my normally easy-going demeanor go and do what was needed to make sure our star got top shelf service, fortunately I did not have to.

The next thing I remember was standing in the waiting room with the Doctor telling us, "She may be blind in that eye." Neither boyfriend nor I freaked. In one of those unison life moments we both said something like, "Don't let that happen." We asked if we could see her. The answer was no. We asked if we could stay in the waiting room until we could. The answer was no. The Doctor then added that she would do everything humanly possible to give our star the best medical treatment. Boyfriend and I looked at each other and decided to try to make at least part of the gig. Before leaving we asked how early we could see her in the morning. The Doctor said any time after 0800. We split.

Boyfriend again drove. I think I remember that we got, or nearly got, a speeding ticket and had to use GI shit to get out of it but I am not sure about that. I do know we got there to the gig just as the second half was starting. Boyfriend briefed management as I settled in behind the sound board.

The second half of that concert tour featured the afore mentioned medley. I had no idea that they were going to attempt it until I heard it introduced. I killed vocal mike number one - I think the Old Man must have setup the board and put it on auto-pilot - and concentrated on vocal mike number two, though it turned out I didn't have to work too hard. Female co-star nailed it! Let me back up a bit...

This was a 6 to 8 minute piece specially written for two female vocalists. The parts were carefully constructed and rehearsed to feature the talents of the singers being featured at that moment to consider range and style, etc. and on the spur of the moment one person was being asked to do all that herself. Well, with the exception of being able to pull off polyphonics and cover the two part harmonies, she did it. I have sat here for over 30 minutes attempting to come up with some analogy as to how difficult that must have been and I cannot.

After the gig, boyfriend and I headed back to Patrick, AFB with the blessings of band management and the well-wishes of the family (band). I don't remember if we stayed on base or in a motel or just stood in a parking lot all night, I just remember the morning after. The lady doctor motioned to me as we came in, 0800 sharp, an unusual time of the day for me to be moving, and asked me if I was the boss or the fiance? I said, boss. That's when she told me that she did not think that our star would ever have sight in that eye again. She then asked if I knew the fiance well enough to tell him that or should she. I was spared from having to say anything because the fiance, other than being a close friend, fine musician and softball player, also had world class ears and had heard everything even off down the hall. He joined us and an uncomfortable conversation was going on which was fortunately broken up by the entrance of our star "In her usual flare" though donning an eye patch - not her usual flare. I signed some papers and we left for the next gig, at the Port St. Lucie Civic Center; Stewart, FL that night.

I remember exactly where that gig was because, well, because of the rather unusual circumstances of the past few days and also because my parents were living in Port St. Lucie at the time. The gig came off without a hitch, except for a few pirate jokes thrown at our star because of her eye patch. It was as if nothing had happened, until the after gig party.

I should explain, an "After The Gig Party" was not necessarily a party. Most of the hoopla of being on the road, unless you were The Stones, is kind of bull. Normally we would just find a boom-box, slap on a copy of the gig tape and critique ourselves while having a modest 200 or 300 beers while dangling a clarinet player or two by their ankles over the balcony of some cheap motel – or some-such. That night was different. That night everybody wanted to check in on our star. That would be us, the TROGs (her closest friends) and our supervisors.

These were the two most memorable sights I had from that party: First, one of my friends who did not have a large heart for what we often called "chick singers" sincerely was interested in her well being. Second, her female co-star just holding her hand. These were two women who by social/musical and/or chick singer standards should have been in a perpetual cat-fight. Nope, not so. Like I said, family.

Coda: Why the memory of this came to me a few weeks before I was to be with most of the people in this post in just a few days after over 20 years, I don't know. But I plan on asking our star how her vision is, next Saturday.

I got to do The Women of the Great White Way (TWOTGWW) for this same cast and crew. That should be a separate post.

Boyfriend did eventually become fiance and then husband.

Unfortunately that did not work out. Fortunately, as I understand it, both found better places to be and are currently very happy.

While researching details pertaining to this post over the past week or so, I found out that our female co-star was particularly freaked about doing "Stony End" in Streisand Medley. Man, really? Hearing her do it that one night I wondered why I didn't put that in her part in the first place...

Posted by Fred

6 + Comments For:

Stephanie said...

> Thank you, Fred, for the kind words and a recollection of this "not-so-much-a-favorite" event. I may be wrong, but it is my recollection that K beat the odds and regained complete sight in that eye. I attribute that recovery to the power of prayer and the persistent, positive, optimistic spirit of a beautiful young woman and incredible vocalist that I had the pleasure to also call a dear friend. I'm looking forward to seeing her this Saturday at the AFB East Reunion. You too, Fred!

Fred said...

> You are more than welcome, you earned them... What are the chances of getting the trio to do "Georgia On My Mind" next Saturday? I bet you guys all can remember the parts... lol

Chris said...

> Works for me...

Fred said...

> I will cover all the band parts...

Stephanie said...

> Got a cheat sheet available for the vocalists?

Chris said...

> Steph, just listen to the recording once and it will all come back!

Fred said... (long after the blog had closed down...)

> While proofing this post for publication it struck me that I had left out one very important part to this story, the injury itself. What was the injury? Well, our star had somehow managed to make eye contact, in the worse possible way, with a hot curling iron. Yes, direct contact with that iron to her cornea. Fortunately, Stephanie was correct, there was no permanent damage.

The Midnight Raid On The Infamous Island Stronghold Of Captain Weekes

This was originally posted as a comment to one of my semi-administrative posts. I am re-posting it as a full post so it does not go unnoticed. This is a gem and a second version of a post from earlier, by another poster. I enjoyed both versions completely. Oh, and by the way, I actually visited the coat of arms mentioned in this post, at it heavily guarded resting place only this past weekend.

Sgt Flattop said:

Sgt Flattop conceived this brilliant, but highly dangerous plan shortly after his advance recon team revealed that the stronghold had sustained major fire damage. Realizing that the usually high security around the stronghold might be temporarily distracted, Sgt Flattop decided to act on this opportunity at once. Enlisting the aid of a trusted munitions/firearms expert, Commando H[*****], the scene was set for the daring adventure!

Shortly after midnight on the new morning of 12 November 1984, while most of the inhabitants of the island were beginning to feel the results of the excess celebrating on the previous day, Sgt Flattop and Commando H[*****] left their brightly lit Headquarters in the old Caravelle Hotel and crept silently through the dark, crooked streets of the island towards Captain Weekes' stronghold.

Approaching their goal, the pair inched forward in the shadows, successfully avoiding the local constabulary's irregular patrols. Through the palm fronds and night blooming frangi-pani leaves, Sgt Flattop's suspicions were confirmed: no patrols watching the entranceway to the stronghold. And, even more incredulous, Captain Weekes' great wooden coat-of-arms was left in its place of honor, and at that particular moment.. UNGUARDED! There was no time for conferring, no time for wondering what would happen to them if they were detected. This was a time for action!

Quickly, from their place of concealment, the duo ran across the open, well lit street and boldly climbed the barred gates to their objective - the great wooden coat-of-arms, an object held in mystical superstition by Captain Weekes' minions because it alone of all the myriad treasures had escaped the fiery holocaust to survive unscathed. Our heroes grasped the great wooden coat-of-arms bearing the sacred image of the infamous Captan Weekes and with superhuman effort, wrenched it free from its moorings and leapt to the cobbled street with their trophy!

Lady Luck was their mistress throughout that night as the made their way back to the Headquarters with the great wooden coat-of-arms. Exactly how the out-of-country transportation of this internationally recognized symbol was accomplished must remain classified, however it is rumored that a "van" and a "transport truck" belonging to the U.S. Army and a multi-engined "C-130 transport plane" belonging to the U.S. Air Force might have been used for certain portions of the journey from the island to its new place of honor at a "military installation somewhere in the southwestern United States". The CIA has consistently denied any part in this event, but in a small town in Texas, there is a retired U.S. Air Force Colonel who just probably knows all of the details.

BYLINE: Lance Sterling, adventurer

Posted by Fred

5 comments:

Stephanie said...

> I hope that the keeper of the Capt Weekes' wooden "coat of arms" guards it well. I think that Chris might be able to appear on the PBS TV program "The Antique Road Show" soon and we can see how much that baby is worth.

> Whaddya say, Chris?

Chris said...

> You talking about me, or the sign?

Stephanie said...

> Sorry, only JoAnn can qualify an answer on the former. I could only be talking about the sign.....

Chris said...

> JoAnn says to forget it... I'm apparently not much in demand, anymore.

> Once the new models come out, nobody wants used anymore.

Cindy, Order Up!

Oftentimes when the Band would be on tour in Florida, we would frequent the local HOOTERS establishment for the guys to enjoy the gourmet female eye candy, uh, I mean, gourmet chicken wings.

At Hooters, when an order was ready to be taken to a patron's table, the guys behind the kitchen counter would shout the waitress's name and "order up!." Then, the waitress called would come to the counter and serve the order to the patron's table.

Upon visiting said establishment one evening, a certain male portion of the Band in attendance were quite taken with the "assets" of one of the waitresses named Cindy.

It seemed way too infrequent for some of the Band guys that Cindy would approach or pass by the Band's table to ask if we needed a beverage refill, or an additional plate of wings.

One of the senior NCO's at our table decided a way to remedy the infrequency of Cindy's "Pass in Review's".

"Cindy, order up!"

Cindy approached the kitchen counter to retrieve the order. Hmmmm. There was no order at the counter. "Oh well, I must have misunderstood." I'm sure she thought. But, for the Band guys, the order had been well served. After another few minutes . . .

"Cindy, order up!"

Cindy approached the kitchen counter to retrieve an order again. Hmmmm. There was no order at the counter. "WTF?," I'm sure she was thinking.

After the third false order, the "Band-its" 'fessed up to Cindy that they were just "giving her a hard time" (pun intended) and then they gave her a VERY large tip.

Posted by Stephanie

4 comments:

Fred said...

`	Dang, I always thought it was the Grouper Sandwich... Cindy? Oh, CINDY!!! Order Up!

Stephanie said...

> No, Fred....but, some of the guys wanted to make a "grope-her" sandwich!!!!!

Fred said...

> Am I a good straight-man or what?

Stephanie said...

> The best!

Swing Low #1

I have been dry for a while now, but thanks to the other posters the blog has not completely died out. As I was sitting here today attempting to get my brain to slow down and process some of the ideas I got from the reunion last week, I paused for a moment to complain, to myself, about the heat. Here in my quaint little sea side place in Southern California, it reached 101 degrees F. today - that is unusually warm for this area. Bingo, August 1981, AFB Overseas.

It was a Change of Command for the USAFE Commanding General. As we were forming up, behind the parade field, people were talking about the weather, another unseasonable warm day, though being Germany, it was probably more like the mid 80's. I remember the Security Police squadron gathered right next to us and one of the SPs made a crack about how "The Band Queers" were going to be dropping like flies in this heat. Hmm... I also remember one of our guys saying something about, "Whenever I feel like I am going to fall out (faint) I always hum a little to myself. That makes me feel better."

About an hour later, after we had been standing at attention in the direct sun in our full Combo One uniforms we could hear, very softly, from about the middle of the band, someone humming "Swing Low, Sweet Chariot". You would have to have had bandsman's ears to hear it so I am sure none of the other flights, also standing at attention, even noticed. A few seconds later the humming stopped and the first SP bit the dust, just collapsing in place although he received points for remaining at attention as he turned into a puddle.

A few seconds later "Swing Low" could be heard again, but from a different place in the formation, as more people dropped in other squadrons all around us. I am not sure if the second humming was needed therapy for a bandsmen or just a heads-up on the pending folding of our comrades from the other "tougher" career fields.

It got so bad that the people on the reviewing stand noticed and they did a good job to finish the ceremony quickly. By the time we got the order to play the troops off, I would guess that over twenty people had fallen out, most actually passed out. Oh, NONE of those were from the band.

Coda: As we were putting up our horns and stuff a few of the SPs came over to our First Shirt and complemented the band for hanging tough. The Shirt thanked the GI's for the complement and a French Horn player, an older fellow, perhaps in need of the Weight Program, added, "It's part of what we do Sarge. If you would like some additional OJT for your troops, I am sure our Commander and Drum Major can arrange some for your people." Half the band cracked up. Oh, by the way, they did arrange for the OJT, but not for just a few. As I recall there were about 90 SP's assembled in the parking lot in front of Glenn Miller Hall a few days later where they were given some, but not all, of the secrets that bandsmen over the years learned to deal with marching gigs. We never got shit from them again and yes, they had more fall outs then we did the next time we got together. Then again, we didn't tell them about "Swing Low."

Posted by Fred

2 comments:

Stephanie said...

> Bandsmen do "Pass In Reviews."
> SP's do "Pass-out in Reviews."

Fred said...

Grin...

A Mile And A Half

I was having a hard time deciding what to post today so I glanced through my pictures from the reunion hoping to get an idea. Well, I did, but it was not the face of an old friend that gave me the idea, it was the picture of building 1316, where the reunion was held, that did it. That building stands only a matter of yards from where the AFB East used to Run Aerobics.

There was probably a proper military name for having to accomplish a mile and a half run (or three mile walk) in a certain amount of time, depending on your age, but we just called it "Aerobics." I mentioned, run or walk. There is a hitch there. If you chose to run, you could break into a walk at any time, though you still had to complete the mile and a half in the runner's time. If you chose to walk, and broke into a run, you would be disqualified and have to do it again, and people would really razz the hell out of you. The official Air Force differentiation between walk and run was a walk was moving on foot while one foot is always in contact with the ground. Running was defined as moving by foot while both feet may be in the air at the same time. Therefore I would assume very fast hopping would be considered running, therefore discouraged as a technique for those who would be walking.

The year for this post would have been 1985, because that was the year that I passed from one age group into another, therefore getting five more minutes to accomplish the run. I was kidded about that by more than a few of the younger troops. I also got ragged about having a fresh pack of cigarettes in my pocket as I got ready to start. Somebody shouted out, "No smoking in formation" and the guys cracked up. So, I ditched my smokes in the trunk of my car right next to the six-pack of beer I had on ice for the post run revival and got back to the starting place.

Normally I don't care where I am in a line, but at aerobics, I always tried to be in the front of the starting pack. Why? Well, if you start a few rows back you have to run that much farther. Hey, I know just a few yards, but a few yards are a few yards. While I may have been an avid Softball player at that time I would never have considered myself an athlete. So, I weaseled myself to the front and got ready to go.

As we started off, I got a few more razzing comments as some of the younger troops past me and I got pissed (not angry, pissed, just pissed enough to know I was not going to let this 30 thing become an issue). So, I attached myself to the butt (figuratively) of one of our younger guys and did everything I could to stay with him. To my surprise, and his, while I fell off quite a few yards I did cross the finish line only a few seconds behind him.

My time was so fast (better than I had run since basic training) that the guy taking our times asked the guy I had paced myself with if I had skipped the loop at the lake. My pacer backed me up and they recorded 13:16, or 6:44 less than the time I was allotted in my new age group.

I made a bee-line to my car, lit up a smoke and cracked open a beer with the official witness (somebody from outside the squadron who made sure we didn't break any rules) standing right there. She commented, "He's gonna kill himself like that." My pacer replied, "He does that every year" as I handed him a cold one and offered him a cigarette. He graciously excepted the brew but passed on the smoke.

I did do that every year, but until that day I never thought of it as being unusual. Oh, but the way, at this moment I am having a smoke and a beer, but I did not just finish a run of a mile and a half.

Posted by Fred

3 comments:

Stephanie said...

> I think the theme song for "Chariots of Fire" playing in the
> background while reading this post would be quite
> appropriate - or should we parody the soundtrack and call it
> "Chariots of Smoke"? ;)

Bill B. said...

> I remember doing the 3 mile walk in my blue duty uniform
> one time. I was too lazy to practice for the run and just did it
> "as is." I even wore my flight cap since I was outdoors
> regulations, you know. I too had a smoke and a beer after the
> walk. I did have to clean/dust off my shoes afterward.
>
> Corfams get dusty real easy!

Fred said...

> Yes. There were three of us that I ALWAYS remember with a
> smoke and a beer after the walk/run. You, me and that guy we
> worked for.
>
> Dude, start writing stories...

Manny, You Ok?

This is actually the first post I drafted when I set up the blog back in
May of 2010. Because of it's serious subject matter, I really wanted it
to be correct. It has taken me this long to get to the point that I have
chosen to post it with, frankly, some disputed points, but I serve it up
to the best of my recollection. This one is not a fun one, but in one
form or another it really did happen.

Autobahn A62 just south of Trier, Germany in the winter of 1981.
The conditions were icy and cold and there was some snow on the
ground. It was maiden voyage of the AFB Overseas brand new
Mercedes bus. Before you get too excited about the "Mercedes " part
let me explain that this bus was outfitted in a very Spartan manner,

complete with hard bench seats that made the motor pool Bluebirds feel comfortable. The only other person that was on this bus that I am in contact with, disagrees with me on this point - and she is PROBABLY right on ALL of the disputed points. She says that the Mercedes was tricked out. In any event it was ours. The gig in Trier was uneventful but the ride home will forever be stuck in my head, at least a few hours of that night.

I don't know how many of you are familiar with the German Autobahns but in the early 1980's it was not unusual for them to have long stretches with no lights and no guardrails. When you add to that the fact that for more than half the year it was common to have what was called "Black Ice" a super slick patch or road that did not require any noticeable precipitation to occur. Somehow, over there, the humidity and temperature combination simply turned the road into a skating rink without any warning. We were on such a stretch of road for a while that night.

I was involved in a Spades game where we used a cooler full of sponsor-donated beer as a table. My guess is that there were probably two or three other cases of said beer on the bus, only because that was a pretty normal thing. I don't remember if I actually saw what started the memorable event or if it was just recounted so often that now, nearly thirty years later, it is an artificial visual memory. Here is what is in my mind's eye.

We are descending a steep grade of a four lane highway, it was after gig time so pitch dark except for headlights. We are in the far right lane. There is no guardrail to our right though there is a severe drop-off only a few feet from the edge of the narrow shoulder. There was no guardrail between the two lanes coming from the opposite direction either. In the left lane, coming in our direction, descending an equally steep grade, was a smaller vehicle which turned out to be a VW microbus. As the VW reached the bottom of the hill, it lost control and started to swerve and spin. My friend remembers this as being a construction site, therefore explaining the lack of lane dividers. It slid out of control into our lanes and was coming right at us, now going slightly up hill. Somebody shouted to hold on to something. Like an idiot (NOT disputed), I grabbed the cooler. Suddenly there was this "THUNK" a sound I had never heard before and we stopped moving.

People bounced around a bit, I heard what sounded like rain and the interior lights of the bus came on. I was perfectly fine, though I may have shifted my position some. Somebody shouted from the front of the bus that help was needed. At least half of the band stood and rushed forward, myself included. I was mostly at the rear of the pack that stopped moving as a bottleneck occurred around the driver's seat. Somebody shouted, "A towel, we need a towel!" that was closely followed by, "JESUS! WHO KNOWS CPR?" Two of our guys, trombone players, pushed forward and exited the bus swiftly. One through the regular door, the other through where the windshield formally was. What I had thought was rain turned out to be the sound of German safety glass disintegrating.

Somebody did come forward with a towel and a few others were tossed forward as well. What the towels were needed for became immediately apparent. Our bus driver, Manny, had taken quite a bit of the windshield glass in his face and hands. I don't remember who manipulated the towel, I just remember the technique. They laid the towel over the driver's face and lifted gently as they pulled it away. Each time coming away with more and more shards of glass. I got involved with rotating the towels and shaking out the collected glass for a short while but soon ventured outside.

As I exited I noticed that the bus was just barely on the shoulder and still just about parallel to the road. There was a steep drop into a ravine only a few feet away. In front of the bus, and partially underneath it, was the completely totaled VW. I remember two guys struggling to get a door open but the finally did and pulled out a very limp body. They immediately attempted to start CPR. They modified their first-aid technique a bit when the guy attempting to pump his chest said something like, "He's got no chest left." They continued to perform mouth-to-mouth on the guy until the polizei arrived quite a while later. I think I remember a third person getting involved in what could only have been a horrible first-aid experience. But, in Germany you were expected to come to the aid of such victims and were expected to continue aid until the professionals arrived. I don't know how those guys did it. I couldn't take it so I went back inside the bus.

Inside, people were helping each other and checking each other out. Everybody other than Manny seemed pretty much OK, maybe some bumps and bruises. Manny was now mostly glassless and somebody was dabbing the blood spots with some sort of German Schnapps (which I am sure had a high enough alcohol content to be beneficial). Then somebody said, "Should we dump the booze?" I don't remember anybody saying yes or no, but within seconds the bus was clear of all beer and schnapps and whatever, all of which was now at the bottom of the ravine.

When the polizei finally got there some of us went back outside. In my case I went towards the back of the bus rather than even consider looking at the action. One of the polizei noticed me and held out a pack of smokes, Rot Hand as I recall, and I graciously excepted his traditional German expression of friendship. He also had to give me a light, I needed one because I had quit smoking some months before that night but have continued to smoke ever since. A few seconds later he said something like, "You are a band. Do you have any beer? I sure could use one." All I could do was point to where we had dumped our stuff. He just kind of nodded and walked off. I could have used one too.

Coda: I don't know if Manny got a medal for what he did that night, or if the person with the towel or those who attempted to save the other driver got any recognition. I do know that there were about twenty people (counting Band Wives) that probably owe their lives to that fine young GI bus driver. How he kept us on the road I do not know.

Yes, unfortunately, the driver of the VW died. As I later heard form one of the first to get to him, he was probably dead even before they got the door open.

Posted by Fred

11 comments:

Stephanie said...

> I would have thought that in eight years in the AFB East, I
> would have at least one memory of some sort of bus accident,
> but I don't. Sounds like a real blessing, huh Fred?

Chris said...

> We were extremely fortunate, considering the massive
> number of miles we put on buses. In fact, the only problems I
> recall during 15 years there was the occasional A/C
> malfunction, and one occasion when the throttle linkage
> came loose on the MCI while trying to go under the bridge at
> McDonough on I75... something that we rarely did, as it was
> the normal food/coffee/smoke/pee break point when traveling
> north from Robins. It only took a couple of minutes and a
> Leatherman tool to get it working again...

Fred said...

> @ Stephanie: Yeah, then log all those hours/miles on the
> trucks. Very fortunate.
>
> @ Chris: I remember McDonough VERY well. I stopped
> there on the way down from Atlanta on the 17th of
> September last year, and then again on the way up to Atlanta
> on the 19th. Chris, in my mind, that (the Flying J) is what the
> Peyton Freight Yard is in my mind in the scripts. I wonder
> how Manny is now?

Chris said...

> I had the same picture of Peyton... only with a Waffle House
> on the side!
>
> Were you with me the trip that the truck started to overheat in
> FL/GA on the way back from Tyndall or Eglin... we had to
> stop in a little churchyard to get water from the standpipe in
> the yard... watched the van blow right past us...

Fred said...

> Yup, I was on that one. I thought we were coming from Gulf Shores (Gulf Point) but, yeah that same back road...

Chris said...

> Come to think of it, it might have been the Shrimp Festival... that might make an episode all by itself, as I remember some of the other stuff that happened that trip...

Fred said...

> You didn't like me blowing up the back porch?

Stephanie said...

> Three words guys... Pink Pony Pub ;)

Chris said...

> And the world's longest crawl back... must have been miles.
>
> Always wondered why we couldn't stay closer, but, then again, it was on Uncle's nickel...
>
> I was remembering the only time I ever blew the lyrics to a DE tune... when the "young lady" walked by in front of the stand. To quote myself that day, "Sorry, folks, I got distracted for a bit, there."

Fred said...

> Yeah, the crawl... That's what goes on with Patrick and Davis followed by Peterson and the Bus Driver) in that episode... Your last comment reminded me of another gig...

4th Movement:

A Musical Life

Late 40s Detroit

Reality check - c.1948 Detroit.

My 26 year-old father was an established musician in Detroit by this time. He played trumpet and flute, a combination that was, somehow, popular in those days. Did a lot of shows at the Fox Theater - he was, at the time, a first call player.

Now, this is the first I heard of racism when I was a kid. My father had a small group in the late 40s, early 50s, that played the usual weddings, bar mitzvahs, etc. So, one day, he gets a call from someone to do a wedding at the Detroit Yacht Club. Of course, he took the job - very prestigious at the time and good for some real money. Unfortunately, one of the better known racist venues. My father knew the drill and often went by the name Jack Roberts when he 'needed' to. But the way he explained how this came down really got me.

They had played the first set and were leaving the stage, when someone came up to them and asked "Where's Sternthal" (someone at the wedding obviously knew him and gave him away). My father answers - "That's me." The guy says "pack up your stuff and get out, we don't allow 'kikes' here." Now - he didn't say Jews - he said 'Kikes.' Pretty brutal stuff.

At any rate, he starts to pack up, expecting to leave and let the other guys play and take the cash. Let's just say, some things are more important than money. They also packed up and followed him out the door. Any of us would have done the same.

Good history lesson.

Posted by Shep

1 comment:

Fred said...

   I wonder if "The Guy" learned anything from it?

From Bad To Worse-er-er

I mentioned in some other post about having the distinct privilege of working with Rob McConnell for a week or so, back in the 1980's. Part of his contract stated (mostly to get the US State Department people to get him a Visa, dang, he's (was) just Canadian, what's with that?) that he was supposed to critique a couple of charts our writers had done.

He performed those duties admirably, sipping a Gin in his comfortable hotel suite while we (his disciples) swilled beer at his feet. Then, with no provocation at all he light into me for the chart I did on "Do Nothing Until You Hear From me" which had the melody and harmonies messed with so much that I simply called it "Do Nothing."

He went on about how to mess with an Ellington piece was sacrilege, and how I had voiced the horns too tight, and that you NEVER have the band play the same notes the vocalist is singing, on and on. Then he tossed me another beer, and all was forgiven, though I did pull the chart from the books before the next gig.

A few weeks later I got a letter from Rob at the squadron. In it he asked, "Can I get a copy of that chart? I have a gig with this vocalist I hate, it would be perfect for her!" Fortunately, I had not destroyed it, though I had considered doing so. It was sitting in the back of my car, so I grabbed it, stuck it in an envelope, score and all, and sent the only known copy to him.

So, one of my major triumphs as an arranger was when a Master Arranger/Musician once requested a copy of something I wrote for his book, because he despised it. Go figure!

Posted by Fred

The Last Train To Clarksville

In the spring of 1993 I had a good reason to visit some "folks" in Clarksville, TN (yes, the town in the Monkey's song – only a few miles outside of Nashville, for those who don't know middle TN). It was a quaint little town, but nothing to make it stand out in my mind. During my visit there was to be a little Jazz Festival at the campus of the local school, Austin Peay University ("Lets Go Peay!" pronounced Pee.)

When we walked into the hall where we were to hear John Scofield with Joe Lovano and a few other not so famous acts, the room looked familiar. But like many university halls it could have been any number of venues. Then the first act came on, Tuck and Patti. Bingo, not only had I played that hall, but Tuck and Patti were on the bill when I (well, the AFB East) played it. I involuntarily cracked up, loud enough to have a nasty glance cast in my direction by Tuck, on guitar.

I proceeded to tell the folks that I had played there before, though I had no other recollection of Clarksville. So, of course they said sure, come on, whatever. So at intermission, before the big acts, I took my friends to back the stage entrance and ran into Tuck.

I got his attention and apologized for laughing during his first chorus. He recognized me and called me that Air Force guy who helped with their PA a few years ago. I had forgotten about that, I guess I did. He said, "Come on back, you should see Patti (his wife) too." So we went back stage, which thrilled the children present and we chatted for a few minutes, and a few autographs were collected.

Then I glanced over to the main power box and had a SERIOUS flashback. "Hold on a second, I gotta check something" I said as I reached for the catwalk ladder a few feet away. When I got just above the power box I looked down there was a dust covered Walkman with a gig tape of the AFB East in it from Knoxville in 1990. I had left that there almost 3 years before. I retrieved the tape, brushed off the Walkman and gave it to the kids. "It's a Small world After All" I like "Take the Last Train To Clarksville" better than that, but it's true!   Posted by Fred

Any Foot-Long Sub Only $5.00 –
Not So In The Music Business

I never knew about Subs, substitute players – though I had eaten a few hoagies, before I got to school in Denton in 1973. I was made clear to me that if you were to miss a gig, or even a rehearsal, even if your Mother did die, you were abducted by Martians, your dog blew up, whatever, you sent a sub. Huh?

At that same school I had the good fortune to study arranging with this amazing teacher named Lew. I am not sure he was a good arranging teacher, but he taught me a poop-load of stuff. One thing that he was adamant about was, "If you can't play it, you can't write for it!" He went on to say "You don't have to become Tony Studd or Cliff Heather, but you have to understand the instrument."

So, I was pretty much screwed. I was so good at skipping classes that I even skipped Lab Band (thought it was almost as good as sex, Lab Band rehearsals that is) and I personally thought that the most important part of being an arranger, which I desperately wanted to be, was the orchestration. So, what, I am gonna have to learn to play everything I hear and find people to cover for me every time I feel like drinking beer or get lucky? GEESH!

So when I wimped out at Thanksgiving in 1973 and went back home like the scared little kid I was, I thought about it, though I did not get a sub to cover the rest of my semester in the 8 o'clock band.

After a few days of feeling comfy at home, mooching off Mom and Dad, I called Phil. He played everything, literally, and played everything about as good as anybody I ever met who only played one thing. Top it off, he was like 16 at the time, I was a worldly 18. He lent me his Oboe, his Cornet and his Transverse Mounted, Rotary Valve, Eb Melaphonium (Man, that looks so cool to read). Oh, its kinda like an untwisted French Horn with Trumpet valves.

I got a gig as the desk guy at the local YMCA at night. During the day I would torture the neighbors with me attempting to learn these new axes; all along neglecting the saxophone, clarinet and flute, (my legitimate doubles). After a few weeks I knew this: Oboe sucks, though I like to write for it. Brass instruments are harder than Woodwind instruments, but I did like the "Transverse Mounted, Rotary Valve, Eb Melaphonium" and wish I had one now.

I have no idea how I ended up back at NTSU the next year but there I was and I signed up for "pedagogy" classes. WTF is "pedagogy?" (I recently heard a comic on cable say that he thought it was an 8 year old girl having sex with a dog. Unfortunately, the true definition was much more obscene.) So, you like got one lesson on each of five different instruments per semester. They made you do long tones, scales (yeah, like I ever did them on sax) or paradittles, or whatever. I made it through 1.5 semesters, with a D.

Then I met this girl form this middle Texas town and we got smitten. Then I met this girl from some place up north who played a "SHIT LOAD" (sorry, there is no way I would censor that one, she was THAT good) of Bari Sax. The first time I decided to dump Lab Band rehearsal in 1974 to just go hang with Ms Smitten, Ms SHIT LOAD covered for me, on like 20 minutes notice (thanks BD). I got an A+ that semester simply for being the first person in history to have gotten somebody from the 1 o'clock to sub in the 8 o'clock.

Posted by Fred

The Midnight Movers Strike Again!

This is a story from back in my NTSU (now UNT) days. It is not particularly musical, but does involve musicians - or at least kids attend a university attempting to become musicians - and a musical instrument. And after Chris' wonderful flashback to the Captain Weekes sign thing I thought this would be OK to post. I shared a house in Denton with a couple of trombone playing buddies and eventually a girlfriend or two. The house had been a Frat house and then sat empty for a while, so you can only imagine the condition of the place. Because of its deplorable condition the rent was $65.00 a month. That's for the house, not from each of us. So, needless to say, we took it!

It quickly became a party house, being in the business district that went to sleep early, we got away with making lots of noise. We had been there a while and somebody wanted to have a jam session, our place was the obvious choice. But, these were the days before really portable keyboards, so not having a house piano we had to use the Save A Soul Mission, so to speak, for that jam.

A few days later somebody mentioned that they knew where a piano that was not being used was, on campus. Eyebrows were raised so a couple of us went to check it out. Indeed, in an unused room in I think the Drama Department building was a piano, that from the layers of dust looked like it had not been used in a very long time. To make it better it was a studio sized upright and was sitting on those big cupped roll-around casters with 4" wheels.

The Midnight Movers were assembled for a strategy meeting and it was determined, because of the wonderful casters, that we would simply roll it out of the building right into the house (only a short stroll away), rather than attempt to load and unload it. This was done under the cloak of darkness as in the VI Commando story. Once at the house, we covered it with old blankets and piled stuff on it so it would not be obvious as to what it was.

We watched the papers, local and campus, for a few days and figured the coast was clear. We took up a collection to get it tuned and fixed up a little (wonderful thing about piano tuners, it is the perfect job for a blind person, so having Eddy work on a piano with a big old NTSU property tag on it was not an issue). Once it was in shape, it became the only piece of furniture in that house to be treated with respect, though there were a couple of cigarette burns on in before too long. It got lots of use for well over a year.

As it happened about that time I was getting ready to go into the Air Force, Danny (one of the original tenants and an important member of the Midnight Movers, due to the fact that he was a freak and a body builder) was going to be moving out too, therefore functionally breaking up the old gang. I don't know who suggested it, but because the piano had been procured on our watch, so to speak, it was decided that we would return it in better shaped that it was in when we "borrowed" it.

The "Midday Movers" were born. On a nice sunny afternoon, with students scurrying all about, we simply rolled it out of the house and back to where we had found it. The dust, seemed to indicate that we had still been the only people in that room. So we moved some stuff around to redistribute the dust and bid a fond farewell to our cherished house piano.

Posted by Fred

My Body Still Nose How To Play

This past weekend I was in Olympia, WA for my elder daughter's graduation. A lake house (well, the body of water directly across the street was actually a fjord, and offshoot of the Puget Sound, but Fjord House looked funny) was procured for Friday and Saturday so a free-form 32 hour long party ensued.

A little before sunset on Saturday a young lady showed up with an Alto Recorder, of the plastic flute-o-phone variety. I wandered over to her and asked her to play something. She popped out a few notes here and a few notes there but nothing that resembled a song then she offered the recorder to me. Figuring I couldn't do any worse than that I tried to adjust the head and foot joints so that they aligned the way I like them (to no avail) and attempted a F Major scale, ascending two octaves. Let's put it this way, I had not done much better than the young lady had, so I offered the recorder to someone else who had been drawn to the plifs and ploofs of the archaic flute.

That person had obviously never even held a recorder before. Right hand on top, fingertips/fingernails attempting to cover tone holes and blowing in it like Dizzy Gillespie going for a double-high C... So I gave a quick lesson on hand position and air delivery. The fingers got better but there was still far too much air for the instrument. I asked for the recorder back so I could demonstrate as I had been shown almost 40 years ago in a little music shop somewhere in Switzerland.

Placing the recorder to my left nostril and closing my eyes, my hands found their positions and a perfect (well, I did crack the high

C) chorus of "St. Thomas" somehow came streaming out of the instrument. I retired to my seat nearer the beer supply to a few chuckles and light applause. I guess it's kind of like riding a bicycle, but I don't recommend steering a bicycle with your nose.

Posted by Fred

5 comments:

Tom P. said...

> I can't pull a counterpoint to that story from my background. It must stand alone.

Fred said...

> I couldn't come up with one for the Bar Ditch either... Must be Monday.

Stephanie said...

> You can lead a nose to recorder, but you can't make it blow.

Chris said...

> Is "St. Thomas" still the only thing you can play on that axe?

Fred said...

> Yeah, but I can play it in 12 keys! Lol

> Actually I can play only about 10 tunes from memory (serious dot player here – but what do you expect from a dot writer). When I did the nose thing I was thinking I would play "Jesu Joy Of Mans Desiring," but "St. Thomas" came out.

> I guess I blew that one. But, who nose?

Sometimes Things Backfire

This one has nothing to do with music, took place with Army personnel, and neither I nor anyone I knew well had anything to do with it. But, as a follow-up to Tom's recent post I think it works.

After I got out of the Air Force I did some odd jobs, like bar back and even Karaoke DJ (there, I said it in public, maybe I can stop going to Karaoke DJ's Anonymous now). Through one of these bar related jobs I met the Johnson brothers, Ed and I don't remember the other guy's name. I got rather friendly with Ed and he invited me to a party they were having to celebrate the birthday of their other brother, Jimmy. I thought that was cool so I showed up at the appropriate time with my party clothes on - that's any outfit I own.

After a few minutes of milling with some of the other bar regulars I asked where the birthday boy was. Ed got a bit somber on me and told me that Jimmy had passed away back in the early 70's. This party was their way of remembering him happily. I felt awful, but how should I know? A beer helped lessen my embarrassment.

Trying to make amends, I ran into the other brother and said something like, "Sorry to hear about Jimmy. Vietnam?" (making that assumption only because Ed had said early 70's with no details). The nameless brother went on to tell me about he and Ed being in the AF and spending all of their time stationed at Robins during Nam. Then the story switched to Jimmy. He worked in the motor pool at Ft. Dix, NJ. He got word that his unit was going to deploy and that freaked him. So, as I understood it, Jimmy decided to try the "Shoot Yourself In The Foot" routine to get out of it.

Well, according to Nameless, Jimmy missed his foot and the round ricocheted up and cleanly went through his left bicep and into some empty boxes as the far end of the bay.

By the way, by this time there was a rather large crowd gathered to hear this story, which was also an annual event I found out later. Hence the need for new blood, like myself, each year to prompt the telling of the story.

Nameless went on to tell us that Jimmy freaked again, hid the gun, wrapped his arm up and went about his regular duties. Just before his shift was over Jimmy's boss notice the makeshift bandage, checked him out and then took Jimmy to the base hospital. Jimmy was at work the next morning even though he had been placed on quarters (had a note from mommy saying he did not have to go to school).

Ed was back at that point and took over the story telling. In his best proud big brother voice, he went on to tell us that not only didn't Jimmy's little prank not get him out of deploying, or even in trouble, it got him transferred to the infantry (it seems Army folks can be impressed by somebody that can take a bullet and keep on keepin' on) where he did three tours in Nam.

Thankfully somebody else asked the next question as the story seemed to be at its end. "So, is that when you lost him?" Ed burst out laughing, "No son, Jimmy went from a heart attack in a Saigon brothel just before rotating home!" The crowd raised their drinks and offered a big "To Jimmy!" before going back to serious drinking.

By the way, I understand that Glenn Miller may have actually met with a similar fate in Paris. I wonder if he had tried the foot thing first?

Posted by Fred

1 comment:

Chris said...

> Wonder how many of the old-timers in the Vietnam era bands got there by trying the same thing? I can think of one Firs Sergeant that we both knew who was supply in Vietnam before Band field... little moustache, sang a lot of Lou Rawls, PIA... you know...

Addled In Atlanta & The Mole People

For a little change of pace I am moving off base and moving into the studio for a couple of short stories.

Both of these things happened at a long gone recording studio in Atlanta, GA. I had the amazing good fortune to spend many hours there and became close with the lead engineer and got to love the owner and his wife. Then there was in inevitable crush that all the guys had on the cute receptionist. So I guess she's up first.

One morning, before rolling tape (remember tape?) I strolled up to the reception area with a serious cup of Joe to chat with the receptionist. She was somewhat disgruntled, moving papers and stuff around and complaining about this "damn new machine." I plopped myself down on the comfy half-sofa and asked her what was wrong.

She picked up an 8 inch Floppy Disk (remember them?), shaking it in the air over her head and said, "Every morning when I come in, it's like I have to re-type (re-enter was not a word yet) everything from yesterday!" Then she took the disk, slapped it against the side of the tall file cabinet and fastened it there with a magnet, that looked to be off an old speaker. You know like notes on the refrigerator.

It took only moments to instruct her in the proper storage of her new-fangled magnetic media.

Now batting, the Master Engineer!

I don't remember why, but I remember being in the room, rather than the booth when this happened, but during one of our sessions came this over the talk-back, "Alright, 'Mole People' it's time for a 'Sun Break'" and the engineer slid out of the booth, excited through the imposing mettle rear door into the lush Atlanta sunlight bathing the parking lot. He was followed by the smokers, lusting to do more lung damage, and non-smokers alike.

Because, like most studios I have ever been in, there were no windows, and "The Room" and "Booth" normally had very subdued lighting, the engineer stated that humans, even musicians and engineers, needed sunlight (something to do with vitamins). I dunno, I just wanted a smoke break, so I never turned him down.

Almost 10 years later, I found myself working for the IT Help Desk at a major metropolitan Newspaper. Only people who worked at a newspaper, capitalize it when making this kind of reference. Taking dozens of phone calls and making desk visits to irate customers every day was stressful, but I began to wonder why I was still SO stressed out, even after getting comfortable in the job.

Then I realized there were no windows (none of the three offices the Help Desk was in had a single window) and subdued lighting (all fluorescent to make matters worse). Bingo, that morning when break time came, 105 on – 15 off, I stood up and proclaimed to my fellow nerds, "OK Mole People, it's time for a Sun Break" and proceeded to the distant second floor balcony - normally called the Lounge or the Back Porch -which had a lovely view of the "Dragnet" building (also the Daley Planet, from the Superman TV series) for a couple of smokes.

Before the end of the day, everybody wanted an explanation of the Mole People thing. Before too long everybody was doing it, and the exiting expression was simply shortened to "Mole People..."

A little added twist, the studio was on Spring ST, Atlanta, GA – the newspaper was on Spring ST, LA, CA.

Posted by Fred

Proof That I Can Write A Short Post . . .

Q: What do you call six or more trombone players in a room at the same time?

A: An Unemployment line.

Q: What do you call a trombone player without a girlfriend?

A: Homeless.

This post was specifically targeted at, well you know who you are. Common folks, inquiring minds want to know what trombone players are thinking too! Well, maybe not really...

Posted by Fred

2 comments:

Bill C. said...

> Hardy-har-har. OK, I'll play:
>
> The other day I met two fellas on the street. One was a trombone player. The other one didn't have any money, either.

BJ said...

> Definition of an optimist... A Trombone player with an agent, and a cell phone....

Fred's War Story #3: An All-Natural Ham

Thanks, Shep, for your "Cowboy Rumble" story. Did you open the next set with "Rawhide?"

Anyway...

July 4th, 1969 – Compo Beach, Westport, CT. This was my first gig ever, 14 years old. Having just recently gotten back in touch with three insaner friends who played that gig with me (they were on the invitee list for this Blog, and while they have given no indication of being interested in contributing, they have reminded me of stuff like this). We were the warm-up act for the fireworks, so I guess there were a few thousand people there? We were on a flatbed truck with my Dad's Big Band (he put that together for us kids a year or so before) and I guess we had about 13 or 14 of the chairs covered.

My Dad started off on the mike and kicking off the tunes. Then after a few tunes he handed me the mike and said "You take over." I looked surprised and said "What do I do?" He said "Tell them what you are going to play, and then play it."

It never occurred to me to be nervous, so I looked down at the lead alto part (that I was barely able to cover, even though the charts were all 2's and 3's) and saw that good old #7 was up next. So I stuck the SM 58 in my chops and proudly proclaimed "We're gonna play Hoagy Marcarkle's Stardust." The audience applauded and the band began a long tradition of giving me serious shit every time I stepped in front of a mike, deservedly so, I might add. Oh, I think I got "Carmichael" right when we played "Georgia On My Mind" later in the set. So, a ham was born.

Later embarrassing moments, like getting the name of the Director of Jazz Studies for the University of Tennessee wrong while performing in Knoxville, willfully performing the "Chicken Dance" on stage all over Europe with the AFB Overseas or spraining an ankle while prancing around the stage in a tutu during a pantomime on "The Twelve Days Of Christmas" (the sprain was embarrassing, I dug the shtick) pale in comparison to that first blunder.

But, as they say, the show must go on. To which that band might have said "Why?"

Posted by Fred

6 comments:

Stephanie said...

    I enjoyed all of these war stories very much!

Anonymous said...

    Over the years we continued to morph your botched intro. By the time we were finished, you had said "Sporky Smorkforkle" or worse.

Anonymous said... (cont.)

> You were very nonchalant (or was that oblivious?) about your announcing duties.
>
> "I'll have something cool and refreshing, perhaps." WPB replying to a waiters inquiry at a country club gig.

Fred said...

> Yes! See, this is why you got an invitation tho this place. It could have been "Sporky Smorkforkle" oblivious is probably more correct. I retained that same announcing style for all those years in the AF bands, where for some strange reason, that allowed me to emcee a lot. Go figure?!?

Anonymous said...

> I like Gil Evans' arrangement of "Sporky Smorkforkle."

Fred said...

> Man, Bill, you got the title wrong. I think you mean "Struttin' With Some Smorkforkle" from the "Roots" album, with Cannonball.
>
> You guys!!! Lol

Anonymous said...

> ...maybe I was thinking of Stravinsky's "The Rite of Sporky," or Bach's "The Well-Tempered Smorkforkle."

Fred's War Story 3.5:
Retroactive Background Info and Foreshadowing

Sorry I missed a post for yesterday. But, as Shep pointed out, you folks can post too. Out list of Contributors has grown, and yet I think so far only Shep and I have posted. OK, some others have commented, but we would like to hear your stories as well.

Anyway...

The last two days have been a hoot for me. It started out with a rash of e-mails from old JHS/HS friends. That was followed by a bombardment of Facebook notices from friends from my HS choir. So, needless to say I have been awash in polyester, bell bottoms, Peter Max posters and sandalwood incense ever sense. (Not actually, but I did go through a bit of a time warp.) So here are a few "Shorts" from my PRE-NTSU musical experiences.

My Dad, who played Tenor and Clarinet in his day, put together a Big Band for me and my friends from the school band because the schools in my hometown only had concert/marching bands, that was like 1967 maybe 1968. The first rehearsal we had only one chart, "In A Persian Market" arranged by Richard Maltby. We played for about an hour then attacked the fridge for soda-pop (yes that's what I called them in those days) and played something like volleyball until the parents came and picked up their kids. I WAS HOOKED!

Of the kids in that, and subsequent iterations of that band (which continued until the mid 80's), quite a few went into music. Of those, I am only aware of one who is still seriously playing, Tad Shull. He has about half a dozen recordings on the "Criss Cross" label, if you would like to hear a guy I used to gig with when I was 13.

OK, I know that was much like my War Story #3, but it was there for the background. Here is some new stuff.

I had no interest in singing of any kind when I got to High School (though I did dig the Hi-Lows, thank you Todd for turning me on to them, and Lambert, Hendrix and Ross, thank you whatever that radio station in Mt. Kisco, NY was). Then one day, somebody asked me to join the Choir, I can't remember if it was a fellow student or one of the music teachers. I remember saying I would think about it, but in the back of my mind I had already blown it off. A few days later somebody else suggested the same thing, it was either Todd or George B., but they added, "The girls are hot!" and ran off a few names. My "Little Head" made one of its finest decisions that day, and I became a disciple of Mr. George Weigle (the choir director) as soon as I could get the paperwork done.

Mr. Weigle was by far the best teacher I ever had, any subject, any possible use of the word. Other than the curriculum, he taught things like how to love music – all you had to do was look at his face when/if we nailed four bars of something, and how to respect your fellow musicians. And yes, in one of his ensembles, even the singers were musicians (OK, for the most part) once he got a hold of you.

Mr. Weigle, even more than my Dad, was responsible for me spending 20 plus wonderful years in the music business. So, if it had not been for him, I probably would not know any of you. So, you can blame him!

Now that you have the background, I can hit you with something a bit more humorous and/or risqué. But I have typed too much for today, so I will hold off until tomorrow for "Tales of Graz."

Posted by Fred

7 comments:

Bill C. said...

> Memoirs of a Jazz Amnesiac... Since we're geezin'-out, here's how I lost my jazz virginity: 3rd grade (1963?), Elmhurst ES, Greenville NC. The high school band directors, James Rodgers and my mentor, Tom Smith, Jr., came to a school assembly to demonstrate the band instruments and recruit suckers, I mean players, into the program. Mr. Smith, a world-class trombonist, played "Lassus Trombone" and it changed my life.

Bill C. said... (cont.)

My father bought me a pawn-shop horn and overnight my musical favorites switched from the Beatles to the Tijuana Brass. The first albums of my record collection were "The Original Dixieland Jazz Band" and Herbie Mann's "Live at the Village Gate" (talk about bookends). The first Big Band chart I paid attention to was Benny Goodman's "King Porter Stomp."

Fast forward to 7th grade ('67?), Greenville JHS: The concert band playing "Night Beat" (a musical portrait of NYC); I really laid-in to the swingin' "Harlem" section. That same grade, GJHS burned (I didn't do it; I swear!): no more bandroom, so we would go to the HS for private lessons. Mr. Smith would pull out the "Dixieland Combo-Orks", and with him on trumpet, we'd play "Basin St Blues", "...Miss New Orleans", "Tin Roof Blues", et al.

Then four different high schools, played lead trombone in four different HS Big Bands. To NTSU fall of '73 and disillusioned to learn jazz didn't begin until Charlie Parker first drove a spike into his arm. Most of you know the rest of the story: 30 years +/-of either being ferociously true to my old-school roots, or a hopeless stick-in-the-mud. That's it: time to drink my Metamusil and change my Depends.

Fred said...

Good story! Hey, don't make fun of your roots. Just consider yourself Wynton Marsalis without as good a tan. You got the hair!

Anonymous said...

I'm not making fun of my own roots, but I will admit preemptive self-deprecation has always been my first line of defense as I refuse to blindly march in lock-step with others of my generation. - B.

Fred said...

> Man, I love you!

Bill C. said...

> How 'bout you other blogistas? When and how did ya'll get the "jazz bug"? SHEP?! –Bill

Tom P. said...

> I was 13 years old. My friends listened to the Beatles, Rolling Stones, etc. That was fine but I had the feeling there had to be something else out there for me. When we moved into a new home I found that the previous owner had a left a 1957 "Best of Brubeck" album in the basement. I hauled down my sister's plastic kiddie record player (with it's five-pound stylus) and spun the thing to see what was there. It was like seeing God.

Shep said...

> I was fortunate to have a father who was a musician (not so fortunate that he was a bloody drunkard and bastard his whole life).

> He would often listen to Puccini, Dizzy, Sarah, and who knows what, in an afternoon on any given Sunday. My mother was a June Christy fanatic.

> So, I grew up with it in the house. When I got my first record player ('67, maybe), I bought Nancy Wilson first, Miles next. I also loved pop and would buy lots of 45s.

Only In The Movies?

We had just finished four weeks at the Hilton in Vegas - must have been '81 - a real sweet gig. Then our brilliant manager books us for the next two weeks at this dive in Farmington, NM. I won't even get into the trailer they gave us to stay in and what was inside, suffice it to say it was disgusting. The first night, we're tryin' to come up with as many country songs as we can. Luckily, the drummer/vocalist knew the entire Eagles catalog. So, we figured a few Willie and Patsy tunes and we're off and running :-)

About 20 minutes into the first set, a fight breaks out and the bottles and glasses start flyin' around the place. Then the bodies start flyin' across the tables. This was a real "cowboys and indians" thing going on right in front of us! I thought to myself, "holy shit - this is only supposed to happen in the movies!" Well, not that night. We calmly retired to the back of stage and waited until the cops came and cleared out everybody.

That was my first and last time in beautiful Farmington, NM.

Next up - Coffeeville, KS. Bet you can't wait.

Posted by Shep

1 comment:

Fred said...

That's the spirit! Duck, Yankee!!!

The difference between a Yankee and a Damn Yankee?

A Yankee is anybody from above the Mason–Dixon Line who happens to be below the Mason–Dixon Line.

A Damn Yankee is one who decides to stay.

What's In A Name?

While I was working at the Help Desk for my major metropolitan newspaper I had one of those phones that would display the caller's name if they were calling from inside the building. By default they would display First Name then Last Name. But, If you wanted to jump through some hoops and fill out the paperwork you could get the name to display Last Name then First Name separated by a coma. Yes, there is a musical twist here...

After a few months there I had chuckled more than once about the names of two regular callers, Carlos Santana and Jimmy Paige, showing up on my phone. There were other celebrity names (we did have a staff of over 5,000 when I first got there) but these were the only musically related names I encountered for quite a while.

By the way, neither of those individuals even vaguely resembled their namesakes in personality. In fact, one of them was quite a jerk and would get all prissy if I mentioned the legendary guitar player.

As time went on, the LED's on my phone would selectively malfunction with some regularity producing some interesting results. Then one day the phone rang and the display read "Little Richard." I had a good chuckle and cleared my throat before I delivered my patented, "Help Desk, Fred speaking. May I help you?"

My greeting was met with a cheerful flamboyant response from the caller who was new to the paper and was just calling to say hi to the people he hoped he would never have to call in an emergency. He was a hoot. We chatted for a few minutes and I let him know where we were physically located in case he ever needed a walk-in.

After he hung up, I had to look him up on the Employee Directory web site. Nothing, no Little Richard anywhere. OK, maybe he was too new? Then I typed in Richard Little. There he was. A skinny extravagantly dressed Afro-American gentleman in say his early 40's with a big old grin on his face. My phone and the quirky LED's had perfectly removed the coma providing me with that memory.

A few weeks later he did do a walk-in, but once again just to say hi. He was more impressive in person, and a lot more, or should I say a lot less, straight?

Unfortunately, I heard about a month later that he had been let go, art critic, for being a bit too, shall we say, flamboyant. I wonder how many times something like that happened to the other Richard,

Little?

Posted by Fred

Let's Do The Time Warp Again – AKA: War Stories In The Making

As some of the regulars here may know, I spent last weekend, in Las Vegas. It was my first time there. Pretty cool (well, it was actually over 100 degrees but you know what I mean). I didn't go for the gambling or the shows or any of the things most people go to Vegas for. I went to hang out with two old AF buddies (and we have finally at that point where I must say that I mean that literally and figuratively – though it must be noted that I was the oldest of the group).

The youngest of the group, K, is local to Vegas these days though we met back at Robins in the mid 80's. Odd, he was not in the band. I had seen K more than once since moving to CA, so I kind of knew what to expect when I saw him last Friday night. On the other hand, R, who I had met earlier and gotten much closer to over the years I had not seen since 1997. I had seen a few pictures of R on the internet and there was one that concerned me when I saw it. The picture I remember seeing of him was of a really old fat guy. So, I gotta tell you I was pleasantly surprised when this dude that looked just like my buddy from Robins in 1997 came through the doors of the Riviera Casino last Friday.

We had all changed, less hair hear, a little broader there, then some "where did your butt go" and stuff like that. All and all, I really felt like I was hanging with the boys (known as the DF's in those days) from even farther back, say 1986.

Our trio was finally reunited at the bar in the center or the Riviera Casino, ground floor, where Ed, from New York (it said so on his name tag – and he lived up to it being a jerk as he provided us with lousy service) was our bartender. Fortunately, even before he could screw up a second order, we decided to move to new bar, in the same casino, that served good imported beer on tap that was on the fringe of the casino, therefore much less commotion going on. Nice decision.

So, on our short trek from Ed's bar to the Queen Victoria Pub our marching orders were vaguely sketched out. K would be the point man (even if he did not know the area, it is in his nature to want to be in charge) R fell into the role of informed second, and I became the road guard (though I did not have a Lackland Laser that weekend) and pulled up the rear.

Once the first round, a Guinness and two Boddingtons. (I had never had one of those so I yielded to R's choice – he is a true beer master) hit the table, the DF convention, 2010 was called to order. Nothing official, but we found ourselves in one of those time warp conversations. You know, where it felt like we had just been discussing this yesterday, when yesterday was actually 25 years ago. Whoo-hoo.

One thing that became apparent to me as the night went on was that I seem to remember 0.5 to maybe 0.75 of things that went on 20+ years before. But, you should know, that does NOT stop me from telling the whole story. I simply make up the parts that I am not sure of and move on. I am not insinuating that R & K were doing the same. In fact, I think they tended to only recount stuff they knew they knew, or pointed out areas of a story where they might have been sketchy on.

With that said, sometime during the evening I was telling some story about some guy who had two stars on the Hollywood (CA, not FL as in some of my earlier posts) Walk of Fame. My story was met with a mixed reaction (I am seldom as funny in real life as I am in my own head). In fact, I think I remember K giving me a "No way" or something like that. I will skip to the following night so this post won't top the word count for the "Last Of The Mohicans" but this is not the only Friday story to be posted.

As we were on our way to diner on Saturday, K began to expound on the research he had done on my preposterous statement about the "Only Person To Have Two Stars..." from the night before. In an attempt to defend myself, I asked K who was it I said that about, as he was lovingly ripping me an new sphincter. Things got quiet. None of us could remember who it was. We could all remember my story being told, just not who it was about.

Maybe 25 years from now we will be able to remember that?

Coda: R broke the silence that our brain farts had caused by telling a wonderful and beautifully embellished call-back joke, based on one that K had told the night before, that cracked us all up. Oh, and the dinner was fantastic! More later.

Posted by Fred

Dissed-illusions Of Grandeur

I mentioned in an earlier post that I had lived a dream and got to play with Ringling Bros. I also had the chance to play the Disney parks in Florida more than once, which was also sort of cool. The only bad part of working in such places is that if you do it long enough, some of the magic may rub off. Here are my two examples.

Disney World in about 1990: We had an afternoon gig on an uncovered stage in the middle of the afternoon in August. If you are not familiar with Florida in August, you may not be able to understand just how uncomfortable that could be. I think it was over 100 degrees with about 99% humidity and I don't think that is an exaggeration.

We lost one guy to fainting in the first set, so the sponsor rushed us into the secret back stage area as soon as the set ended, another to follow in 30 minutes. The back stage area was filled with beverages, no beer, but stuff that would help you recover from heat stroke. The guys dove in.

Once we had regained some of our senses and tossed around a few phrases like "Who booked this gig?!" and "Yeah, but it's a dry heat..." I realized that the regular park performers were also there milling around. I don't know about you, but for me to see Goofy walk in, yank off his head revealing a very tall young black woman was a little strange. Then when she clearly uttered "It's F**KIN' hot out there!" one of my childhood bubbles burst. I never really dug amusement parks after that.

Part two, The Weirdest Show on Earth: Albany Civic Center, Albany, GA with Ringling Bros: This was show number eight for me, so I was feeling pretty comfortable, and no longer bleeding. For this trip I had made a big batch of chili for myself and the guys from Macon that all carpooled down together to the gig. So after dragging in my horns I went to find a place where I could plug in my crock pot. There was a nice empty table right near the Mens room with a convenient plug so I set the grub up there.

As I was turning the crock pot on, around the corner came three clowns, real ones, not band guys. They were in full wigs with face and hand makeup, but wearing only blue jeans and sneakers other than that. What made the topless part a surprise, though a pleasant one, was that two of the clowns were defiantly female (and fine representatives of their sex). My smile was quickly turned upside down when the three of them erupted into a HUGE argument, complete with words that Richard Pryor would never use. There went another bubble.

Coda: On the way in for the show the next day, I got to see this HUMOGOUS elephant take a dump. Well, not like a stood in line to buy tickets, it just happened while I was walking in. Wow they make lots of POOP! The magic, at least for the circus, was restored!

Posted by Fred

Getting Karaoke-ed Away

My buddy Keith sent me a Facebook message with a link to a video about the pop singer, Jewel, doing a setup Karaoke performance which was really pretty cool. It reminded me of two Karaoke experiences I would like to share here. OK, OK, I know what you are thinking, "Karaoke and Music" isn't that like Jumbo Shrimp and Military Intelligence? Just read a bit.

I think I mentioned before that after getting out of the AF I did some odd jobs, one of those jobs was playing Karaoke DJ, or KDJ as those in the business like to call it. (I have long sense gotten over the stigma attached to that.) One of the jobs of the KDJ is to fill in when it's dead or to cover a duet when somebody could not find a partner. Those were rather uncomfortable and sometimes embarrassing for me, but being the ham I am I managed to get through that will a little help from Uncle Bud - which was normally all I made for the gig – free beer. Which brings me to the bars I worked.

90% of the KDJ I did was at a place called Rosa's later Fortunes. To call it a Redneck-Cracker Bar would be pretty accurate, but you must understand that I mean that in a good way. The other bar, the name escapes me for a good reason, that I did a few nights at was a little more up-scale, but then again this was Warner Robins, GA, so still pretty Cracker.

One night at Fortunes a tiny Filipino woman filled out a request slip and handed it to me. Being just outside the back gate of Robins, AFB Fortunes saw quite a few Filipino customers. She then leaned in and asked that I take the pitch up a half step when she sang. I have to tell you that conversation took quite a while because the club was loud, her accent was VERY thick, and her English was not that good. But, I marked her card and she got in the queue.

Fortunately, the lady's name was easy for me, Patty (I had run into some Filipino names that I murdered) so when I called her up there was no problem. As I cued up the CD and raised the pitch, I noticed for the first time what song she had chosen, Barbara Streisand's "Somewhere." Yikes! I had heard a couple of the regulars, pretty good singers by Warner Robins Karaoke standards, fold on that before so I kind of sighed as she stepped on the stage, looked away from the monitor with her eyes closed.

When she started to sing, there was NO ACCENT. Not only that she actually sounded a lot like Barbara. She never moved, except to breath like a trained Opera Singer, and never opened her eyes as she NAILED every note! It was so damn good that there was a moment of silence in the bar, not a normal thing in a redneck bar, before she got her standing ovation.

She left right after that song and I never saw her again. I asked around but nobody seemed to know who she was or why she never came back. I was disappointed. She had given me goose bumps!

The other story took place at The Bar With No Name. The KDJ booth at that place was right between the door and the tap side of the bar at that place so I could see everybody coming and going and get my free drafts easily. That night this kid who looked to be about 15 years old, walked up to the door guy with his ID in hand. I guess he was ready for the inquisition that was about to unfold. He got more crap than usual, not only because he looked so young and had an NY State drivers license, he was also black. "Black Yankee in King Bubba's Court" just didn't ring true to me. But eventually they let him in. About five minutes later he was given more shit when he ordered his first beer.

I think he was pleasantly surprised when he asked for a request card and I handed him a stack and said, "Here, what ya gonna sing?" without any shit accompaniment. He asked if we had "Sir Duke?" I actually had to check the book. If he had asked for some Elvis tune or George Straight, I would have known, but Stevie Wonder in a Cracker Bar? Fortunately, we did have it.

When it came his time to sing, the kid looked like the proverbial deer in the headlights. I could only imagine what he was feeling while the horn intro was playing and he was stared at the monitor. The first few words were a little weak, but by the time he got to "understand" at the end of the first line, he put some air in it and even added that cool little Stevie vibrato to it. He was on! By the time he got to "in the groove" he was, and then some. Then he started movin'. Then he started to dance during the horn breaks. The crowd was really into it. By the time he finished the room full of a couple hundred Crackers and one very brave young Afro-American singer looked like a remake of "We Are The World." He also got a standing-o.

The kid stuck around. People bought him drinks (and he didn't even have a cool bird shirt on) and he sang like five other things, including some C&W and Cracker Pop. Just before last-call, the bartender asked to see his ID again as he served him his last beer, though he was very polite about it this time. The kid handed him the license and the bartender said something like, "Cool. So It's your birthday." The kid smiled as the bartender slid the card across the bar towards the kid. At that point the kid waved at me and said thanks and calmly walked out the door, beer and mug in hand. I shouted, well a little shout, at him and mentioned that he had left his ID on the bar. He looked back and said, "They can have it. It's a fake anyway" and kept right on walking.

Now, that took balls!

Posted by Fred

The Bombs Bursting In Air

I know it's not the 4th of July, actually it's the 14th of July as I type this, but yesterday was another National Holiday, at least it is to me; the Baseball All-Star Game (ASG). I never know how I am going to react during the ASG, but I normally start to cry about the time they introduce the Coaches and Reserves and get my stuff together just before First Pitch, when I offer a toast, with a special beer, to the home team pitcher. After that, it's anybody's guess.

Sandwiched between the intros and First Pitch is normally the anthem, sometimes two, Canada and USA, but yesterday it was just the US anthem. The girl (and I mean girl, perhaps 18, is on some TV show) who sang it gets about a B from me, though she did finish strong (up until that final Soul Train lick at the end). So, I mused a moment about good renditions of the US National Anthem, and came up with a few associated and some not really related things to share.

First, my buddy Barb told me this story of the time she was on a bus with the band in the PI and one of her friends, a singer by trade, stood up and just started singing the anthem. Remember, this is a bus load of GI Bandsmen who probably don't want to hear that tune any more than they have to. As I remember Barb's story, in just a few bars her lady friend had the attention of the whole bus, though I hope not the driver. When she got through there was a bunch of silence, as I recall. For those of you who have e ver been on one of those bus rides you know how much of a tribute silence can be for such an event. For those of you have not, it's kinda like winning the lottery without having to pay taxes. I wish I could have heard it, both the performance and the silence.

Second, I flashed back to the version of "The Banner" by Igor Stravinsky he wrote in 1939 or 1940, not sure. If I didn't, and there is any interest, I can post a link to both his original Orchestral version and a Vocal version that was done later. I had never heard it until a few weeks ago, but when I did I was blown away. He didn't do a theme and variations, normal when a Classical Composer is credited for an Arrangement, he did a chart. Very respectful and one time through.

All I could think was, what a gift this Russian immigrant has given his new country. Then I found out he got busted for screwing with it, or whatever the official charge was, in Boston on the 14th of July 1940. Why he stuck around after that, I don't know. But, I am glad he did.

Third, I then remembered the version of the anthem that was popular in the 80's done by Amy Grant which had these prolonged extended phrases between the early part of the first verse. The one that came to the front was the use of a Symphonic Bass Drum to punctuate "The Bombs Bursting In Air" that part always gave me a, well, shall I say, pleased me. But that was not the first time, or even second time I had heard such a sound and had that kind of reaction. So, out of order...

Fourth, would be this first time I heard the cannon shot sound, and it was not even a cannon (they really don't sound that cool in person) nor was it a Symphonic Bass Drum. It was a clap of the most unusual thunder I had ever experienced.

I was in Graz, Austria for a music festival with my HS Choir in 1972. It was our second night there, so I had gotten over (a bit) the first time away from home thing and was up in my dorm room (where they billeted us) all by myself when I could hear the sound of a thunderstorm rolling in. The low rumbling was pretty cool and just added to the feeling that I was in a Frankenstein or Dracula movie.

But, my room had only a tiny dingbat window, you know into the slanted ceiling, being on the top floor so I when out to the hallway to find a window so I could see the lightening, I mean, what is Donner without the Blitzen?

When I got to the hall the rumbling stopped. I hoped that I had not missed anything and ran down the hall to where I knew there was this big inset window about three feet off the ground and hopped up on the ledge to pear out. I could see AMAZING driving rain, I would not see rain like that again for years, Florida in the 80's. Then I saw a flash. No time to count, BOOM. It almost knocked me off the windowsill. Being 17, and just as stupid as I am now, but far less experienced, I stayed on the sill but I grabbed the cool European window handle for support. Then another flash followed immediately by a BOOM, the storm must have been right overhead, no lag. Then I realized, there I was in the Alps, and there was NO ECHO, just a little reverb from the glass shaking. I don't know if it was the acoustics of the 200 year old stone building I was in, or if that's just the way it sounded there, but I was really impressed. A few more flash-booms (they were so close together that needs to be one word) and then things started to lengthen out. The rumble was back and the rain was letting up. I ran down the stairs, about six flights as I recall – but I was 17 at the time, so I could rush out into the street and smell the air (you know that smell). I wasn't trying to sneak out or anything, which I did try later in the trip with little success, I just wanted to smell the air.

I got outside and the rain was now that fine mist and the street looked like something out of a Dickens novel (something you could only see in a dream, that couldn't have been real, but it was). I did a little Gene Kelly and before I got totally drenched I ducked under the awning of the establishment next door and peered in the window. I was like a kid in a candy store kind of happy but I was not looking into a candy store but a Pub, I didn't know they were called Gausthouses then so I substituted the closest term I knew. So what the heck... I had some local currency, why not go in and sneak a beer not realizing that I was perfectly legal there. So, I did.

It never occurred to me that there might be a language barrier there, remember, in my mind I was in an English Pub so after passing a few people with these amazing looking drinks that looked much like the deluxe version of what my Uncle Art drank I asked the barmaid for one of those please, pointing. She smiled, walked to the tap and started the beer.

She came back in a few seconds and attempted to teach me how to order a beer in German, but it was pretty far over my head that night, remember I was in an English Pub, it might as well been a dream. When she brought this flagon out she said something like, "Two and twenty" I must have grimaced or something so she just walked away. I never did pay for that beer.

I had about three sips and realized I was in over my head. I grabbed the coaster, those cool European beer coasters, under the mug and asked her if I could keep it. She smiled again and handed me a handful of dry clean ones and said, "Sleep well tonight." Man, did I... I still have the coasters she gave me. The bear was called "Puntagammer." I have no idea if it was any good, but for that night it was the coolest thing I had ever experienced, after the BOOMS.

Fifth, and final. Fast forward about ten or years. The AFB East Concert Band has a gig at this place in Sarasota, Florida that we used to call the "Purple Cow" (officially known as the Van Wezel Performing Arts Center). It was a famous building designed by Frank Lloyd Write (and part of the design required that it be painted purple, as I understand it) that had the best acrostics of any hall I had ever been in. Because of that we did not use our normal road PA system, just the house stuff which as I remember meant just a few mikes for the vocalists, everything else was acoustic. Being the sound guy, that basically meant all I had to do was sit and listen to the show, sweet!

Being in Southwest Florida, the show was mostly patriotic and ended with the usual, "A Tribute To The Armed Forces" medley. We had played it a million times so the charm had worn off almost as much as the charm of the anthem. But, that night, something happened in that hall with that percussion section that sill makes me cry like I am listening to the All-stars being introduced when I think about it – which I did last night.

More than half way through the medley, just before the Coast Guard Song, there is this hit in the Marine Hymn from the drummers. That particular night there were five, two Snares, one Tymp, one set of 20" Marching Cymbals and a Symphonic Bass Drum. I don't remember who was on what except that "The Krotz" or "Krotz" as his friends called him, was on Bass Drum.

So it got time for that hit, ho-hum, the Major pointed at the percussion section and there was that sound again. Time stood still for me. I was back in Graz, and now can transport myself to that over produced 80's album (yeah, still on vinyl in those days) and it was there. Five musicians struck, sustained and choked PERFECTLY! For those of you who have not taken a percussion pedagogy class, that means they nailed it.

So, if I were asked if over a 20-plus year career in music I can remember the ONE best note I ever heard, I can say yes.

Coda: there was one other story that involved "Bombs Bursting" that came to mind last night, but I will save that for later. Rick and Ron, you may have to help me with that one.

Gort!

Posted by Fred

Cat Litter

Another early musical memory. I don't remember exactly when but it had to be before May of 1974 when this came down.

Todd, Bobby, Jack, perhaps others and I got tickets to see the Ellington band at Alice Tully Hall, Lincoln Center, NY, NY. To mark this as the greatest musical experience of our young lives, we all went down to Ed Mitchell's, a local clothing store, and rented Tuxes for the event. Remember, we were like 16, maybe 17 or 18 at the time, so that was a big deal. We caught the train from the Saugatuck station and headed to "The City." When we came out of Grand Central Station a pigeon did his/her duty on the right lapel of my rented Tux. Eventually the cleaning bill cost more than the rental. Having been raised in my household, I had a handkerchief and attempted to wipe it off - probably causing more damage than good. Then we started out walk up town (about what, 50 blocks? More like half that...) to the center.

We got there after the concert had started and we headed to our cheap seats, like second balcony or something. As we went through the door from the hallway there was this mass of sound pressing us back. It was not 18 guys blowing into a bunch of mikes plastered over a KA PA. It was just the rhythm section, a quartet (Wild Bill Davis was with the band that night too) accompanying a solo trumpet (playing off-mile) on "Satin Doll."

I had heard this guy before on records. The guy who played high but had such a little sound. I knew him, that Anderson guy. Then he took it up. Davis cranked the B-3 and it was just the two of them. I think I spotted myself (though that may not have figure into the cleaning bill) right there.

So, there I was over 100 feet away from this Cat, excuse the pun, with no mic, killing me. Oh, by the way, his notes worked just fine, thank you . Yeah, I cry a lot, that was another time.

After "Satin Doll" we finally shook out our shorts and got seated amongst our fellow Duke-ites. It turned out that we were not over dressed at all, though out haircuts may have been a bit shabby. The concert continued and we got to hear Duke speak in person. It was like listening to God, even better than Morgan Friedman or James Earl Jones.

At the end of the closer, right, the house erupted. Personally, I could not even stand I was that blown away. Then came the encore, a little thing called "Cottontail." This was not the 1938 "Cottontail" this was the one he wrote in the 50's where the sax section played the Webster solo and Cat did major 10ths instead of major 3rds on that out-figure. So they went at it. Cat, Rabbit, Harry, Gonzolves, Russell Procope, Ralph Erikson, those guys and we just stood there (I finally found the motor skills to stand up). Before I go on, let me remind you that this was an encore to a two hour concert.

I was already drenched by the time it came to those 10th figures just before the out-chorus and then it came. Cat didn't stand up, he hardly even moved, he just played. "Daba-dot-a-dee-bah-dop-be-dot-daba," "Daba-dot-a-dee-bah-dot-be-dot-daba," "DABA-DOT-A-DEEBAH-DOP-BE-DOT-DABA," "DABA-DOT-A-DEE-BAH-DEEBE-DOT-DADA" OMG. What happened there was probably on the cleaning bill.

I remember thinking at that time that it was odd that my friends and I were the last people out of Alice Tully Hall, Lincoln Center that night (they actually had to come and ask us to go) but not anymore. Now I understand that I have always been lucky enough to have smart friends. These dudes where just as blown away as I was.

Soon after that concert, that band began to break up in the only way that, "THAT" band could possibly have broken up, the cats started dying. How lucky was I to be at that concert? I still wonder what it would have been like to hear the in their prime? It's OK, I'll take my memory of those crusty old dudes passing along their legacy to a handful of puppies, and perhaps a few hindered others, that day and cherish it forever.

Coda: OK, OK, I got home at about 3:00 AM (we had stopped in Time Square at a couple of Adult type establishments). Dad was waiting for me, shit! I think I was ready for Mom being up, but not for my Dad. By the way, that house, the house I grew up in, had a gravel driveway. I believe to this day that my Dad had that put in as an alarm system. No way you could drive in without him hearing the crunch of tires from his ground floor bedroom. Standing on the linoleum floor that looked like a Jackson Pollard painting he asked, "How was it?" Forgetting who I was, all I could say was, "F**king fantastic!" He nodded and said, "Then get some sleep and we will talk about it later."

I had never said a curse word in front of my father before that moment. But at that moment, f*** was not a curse word, and he understood it. Perhaps "Growing My Father's Finger" is a good thing (thank you Paul Reiser).

Later turned out to be like almost twenty years later. When I came to

California to help out with my Dad, he was pretty sick but pretty well aware of what was going on though he had trouble communicating some of the time. But, when he and I were alone together he couldn't stop talking and all he wanted to talk about was music. OK. I'm the son and you are my Dad, like what could be better?

A few days before he stopped communicating completely he asked about the Ellington concert, by the way he paid the $13.50 tux rental and the $25.00 cleaning fee. I had not thought about that night in years. So, rather than try to recount the tale right off the top of my head I decided just to bring in the "Duke Ellington 70'th Birthday Concert" album, and play "Satin Doll" (I didn't/don't have a recording of THAT "Cottontail) for him. When it was over he smiled and said, "That was f**king fantastic!"

Thanks, Dad.

Posted by Fred

Throw Another Hog On The Fire – Part One

It was the spring of 1996. My husband and I had a music duo act and performed for private clubs, private parties and wedding receptions. We had a country club manager that had caught one of our Elks Lodge performances, and hired us us to provide the wedding and reception music at a small agricultural community in southwest Georgia. Needless to say, it is a southern, down-home kind of place.

We arrived at the country club about 4 pm to set up our equipment which included MIDI file accompaniment to my live keyboard and vocals and my hubby's live sax, flute and vocals. Everything seemed to be going well as we finished set-up, changed clothes and prepared to play the prelude music and ceremonial music. The wedding was scheduled for 6pm.

We had been invited to join the guests at the reception for food and drinks before starting the dance, so while we were waiting for the ceremony to start, we checked out the food table.

The ballroom had been partitioned with the reception area on the south end of the space. As we entered the reception area, you would have thought you had entered a barn social....plaid table cloths, paper plates and napkins, plastic silverware were arranged on the tables. There were wire chickens with flowers in them displayed as center pieces on each table. Then, the main event of the food spread caught our eye.

You could see through the large, full-length plate glass windows at the back of the room, a rather large, black barrel smoker grill on the patio, covered with the full carcass (head and all, no joke) of a rather large hog. The food table included all of the appropriate accessories to a traditional, southern barbeque. My hubby looked at me, I looked at him.... blink.... blink.... Don't get me wrong!!! Like any sane, healthy, red-blooded, born-and-raised southern girl, I love barbecue.... But.... for my wedding reception??!! A WHOLE HOG DISPLAYED IN ALL IT'S GLORY ON THE BACK PATIO?

REALLY!?. I looked at my hubby and said, "You know.... I've got a bad feeling about this gig....."

About 20 minutes before 6, the Country Club Manager approached us and said, "I don't want y'all to worry, okay? Y'all will git yer money no matter what! But, it seems that the groom's family cain't find the groom." About that time, the hysterical bride, and several of her female family members, enters the hallway leading to the ballroom where the wedding would take place. This woman seemed to be in her late-40's, wearing a white wedding gown styled as a clogger's dress with silver cowboy boots and hat! From the looks of her, I got the feeling that this woman had seen the bottom of a few bottles of adult beverages over the years and today was no exception. Her make-up was smeared with tears and her smile had a few gaps which were visible with every sob. She had a few choice words to slur about the groom and his tardiness, but her entourage and the CC Manager reassured the Bride that all would be well, and the ladies guided her as she teetered away to go and freshen up for the ceremony.

Finally we received the news at 5:45pm that the groom had arrived. We started the prelude music at 5:50pm and as 6:20 approached, we were worried that we would run out of syrupy love songs to play while everyone waited to start the wedding.

Finally, the groom entered the ballroom, a man most likely in his late 70's (maybe early 80's) dressed in a black suit with western string tie, black cowboy boots and matching black hat. He was accompanied by his brother, the best man, dressed in blue jeans, plaid shirt and NASCAR baseball cap. The groom had seen the bottom of a bottle, too on this momentous day and was quite intoxicated, leaning on his brother for balance, and reassuring everyone that he was, "Fine! I'm just fine, G--damn it!... I'm heady to get hitched, where is she?", he slurred, loud enough for the whole town to hear.

As we started the wedding processional, the bride entered the ballroom on the arm of a man (don't know what relation he was to her, but he looked too close in age to her, rather than the groom to be her father) dressed in similar garb to the groom, except he simply wore a white shirt buttoned at the neck, without a string tie. The groom managed to stay upright for the ceremony and to say "I do" at the appropriate time, consonants and vowels all in the right place, with the bride echoing her willingness to hitch herself to this fine, "upstanding" gentleman. The bride gave her groom a gapped smile as the preacher pronounced them husband and wife and all was well, for now.....

Posted by Stephanie

1 comment:

Chris said...

> I've been to many a fine, southern wedding where the groom, best man or most of the male attendees wore jeans and a NASCAR hat (or John Deere, or Summit Racing... you get the idea). Most, if not all, also showed the propensity for fine adult beverages consumed before, after, and in at least one case, DURING the ceremony.

Throw Another Hog On The Fire – Part Two

Previously in our story, the happy couple had just been pronounced "hitched".

Let the party begin!! The whole hog was brought in off the grill and proudly displayed on the main buffet table, along with three BBQ sauce choices, and the aforementioned accompaniments.

As expected at such a gathering, country and western music was heavily requested and we pulled out every Waylon and Willie, Patsy Cline, George Jones, Johnny Cash and Conway Twitty tune (to name a few of the legends performed) that we could find in our MIDI files.

Things were going quite well. The $20 tips were piling up with each request. Cowboy boots were tapping, cowgirls were twirling and a good time was being had by all...

We took our second break and walked over to speak to the Country Club manager who was greatly relieved that things had worked out as planned (well..... as close as possible under the circumstances......) and thanked us for the music. Ken (my fine sax playing husband) glanced over at the bandstand where a certain cowboy stood poking at the keyboard/computer that played our MIDI accompaniment. Ken goes over and asks, "EXCUSE ME, but can I help you?" "Does this thing have any Garth on it?", the cowboy slurs, as he teeters over the keyboard.

Ken tries to explain to this guy that he can't mess with the equipment because it is playing the break music he is now hearing. This didn't go over real well with the guy because he's dying to prove how good he could sing some "Garth" for everybody. But Ken manages to persuade him to leave the equipment alone and we let the dude sing "I've got friends in low places" during the next set. All goes well after he gets his 3 minutes of fame, and we finish out the gig.

About fifteen minutes after we start tearing down the equipment, we witnessed very bright headlights to a very large, jacked up pick-up truck glaring through the side windows of the ballroom. The truck managed to clear the country club ballroom, but came barreling across the practice putting greens which were just off the patio at the back of the building, and then proceeded across a cart path and onto HOLE 9 of the CC Golf Course......

We later found out just before we left, that the same dude that did his "Garth" impression thought that he was driving home on the main drive exiting the Country Club, but instead he was driving across the Country Club's Golf Course. I think he had had a beer or twelve!

The CC manager told us later in a thank you letter she sent us for the gig, that this guy's truck did $1,700.00 worth of damage to the club's golf course!

Posted by Stephanie

And The Winner Is . . .

This is a pre-GI days story. It was brought to mind by a friend's Facebook post which included a review of a performance by a number of bands at the conclusion of the Girls Rock Camp Houston the other day. This camp was for girls aged 12 to 14 (as I recall).

Their task was to write an original song and learn it in five days and then perform it in a real club in Houston in front of a packed house. Do the math, no small task.

The reviewer (not a parent of any of the girls) was lavish with his praise of the performers and polite with his assessment of the musical qualities of their performance. If I knew more about the genera I could probably better expressed that, but I know nothing about current "Pop" (if they still call it that) music. The reviewer went on, at length, to point out how the bands cheered and encouraged each other on the gig. He plainly stated that the young musicians exuberance transformed what could have been a rather overbearing and frustrating competition sort of thing into an artistic collaboration. I wish I had been there... So, what does that have to do with me?

In the summer of 1972 my High School Choir partook in an international music festival in Austria (I did post something about that earlier). The festival revolved around a competition to select the three best pre-university level choirs form the fifty or so choirs in attendance from around the world. Each choir had an adjudication performance which was attended only by the judges. They also had a free/open performance that the judges attended but was also open to the public.

I attended two of the open performances, one by the University Of North Carolina Choir (they were the "Resident" choir, not competing) and a second by a High School form Oklahoma City, OK, USA. Personally, I thought my HS Choir could blow away the one from UNC, but the kids from OKC were AMAZING! Their free concert consisted of 99% Spirituals and one Broadway thing. In contrast, my choir did 15th century madrigals, pieces in Old French and Latin, you know, real high-brow stuff (which we nailed if I may so boast). Not having seen their adjudication, which did require all that high-brow stuff, I could not tell you where I thought they would have stood among the rest of us. The next afternoon I was to find out.

We were told that if your choir won the competition that you would be informed the night before so you could prepare a piece to sing at the end of the ceremony. Morning of the ceremony, and we had not received any notice. So we headed off to the beautiful hall to see who got what.

They were to only announce the top three (though I understand that the choir directors of each choir did receive their choir's rating along with a critique from the judges). Third place went to a Boys Choir from someplace in NJ, USA. When they were announced they squealed a bit and polite applause was given. Second place went to the Orphenians from Staples HS, Westport, CT, USA. Once again a polite reaction from the crowd for my little choir.

The first place choir was not actually introduced. The speaker simply pointed to stage right front and in unison 60 or so, mostly Afro-American, high-schoolers stood and filed onto the risers on the stage in total silence. These guys looked familiar. Once assembled, I noticed some things were missing, no piano to crank out the spiritual backup, no music in their hands and no conductor. This tiny dark-skinned soprano stepped a few feet in front of the choir and in this huge voice sang; "It is good to be merry, 'tis good to be merry and wise..." The rest of the choir joined in bar six and continued as published (I found out later when that piece became one of my favorites and a regular encore piece for the 1973 Orphenians). There was still no conductor. Instead, the opening soloist directed the choir mostly with her head but used some body-english when appropriate, all the time looking right at the crowd and singing.

Upon completion there was an instant standing ovation from the competition and we were informed that first place went to this choir from Oklahoma City, OK, USA. People started shouting for an encore, myself included as I thought what do you top that with (Google it, you will see what I mean). That's when their director finally got up on stage. She quieted the crowd, but we were all still standing. She was gracious and agreed to do one more on the condition that anybody who wanted to sing along should. She also added a little shtick, asking the crowd if anybody had a pitch pipe.

About thirty pipes squawked out random pitches. She asked for an Ab and got one. She pointed to the basses and out came "Ezekiel Saw De Wheel."

In moments there were hundreds more voices filling the hall. Lots of the kids who were seated in the orchestra level wandered up on stage and joined right in, many in wardrobe not native to places known for Negro Spirituals, but they were singing their hearts out.

Everybody won that day!

Posted by Fred

Just The Facts, Ma'am

I continue to receive queries as to the validity of some of my posts. Strangely few of them have been through the blog's comment feature, which is what I had hoped for. You know, get a discussion started, get the story straight, that kind of thing. Instead I get e-mails and even phone calls from people asking if this or that is (was) true or even a few, "That's not how I remember it" comments. Unfortunately, the people who have told me that they have different memories of the same event have not given me their versions. So you can see my dilemma there.

Also, remember that the most of these stories are over twenty years old and have been played through in my head countless times, therefore having gone through the "Telephone" process (you remember that game... you line up people and one whispers something and they pass it on, then you compare what it started as to what the last person remembers...) an equal number of times.

OK, then there are the times when I have intentionally chosen to change certain aspects of a story, in an attempt to lessen the embarrassment factors and such. And, there are other times when I have taken credit (debit) for doing or saying something that was actually said (done) by someone else for the same types of reasons. I have no problem making fun of myself or making a fool of myself. Anybody remember the "Twelve Days Of Christmas?"

It has also been brought to my attention that is looks like the most recent posts are more fiction-like than the early posts. I can see why it might seem that way, but I have a good explanation for that.

When I started the Blog, back in May of 2010, I jotted down a bunch of "Hooks" to remind me of stories that I would consider turning into full posts. I had well over 100 before I ever posted anything. Then I started working the strongest memories first. Now add to the mix that writing this kind of stuff was not natural to me. I have read very little these days except for technical manuals (Computer Nerd stuff), never was good in English and tend to start writing posts after a beer or two. So, what is showing up recently are posts that I had to think about or even research before putting them together. Oh, and my overly wordy style has also evolved a bit.

But I am still having fun writing and according to the hit counters people are still reading. So, I'm going to keep getting on the bus every day (well, most days) until I run out of undeveloped hooks. I hope you keep reading.

Posted by Fred

4 comments:

Stephanie said...

Just keep doin' what you're doin', Fred!

I say accuracy is way over-rated, don't you?

It's the soul essence of the story and the overwhelming accuracy of the much anticipated punchline of each story that is important. So those who are giving you grief about post accuracy need to remember to lighten up! And if they get offended, I say, Joke 'em if they can't take a f---!

Fred said...

Will do, co-conspirator...

Chris said...

Since when has 100% accuracy done much for a good story? I mean, like the difference between a fairy tale and a war story - the fairy tale starts with "Once upon a time", and the war story begins, "Now, this is no shit..." - there is a fair element of artistic license in any good story. What Steph said...

Fred said...

"Can you dig it? I knew that you could!"

On the other hand, I could offer up your band (DE): "8 foot 2", "Don't Buy The Liverwurst", "Bourbon Street Parade",

Fred said... (cont.)

on and on. 100% accurate every night, except that you never did one of them exactly the same ever, not even Bob.

It's nice to know that I knew some Jazz musicians.

Brushes With Greatness

Clearwater Jazz Festival, Clearwater, FL, early '90's. I have no idea what I was doing on that gig. I may have been playing or I may have been on sound. But for my memory from the gig, it doesn't really matter because the cool thing actually happened to one of the other guys. This band, the AFB East jazz band, had a world class Jazz player (or two or three, depending on the time) this particular story involves Dave, a world class Tenor player.

Dave was a gregarious dude, so mixing with the heavies at a festival like this was no big deal for him. That day one of the heavies milling around in the backstage players-only area was the middle brother (chronologically) of the famed Heath Brothers Jazz family. This dude's press (remember, journalistic interest in Jazz players really fell off after Elvis started gyrating in the '50's and this was the '90's) or, reputation, if you will, was that of somebody that was not too fond of Caucasians. So, as I saw Dave heading over to this dude with the festival t-shirt he had be getting people to autograph, sharpie in hand I kind of winced. A few seconds later they were cutting up and laughing and the dude was signing Dave's t-shirt.

After the gig I asked Dave what it was like to meet that dude. He said, "Great man. He's just a DF like the rest of us." Bad press strikes again.

Same festival, after-hours jam session for the heaviness. A few of us headed over at the invitation of Nick Brignola. In the main room at that hotel there was kind of a reception thing with a bar. We grabbed drinks and headed to the smaller room where the blowing was about to take place. Once in the real room one of the guys spotted Nick and said something like, "Dig what Nick's holding." In his hand he had a Tenor with a bright red rubber mouthpiece.

Nick was blocking the view of the guy he was talking with, but when he walked away to join the band on stage we could clearly see that sitting at the back table was McCoy Tyner. There I was in a room full (OK, two or three) of Jazz legends and I felt quite comfortable. Just a bunch of DF's after all.

The Red Barn Dinner Theater, Westport, CT, 1972. I got a one night gig running a Follow Spot but had no idea what the gig was. When I got there around 4:00 for the Tech Call, the head tech recognized me from the HS Band. He said something like, "Hey, you know the music stores and something about moving instruments. Would you go along when with the truck to pick up the rental bass we need for the gig for an extra $20.00?" Sure, whatever, I was just happy to be working at a theater.

We picked up the bass at Zara Musicland, Fairfield, CT and got it back to the hall and set it up on the standard type Upright Bass Stand that they had at my HS. Then I headed up to the lighting booth. In the booth I was informed that all I had to do was make sure I covered the Band Leader with a Bust Shot (head and shoulders, don't get the belly) all night. So, I asked which guy was the band leader, he said that would be the bass player.

I went over to check out my light, a little different that the ones I was used to, but not a problem. The board guy put on his headphones, the lighting booth was basically sound-proof, so I looked for mine. Nothing, so I asked the dude, "Do I get some of those? Pointing to his gear. He replied, "Not unless you brought some with you." Nope. "It's OK. I'll cue you" which he did just fine.

House goes down, stage comes up and the drummer and piano player enter from stage right and take their seats. The board guy holds up his hand as counts down from 5. I had neglected to ask, and had not been informed, where the band leader was entering from, so I pulled the focus all the way out and winged it. Board guy pointed, I hit the spot, Charles Mingus stepped through the curtain in center stage, and I tightened to the Bust Shot as he walked to his rental bass and sat on his stool and they started to play.

I cannot tell you what they played, remember, sound-proof booth, but I do remember commenting to myself about Charles Mingus was playing a rental Kay Bass from Zara Musicland playing to a bunch of Honkies in Whitesville USA. He moved so little I really didn't have to do much of anything that night.

It was just one set, they went a full hour. When it was over they got a standing ovation (I had no idea my home town was so hip) but they did not do an encore. The board guy again raised his hand and pointed at me. Charles got up, smiled this enormous smile, bowed and walked off with the drummer and piano player, stage right. That was it. I had just SEEN Charles Mingus live, but not heard a note! I was almost shaking I was so mad/disappointed. My pay envelope helped calm me down.

I don't know why I did it, but I just headed down to the stage at that point and started to pack up the bass. I must admit that it looked like a much finer instrument at that point, having just been held my a master for an hour. I was folding up the stand when the trio came from the dressing room. Charles Mingus says to me, "Nice job with the bass kid. Maybe next time you could tune it for me too?" He laughed and waved as he headed out the back.

Though I didn't know what a DF was at that point, I had just met one. What a cool thing.

Holiday Inn, Norwalk, CT 1971. It was an afternoon concert by the Basie band, when all THOSE guys were still alive. It was a Sunday so we had to do the church thing first, so Mom and Dad and I got there in the middle of the Opener. It was a burner on "Summertime." Try to imagine "Summertime" at MM 260 or so, mind boggling. As I sat down Bobby Platter, 2nd alto, stood to blow. Wow! I don't think I had ever heard him take a solo on an album, and believe you, I had ALL the Basie stuff. OUCH! He was GOOD. Well, OK, then Lockjaw (Eddie "Lockjaw" Davis) stood up and, well, Bobby did not win that one...

At intermission I had a bit of trouble locating a restroom, which I sorely needed. So, once I found it, I was not paying much attention to anything but pointing my business to the puck and getting things started. Once I did, I think I said something like, "Wow" or at least something that could have been taken as me expressing my opinion of the concert but also could have indicated my relief at finally getting some relief. In what I now assume to have been a reply to my innocent comment this beautiful rich male voice said, "So, I guess you are enjoying the show?" I didn't have to turn my head, as many times as I had heard, "One Mo' Time" I knew exactly who had said that, but I did. There zipping up was the Kid from Redbank (William "Count" Basie) smiling. As he passed me he said, "Stick around for the second half. We'll play some new stuff for ya."

Years later I heard somebody tell a joke about meeting John Wayne in a men's room where, well, I am sure you have heard it... I chuckle when I think about it now. Maybe if Basie hand not spoken first I might have been startled enough to have carried out that punch line on him. But that voice... How could you be anything but perfectly relaxed after hearing that voice.

Some nice hall, NY, NY, 1973. I don't remember where the gig was or who I was with but this was my first time to see Thad and Mel (the Thad Jones - Mel Lewis Jazz Orchestra). I also can only remember about the first three minutes of the performance. The band was on stage when the house came up, less the drummer, and an off stage voice introduced the co-leaders. As they walked out I remember thinking that's an Odd Couple. Mel sat down and did some rudiment. Then Thad grabbed the mike and started talking. WHERE DO THESE GUYS GET THESE VOICES went through my head. Basie, Ellington and now Jones (placing them in chronological, not posting order)... He could have stood there and read a shopping list for an hour and I would have dug it. Fortunately, he didn't.

Instead he introduced the new guy on the band, and up stepped a VERY YOUNG Jon Faddis. Thad then said, "Ladies and gentlemen, we would like you to hear Jonny's first note with the band." He then shouted off mike to the band "Blues In A Minute," gave them a second to adjust the parts and gave the downbeat. "BAAHAT!!!" and then cut off the band. The crowd burst into applause. Thad then waved us down and said, "For those of you without perfect pitch, that was the G above Double-High C." Turning back to a grinning Faddis, "You can go sit down now Jon." Then came the official introduction of "Blues In A Minute" which did start with that same kick, but then went immediately into two choruses of unaccompanied, Richard Davis, bass, and went on with the chart.

I saw the band about a year later, at the Vanguard, They used the same shtick to open that night too. So, it may not have been Faddis' first note with the band I heard, but it was the first, though not the last, note I ever heard him play.

Ft. Valley State University, Ft. Valley, GA. It was like in the Gym, yikes, but who cares, it was Joe Williams!!! Oh, and a trio. Susie and I were so excited when she found that tiny ad in the paper.

I know we discussed the fact that this thing is going to sell out fast so we better get tickets quick, which we did. I don't remember discussing it with any of my band buddies, until after it happened, but it turned out that tickets were not in short supply.

We pulled into the parking lot. I had played there before with the AFB East so I was pretty sure I was in the right place but there were so far cars. Were we early? Was this the right day? We went around the corner and there were the signs to the show that said we were right on time and a guy took our tickets so... When we got in, there were about 20 young Afro-American music students (I assumed the music student part the other part was rather apparent - Ft. Valley State was a predominantly Black School). Scattered around the rest of the hall, which I would guess could have seated 500 or more, were about 20 more people, about evenly split on the color line. Susie and I took our seats, quite away from the stage, but we had numbered tickets and all...

When the guys were introduced the crowd did what it could to give them a big welcome but even with the exuberant 20 year-olds down front we were a bit week. It didn't seem to bother Joe, he smiled that big toothy smile of his, bowed and kicked off a medium-up Blues. While the trio was vamping, he turned back to them and said something and the key changed and the tempo came down to about a medium. Out came "Every Day I Have The Blues." We did better with the applause when that one ended.

Then he started speaking, WHERE DO THEY GET THOSE VOICES?!?!? He said, "Well, maybe not 'Nobody Loves Me' you people seem to care" paraphrasing the lyric. Then he said, "Let's let the late comers, if there are any, take the cheap seats." Waving around he said, "You folks come on down and get close. Let's make this casual tonight." Then he looked into the front row and asked one of the students, "What would you like to hear next?" I couldn't hear exactly what the kid said but I got the impression that he was not all that familiar with Joe's repertoire because Joe laughed and said something like, "Then class take out your notebooks and clean out your ears." He turned to the trio and kicked off the nasty slow late twenties stile blues that I had always thought of as a Jimmy Rushing thing, though I can't remember the name. At that point all I can remember about the gig was holding Susie's had for the rest of the night.

The next day at the Squadron I gave shit to each and every one of the guys in the J-Z for not being there. Oddly enough the two most common cop-outs where "I didn't hear about it" and "I didn't think we could get tickets." I guess I should have made a bunch of phone calls. To try to make up for it, the Chief programmed as many GOOD Basie tunes as he could cram into the book for the next tour.

Posted by Fred

Hunting Wabbits

I don't mean to steal Gordon Goodwin's song title here (yes I do) nor do I mean to rip off Elmer Fudd (yes I do), while at the same time I am attempting to incorporate both of those references into a new (old) theme. Keeping with the theme I will add that it also involves a immortal Lead Alto player who's nickname was "Rabbit." Others that sat alongside "Rabbit" at one time or another, like Harry Carney, Ben Webster and Paul Gonsalves are also involved. From that lineup you should be able to construe that Edward Kennedy "Duke" Ellington was also a major character. But, the actual star of this post is a feline, not a lagomorph. That cat's name was "Cat." William Alonzo "Cat" Anderson to be more specific.

Sometime during the early 1970's I was riding in our 1956 Dodge Custom Royal, gold over black with one of those push-button automatic transmissions listening to WRVR, 106.7, NY. That car and that radio station were very important to me as a kid. On this particular day, I think I was on my way home from school so my Mom would have been driving. Over the radio came a familiar tune, "Cotton Tail" but this version was a bit different, right from the start.

First of all it was faster than the versions I had heard and it sounded like it was a live performance, you know that kind of ambiance you used to get from live analog recordings, so I turned it up as loud as Mom would let me.

I remember thinking how hot Paul Gonsalves' and Harry Carney's solos were and then was truly blown away by the sax section, lead by John Cornelius "Johnny" Hodges, AKA "Rabbit" on the soli. I was not prepared for what came next.

The eight bars that came just before the DC (return to the melody) had always been one of my favorites, right along with the "A-Train" pyramid, Buddy Rich's fill just before the final key change in "Love For Sale" and Thomas "Fats" Waller uttering "Your... your pedal extremities really are obnoxious. One never knows, do one?" prior to the coda of "You're Feet's Too Big." (There I go again, digressing...)

Anyway, that eight bars was a brass lick that kind of ascended in Major Thirds, except this version. In this version the lead trumpet ascends in Major Tenths. So, instead of the line ending up a Sixth above where it started, it ended up...

FOUR OCTIVES and a Sixth higher!

In bar three of that lick, that version, it was clear what Duke (Cat?) was attempting to do, but I thought to myself, "No way!" WAY. To this day I am amazed that the recording equipment of that era could have even recorded that. I was also impressed that our simple car radio could reproduce those sounds. Oh, yeah then there was the performance.

Coda: For over thirty years I have been searching for that recording, I had a cassette tape of it that my buddy, Jonny, made (probably by holding up a recorder to a speaker and pressing go) that I cherished for a long time. But, that disappeared buy the 1980's. So, needless to say that when I stumbled upon it last night (August 22nd, 2010) on YouTube, I was pretty blown away.

During my search, which started in record stores around the world well before the Internet, I compiled quite a bit of Ellington material. Basically I bought any album that didn't look familiar (that I could afford) containing "Cotton Tale" or even just something to do with "Live In Paris" which I think is the album the DJ (Ed Beach?) said contained that recording. Lots of nice stuff, none with that version.

As the internet evolved I expanded my search and regularly scrounged for it. Again, lots of nice stuff, not that version. So I would like to thank "DarkShark190" for posting it back on June 2nd, 2010. I would like to think that the 475 views it has received up until just moments ago will rapidly go up. Everybody on the planet should hear this at least once.

So, now for a plea. Anybody know anything more about that recording, WRVR at that time (it went Country in the 80's so current info would not be pertinent) or the DJ, Ed Beach (other than knowing that he passed away recently at the age of 85)? If so, please pass that information on through the blog or shoot me an e-mail, call me, drive cross-country and deliver it in person - I will buy you a beer or whatever. Thanks in advance.

I think I am going to listen to it again. And, again, and again...

Posted by Fred

Old Friends There Are Not Forgotten

For those of you who are from the South, the title brings back memories of a song learned in elementary school (for those of us who grew up in the 50s), or one almost universally vilified in the 60s and 70s... to me, as I am writing this, it is a heartfelt remembrance of a friend that I never served with in the Air Force, as he had retired before I entered (heck, he entered before I was born), but had the distinct honor and privilege to play alongside in a variety of venues both during and after my term of service to Uncle Sam.

The first time I met this character, he came to my college campus, having recently retired, and was soliciting business for his new endeavor, an instrument repair facility. I remember talking with him at some length, and eventually buying a can of "Spitballs" to clean out my Farkas model horn... I was sold after seeing the incredible amount of schmutz the first pass-through produced. Imagine my surprise when I found myself sitting next to him n the local orchestra later that same year! I found him to be a funny, earthy, surprisingly good section player, no matter what the genre. He was, at least in part, responsible for my choosing to join the Air Force music program upon graduation from college with a performance degree. It was only later that I got a chance to see the real genius behind his talent.

Flash forward 15 years... frustrated with a commander whom I had not liked when we were airmen together, sergeants together, or Staff Sergeants together, I made the decision to leave the service prior to retirement time.

After severing my ties with the military, I got a call from Fred with a gig offer... all I had to do was acquire a banjo, and I was ready to play downtown. I had to laugh when I walked into the room and there he was; this same trombone player whom I had played next to in an orchestra 15 years before, and had dealings with, in the repair business, ever since. For the next couple of years, I played Dixieland music with this guy, loving every minute! Not only could he play, he could arrange! Fun, fun, fun... until I had to take a job that took me away from the regular Wednesday night jam.

Now, I am mourning the loss of my friend, who passed away from complications of diabetes last night, probably as I was resolving to go visit him this week, more's the pity.

Roger, I'll miss you terribly, and will raise a glass to you at our reunion in September, which I know you had planned to attend. I'll even ride the Harley to the gathering in remembrance of the times we were going to ride together once your foot healed.

Slainte!

Posted by Chris

Unforgettable

As Chris pointed out yesterday in his "Old Friends There Are Not Forgotten" post of 7/25/2010, we who were fortunate enough to have known and worked with him, lost a friend and truly fine musician the other day. I had posted a Roger story earlier, about him realizing that the circus tune we had just played was "The Mexican Hat Dance" before I knew what it was, so you know that I also had the good fortune to sit alongside of him a few times. I was also part of the Dixieland band that worked The Cellar and more than once had him work on each of my horns, so our experiences were similar. Now for a couple of quick unique things that passed between Roger and myself.

One night at The Cellar the Atlanta Braves were on TV and both of us being avid fans, we were a bit late returning from our break because we had to wait for Chipper Jones to finish his at-bat. When we hit the stand Roger just started the Braves chant and the Tomahawk Chop.

That got the best crowd reaction we had ever received up until that point. Smiling with his huge twisted-tooth grin of his, he proceeded to signal "two down" (that's either a curve ball or the key of Bb) and started to play the Braves Chant on his trombone, coaxing the crowd to fall in line to the pitch. We joined in. A few bars later he cut us off with a sharp movement of his slide and broke immediately into "I

Found A New Baby" where he played unoccupied for 8 bars. Second time through the chorus everybody kicked in. The "Chart" continued and the crowd really dug it.

Obviously everybody in the band knew that tune but, as I recall, we had never played it together in THAT band. From that night forward it was part of the book though not a note of it was every written down.

Another Roger, The Cellar and Baseball story... We were only a tune or two into our first set and Roger turned to us and said, "Guys, break time." That band didn't really have a leader. It was more like a Dixie By Committee thing, which worked just fine. But there are some unwritten laws about upholding the 45-15 rule when it came to bar gigs so I think each of us had some apprehension about walking off the stand at that point. Roger then shouted, "I'm buyin' a round for the bar!" We all followed like the happy sheep we were. Oh, by the way, at that point the six piece band outnumbered the audience by two.

We settled in under the TV set which had a nationally televised Baseball game on. Roger reached over the bar and grabbed the remote and cranked the volume up so that it could be heard all over the room. At that point you could hear the PA announcer say, "Now batting, Cal Ripken Jr." This was the at-bat that signified Cal's 2,131st consecutive game, therefore making the date September 6, 1995. As I was turning to Roger to thank him for making sure I got to experience that when I noticed he had his wallet out and was looking at two baseball cards. One was Ripken's 1981 rookie card and the other was a current Chipper Jones card. All I could do was hug him.

Last one, for now... We had a gig on base, AFB East, for some reason. It was pretty odd, six former AFB East Bandsmen playing at the Officers Club, all as civilians, but it was fun. It was a Sunday afternoon thing by the pool.

I don't remember what the tune was but I remember it was kind of up and was in A-flat. I totally kanked the clarinet solo! Splooooft, squllmak, SUCK! Roger just gave me a poke and smiled. I said something like, "God, I just hate up tunes with all those flats." For you not transposing folks out there, the clarinet being in B-flat meant that I was only in B-flat therefore only having to deal with two flats as my functional key signature. The gig went on with little or no more bleeding.

Come Wednesday night our regular Cellar gig came around and in walked Roger with two new charts. Again, I don't remember the names of the tunes but they were both up and both were in D-flat that's five flats for him, four flats for me. Fortunately, as he handed me my parts and laughed a big old Roger laugh he also handed me a cold draft. He knew I would take the ribbing far better slightly lubricated. Side note, those two charts were good, and did NOT have clarinet solos. Saved by the arranger.

More to come...

Posted by Fred

Ride, Clyde!

Two more quick Roger stories... I got a last minute call to fill in on Tenor for a garden party gig from the one cat in Macon, GA, who regularly worked and hired horn players. It was a break for me but I did not have a tenor and with the gig only an hour or so away, and a 20 minute commute I had to tell "Narcoleptic Bob" that I only had an Alto and a Bari. He "harrumphed" a bit but said, "That's OK as long as you can transpose." Never ever having done that, Bb to Eb transposition before sight reading on a gig, I lied to him and said, "Sure. I can do that." So off to Macon.

So I got there about 10 minutes before the downbeat with my bari gig bag and my Manhasset (music stand). There were Roger and Gerry (fine trumpet player and very good friends with Roger, from "the day"). I quickly unpacked my horn and asked where the book was. Roger handed me this manila file folder with Tenor scribbled on it. Inside were two sheets of notebook paper with the names of about fifty or sixty tunes and their keys.

I looked at Roger and said something like, "What am I supposed to do with this?" He said, and I know this to be an accurate quote because Roger himself was quoting the bible (mine and his - not that other one) when he said, "That's where you take over on the Adlibbzaphone" and smiled. (I will leave it to Bill C. to cover the "Adlibbzaphone" story in a separate post.)

I got a call from the Macon musicians union one day. I think is was Gerry that actually called, but I could hear Roger cutting up in the background. A REAL gig! Cool, one show backing up Ray Stevens (remember "Ahab the Arab" and "Gitarzan"?) at the Macon City Auditorium. COOL.

We showed up for the 20 minute rehearsal for the 90 minute gig and ran down some of the charts. About half way through the rehearsal, Roger asked if he could move over and stand next to me for the gig. Ray said it was OK and Roger schlepped his stuff over next to me and the rehearsal went on. When we broke Roger stuck around to look over the book, both his and mine (good bari book, by the way, not something I was expecting) as the rest of us split for the smoking area.

I remember nothing about the actual show except that Roger not only covered the rather boring trombone parts but also about half of the bari parts too. He had moved over so he could see my part and join me for the cool parts. Oh, and he silently mouthed every word of ever one of Ray's songs, when if horn was not in his chops and knew all the pantomime moves Ray used from his old TV show and videos, including the bumpity-bump movements of Clyde as he rode across the desert carrying Ahab to meet his Fatima...

Posted by Fred

1 comment:

Chris said...

> I do remember Roger telling this story... he broke me up with the account of how Ray would drag out the dialing portion of his shtick on "It's Me Again, Margaret" until he had the band

Chris said... (cont.)

cracking up, and then, quickly, go on with the cue for them to rejoin... Rog said he almost knocked his remaining teeth in trying to make the entrance on time...

Oops, Maybe Not

Yeah, another Roger story. (Chris, keep reminding me, I will keep writing!) Another place that Roger and I worked together was with the Macon College Big Band. That band was run by another Bob, but not the one who would fall asleep at the keys, who's name I cannot remember.

At one rehearsal, Wide-awake-Bob handed out a new chart on "Sister Sadie" by Horace Silver. It was a chart by the chick piano player that spent some time with The Note (AKA The Airman Of Note Jazz Ensemble of the Air Force Band, Washington DC). Bob read the MM at the top and kicked it at about Quarter Note at 120, and we read it down pretty well. After we got through with that first pass we took a break and a bunch of us piled out to the smoking area, without Roger. He instead raided my book (Bari) again and joined us after he had a photo-copy of the first page of the Bari part. He started bitching about how come the trombone parts are so boring and all and we gave him shit about trombones in general, having a wonderful time. When we went back in Bob called "Sister" back up but this time kicked it off at the real tempo, Half Note at 120. Not to be swayed, Roger hit all the trombone notes in the intro and then dug in on the head, from the Bari part he had copied, as we went on.

The button dudes (the sax section) were even scufflin' but Roger kept going. After about seven bars we got to the turn-around where we heard, "OOPS! Maybe not?" and he stopped trying to play the head. We lost it so we needed another break to get our stuff back together.

At the next rehearsal with that band Roger came in and NAILED the head to "Sister Sadie" without even opening his eyes. It was a onetime deal, we all smiled and he went back to the boring Trombone part from that time on. What a hoot!

Posted by Fred

Maybe It Was Hereditary?

I have previously posted stories about landing gigs simply because I was the only bari player handy and something about the importance of subs. Well, a friend sent me a Facebook invitation recently to a new page that celebrates the Jan Savitt Big Band of the 30's & 40's. In case you are not familiar with that name, they were quite good. One of the truly hip "White" bands of the day and a band that integrated early, though Benny may have beat Jan to it, I don't remember.

Here is another quirky thing. Once back in contact with the friend that hipped me to the Savitt page she mentioned that she will post something about a live jazz experience of hers that featured a drunken audience member. For some reason that all bounced around in my head for a day or so then it came together.

I waded through my trashed garage out to where our old big band library still sits and went for the last file cabinet. I reached to the back of the bottom drawer and pulled out numbers 720, 720A and 720B. That library only has about 250 tunes in it, those numbers were special, reserved for the three different arrangements of Savitt's "720 In The Books" Dad had reason to like that tune. I just liked it because it's a good tune. Here is my Dad's reason and a chaser...

In the summer of 1970 my Mom and I went along with my Dad on a business trip to Rochester, NY. I have no idea why, but we did. While on that trip the Buddy Rich band had a gig at the hotel where we were staying. As soon as my Dad found out he got us seats in the restaurant/bar venue. Dishes had to be cleared before Buddy would take the stage (Can you say attitude?) so I was rushed through finishing my chocolate ice cream and dripped some on my brand new $8.00, dry-clean only tie. My Mom was very angry! Once the band started, we were all OK.

The first set was fantastic. I don't remember the whole band but Ernie Watts and Jay Core were definitely there (I idolized those two at the time, so I DO remember them). As the second, and final, set was about to start a drunk from the back, bar area, started shouting "Play '720 In The Books'!" He caught Buddy's attention the first time he shouted. After about the third time Buddy shouted back at the drunk. After the drunk continued Buddy slung a drum stick over the heads of us in the table area which landed very close to the drunk, clattering between bar stools.

Buddy then shouted some expletive and stated very clearly, though not in such polite terms, that if he was not removed, the band would not play. At that moment I began to believe the myth about the existence of "The Buddy Rich Bus Tapes" that I would not hear until years later.

Buddy and the boys did not play "720 In The Books." I do remember that the band closed with "Channel One Suite" FOLLOWED by "The Westside Story Medley." I was ecstatic, the trumpet players were pissed.

Back at the rooms, I had a single adjoining my parent's room, there was a knock at the door between our rooms just after I had gotten into bed. It was my Dad, vodka in hand and his unlighted cigarette he did quit smoking them, but not carrying them around. That's when I found out about HIS first unusual subbing experience.

He asked if I knew the tune that the drunk in the bar was shouting about that night. I said, "Yeah, '720 In The Books' Jan Savitt..." Dad, therefore we, had multiple recordings of it. Then he said, "Let me tell you about the first time I ever played it..."

My Dad played tenor and clarinet and was pretty good in his prime. He mostly played party gigs with a local small band in Schenectady, NY. One day he got a bang on his door at the Y.M.C.A. he was living in telling him he had a call on the phone in the hall. Dad picked it up and on the other end was a buddy of his who worked at the local AFM Local (though my Dad never was a member). His friend needed a sub that played tenor and clarinet, not an uncommon set of doubles in those days. Dad asked why not get a union guy. The guy told him that they needed somebody in about twenty minutes and none of the union guys he knew could get there soon enough. It turned out that the gig was at the hotel right next door to the Y.M.C.A. Dad just lucked out.

About fifteen minutes later Dad wandered into the ballroom, walked up to one of the alto players and said that he was the sub, tenor and clarinet in hand. That's when Jan Savitt came up behind him with a band jacket and welcomed him. He did four sets that night and four more the following night. I could see from his face that he was still as impressed with that memory as I was, and would become later in my life to similar things I lucked into.

As he was leaving, I did a Fred Savage from "The Princess Bride" and said something like, "That couldn't happen again in a million years." He said something like, "Oh, yeah it could. I know because it did." He sat back down...

A few years later, but still before he was married, Dad got another call on that same hall phone from the same guy. The circumstance were similar, but not so time sensitive and would have a larger impact on Dad. The Goodman band (yes, THAT Goodman, BENNY GOODMAN) had a few gigs booked in the Schenectady, Albany, Troy area (or as we Upstaters liked to say, the tri-cities). It was the middle of the winter and one of Benny's tenor players missed the band bus in Manhattan and could not get through the snow to make it up north. The guy from the union called my Dad based on two things. First, he was pleased with the sub work Dad did on the Savitt band. Second, he knew my Dad well enough to know that he, my Dad, knew EVERYTHING in the Goodman book by heart. He did until the day he died, I know, I was there and we were listening to "Benny Rides Again" and he was smiling.

Having just seen Buddy throw a tantrum that night, and knowing that Benny was known for being a bit of an AH himself, I asked Dad how it went. He said, and this is a quote; "I don't remember. It was all like a dream. A good dream, but I can't remember any of it." That's not a line you would forget your father saying to you.

Coda: A few days later, back home, I was sitting in the basement playing the piano and Dad came in, Vodka in hand, no cigarette never in the house, but he did have an old faded envelope. He put the envelope on the piano and said something like, "This is the only way I know for sure it ever happened" and he walked back up the stairs. On the envelope in nicely printed letters was "$150.00 – ROBBY" then scribbled (it took me about five minutes to decipher it) was, "Thanks, Benny Goodman."

Posted by Fred

The Envelope Please

No, I never played in the pit band at the Oscars, though I bet that would have been cool like back in the 70's or 80's. It's just a post title that I hope I can wrap up pointing back at it's foreshadowing. This post actually has to do mostly with the term, or acronym, OJT. I know that OJT (On The Job Training) is not necessarily a musical term or a military term, but that's where I was first exposed to it, so I personally attribute it to GI bands. Here are a few of my OJT experiences, though not in any sort of chronological order.

Three Down: I know I should have known this before the age of 25, but remember, I was mostly a big band sax player so small band settings where they just called tunes and started playing were rather unfamiliar to me. To make this one a little more uncomfortable for me it was my first gig with the Protocol Trio (Cocktail Music group) for the AFB Overseas, so therefore sometime in the early 80's. I was on drums due to an unfortunate staffing problem.

The first tune went OK. I remember it as "A-Train" at a reasonable tempo. I don't remember what the name of the second tune was but I remember the hand gestures that went along with it being called blanking everything else from my memory due to embarrassment. The piano player, our Chief, called the title then placed the first three fingers of his right hand over his left forearm and tapped them three times. He then counted, "One, Two, One, Two, Three, Four." I started playing a Jazz Waltz, the other guys started a 4/4 swing tune in Eb. Oops. Fortunately they went with the fool who didn't know how wrong he was and we ended up finishing perhaps the first rendition of whatever that tune was performed in 3/4. At the break the Chief explained the fingers thing. Check the blog glossary if you need more of an explanation.

Follow The Leader: There is no way to set this on up or to explain how 17 people did what we did that afternoon in Clearwater, FL so I will just tell the story.

It as a cool Jazz Festival gig and the AFB East had a phenomenal guest artist with us. Our normal director allowed me to direct the band while the guest artist was performing, considering I had written all of those charts. (I don't know if I ever thanked the Chief for that? Thanks, Chief!)

The stage setup was way funky. The rhythm section was kind of in the back, up stage-right and the horns could not see well and there were these poles holding up the tent above us all over the place and in the way.

I had done this chart on John Coltrane's "Naima" to feature my buddy Dave, from our band. Our guest soloist had heard us (Dave) do it at another festival and asked to do it with us that day with him on soprano, though it was written for tenor and our guest performer was known as a bari player. Not a problem. The problem was the nebulous intro and recap of the intro that preceded the shout chorus.

The intro was intended to be a classic "Intonation." An Intonation was the term used to explain an Organum type of sketch of the tonality that often precede acappella vocal pieces in the Middle Ages (yeah, OK, I did pay some attention in Composition classes at NT). In this case it was mostly like Antonio Frescobaldi meets Gill Evans. It was kind of rubato (out of time) and was pretty stupid to try on that stage at that time. But, hey, we are making up OJT as we go along.

On the intro the time fell apart just as the soprano sax and french horn (cool, yeah that band let me have a french horn in the brass section of that band) lead into the head (melody). Oops. Fortunately, the soprano player realized the problem and even though his part called for a drastic diminuendo, he took over and reestablished the time. All was well.

After the two choruses of the melody (Head) the intro was recapped and we ran into the same problem. This time though we were leading into a full ensemble nightmare, well at least until "The Workhorse" took over.

Our lead trumpet player sensed the same problem that the soprano player had sensed only 16 bars earlier and filled his Getson up and just fixed it. I mean, there I am down stage-left attempting to conduct a bunch of people who cannot see me and out of nowhere comes Gabriele wielding heaven's trumpet and all of us sheep just falling into place. I didn't even bother to conduct any more of that one. For some reason there were a few cats on that stage paying attention at that point. The two other rubato sections went just fine with me covering my part. All I had to do was cut them off at the end.

The Envelope Please: This was in San Antonio, TX in the late 70's. I had two pay gigs (stuff not with the Air Force band) while I was there in 1978-1979, this was one of them.

During the break between the third and fourth set of a dance gig, I ran into the band leader back stage. He was going through this thing, ritual, that I could only perceive as the same kind of preparation I was instructed to use for preparing the Host while in altar boy training (flunked miserably by the way). I had to find out what was up so I went over and asked him. He said that he was preparing the Pay Envelopes. I paid attention.

He explained that the envelopes had to be brand new and white. He explained that the bills had to be in order from largest denomination to the smallest with a good looking bill in front. He explained that the envelope must be clearly marked, printed not script, with the amount and the player's name, in Sharpie, on the front. Then he licked the tail, just a little bit of the gum, not the whole thing, and sealed the one he was working on.

Later that night I got my Pay Envelope, and there it was; "$45.00 - Robbie" inside there was a twenty a ten and a five, in that order with the twenty looking sharp. I felt respected even though I didn't play that well that night and was never asked back with that band. I never forgot that formula.

Posted by Fred

6 comments:

Chris Said...

> Math never was your strong suit, was it, Fred?

Stephanie said...

> That's okay Fred! Musicians aren't mathematicians I'm living proof of that!
>
> I just hope you messed up in your math here in the post and that you didn't get stiffed a twenty at the gig!

Chris said...

> What Steph said...

Fred said...

> LOL... No, SPELLING is where I suck the most, followed by grammar.
>
> Actually I only got $35.00 of the $45.00 I was booked for, a twenty a ten and a five, because I really did NOT play very well that night. But, I still felt the respect of having the bills compiled nicely in a fresh white envelope... lol

Stephanie said...

> See? I told you I sucked at math. In my original comment, I said I hoped you weren't stiffed a TWENTY instead of a TEN

Stephanie said... (cont.)

.... MY BAD!!

Don't shoot me, I'm just the vocalist.....

Fred said...

Hon, take two "Ken Hugs" and call me in the morning... lol.
Oh, hug him back for me, please...

Like Father Like Son?

OK, I thought I was going to come up dry for a post for today,
obviously not. And, no, this post has little to do with me and MY
father. This all came about because an old friend of mine posted
something in Facebook that concluded in us bantering about a book
that Miles Davis' son wrote about Miles. Oddly enough, I had been
introduced to my old friend's son today (through e-mail only) too.
All of that triggered all of this in my memories. I think I should do
this one in chronological order...

1969, Longshore Country Club Ballroom, Westport, CT. They were
throwing a "Dixieland Brunch" and my Dad got us tickets. I was not
a Dixieland Fan at that time so I thought of it as more a chore than a
delight to be on the short guest list. And, it was in the morning, the
band was to start playing at 11:00 AM. But, it got me out of church
for the day, so what the heck.

When we got there, there was a poster out front that listed the guys
in the band. I cannot remember the rhythm section but the horn line
stuck with me. On trumpet, Clark Terry. On tenor saxophones; Zoot
Sims and Al Cohn. Holy Cow!

We got there early and the place was almost empty so we went right
up to this big circular banquette table near the front and took a seat.
A few minutes later an older gentleman joined us, there were like 20
places so he was not elbow to elbow with us. The older gentleman
had two of these cardboard signs that said band on them and placed

them in front of the seats on either side of him.

At that point my Dad introduced himself and the older gentleman turned out to be Al's Dad. How cool! My Dad said something like, "You must be really proud of your son." Al's Dad replied "Well, when he learns to play as well as Johnny (Zoot) then he'll have made it." We all cracked up. Oh, nothing cool like hanging out with Al or Zoot, but the band did KA and played mostly Cool School, Hard Bob, not Dixie! Dads...

Late October 1974, Bruce Hall Lobby, NTSU, Denton, TX (I remember the time of year because of the Halloween decorations). My roommate and I decided to play a phone prank. We decided we would call Directory Assistance in NY, NY and ask for the number of Thelonious Monk.

So, we piled into the phone booth, dialed the number and got a HUMAN OPERATOR (remember them?) and my roommate asked the question of the day, "Do you have the number for a Thelonious Monk?" Without missing a beat the operator said, "We have two." This is before the days of computers and there was no way she could have looked up that number so quickly. We were amazed. I can't remember how we ended up with the number we got but we called it. A male voice answered, my roommate asked, "Mr. Monk?" The male voice said, "No, that's my Dad." He did give us that number but we did not have the balls to call it...

Mid 80's, Jacksonville Jazz Festival, Jacksonville, FL. That day the show was to open with "The Dirty Dozen Brass Band" on Stage A (the good stage) followed by us, the AFB East JZ, on Stage B (the stage for the local and free acts) so that they could reset Stage A for the Ellington band, under the direction of Mercer Ellington.

I don't know why, but the back stage area was packed right from the time they opened the gates, about 10:00 AM. OK, it was probably because of the free food and drinks for all performers (even us AF dudes) all day long. I must admit that I was quite surprised to see the likes of Mercer Ellington, Art Farmer and Benny Golson (the Jazztet was the closing act that day) there so early, but they were.

As we will all milling around waiting on chow, this tall young black man walked over to Mercer, who was less that ten feet from me, extended his hand and said, "Mr. Ellington." Mercer did shake his hand but replied, "That's my Dad. I'm just Mercer" in a playful manner. Not to be out done, the tall dude replied, "I know who you are. I am just proud to be meeting the composer of 'Things Aint What The Used To Be'." They both cracked up and chatted away while I sipped coffee.

A few minutes later the tall dude wondered off. Having seen the friendly nature of the superstar still standing just a few feet away I got up the nerve to go over to him. I walked over extended my hand and said, "I like 'Things Aint What The Used To Be' too." He looked me right I the eye and said, "That's Mr. Ellington to you" and cracked this HUGE smile and slapped me on the back, just about knocking me over. We didn't chat or anything, but I did get to shake Mercer Ellington's hand and had no spinal injuries.

As the show was about to start, that same tall dude came back carrying a Sousaphone. He stepped up on the stage and moments later out came "My Feets Can't Fail Me Now." I had never even heard of The Dirty Dozen Brass band until then, let alone heard them play. I was an instant fan, well, okay, it took me five bars...

Our set was inconsequential to anything.

The Ellington band was very good. Having heard the original band with many of the original players I cannot say that it was THAT good, but Duke would have been proud. As the crowd called for an encore, Mercer turned to the rhythm section and they started Satin Doll." He stepped to the mike and simply said, "Some of you might remember this" and slipped into his father's voice. Out came the "I Love You Madly Speech" exactly like Duke would have done it (my favorite being the 70th Birthday album). They segued right in to "Things Aint What The Used To Be" for the encore.

When the Jazztet finished up that day's performances they also were asked for an encore. I think it was Curtis (Fuller) who took the mike and said, "We don't have any speeches, but we would like to close things up with one of the best tunes Duke Ellington never wrote."

They finished with "Things Aint What The Used To Be" too...

Coda: As I told my friend, on Facebook, I try not to find out too much about musicians other than their music, in the hopes that I won't turn up something that would diminish my appreciation for them. So, no, I had not read the book on Miles by his son. I also have not read the book that Mercer wrote about his father. I had heard some rather unflattering things were written there and though I am not sure when Mercer's book came out. I do not want to change my memory of Mercer or Duke so I have no intention of even considering reading it.

I am sure there may have been issues between Mercer and Edward, heck I had stupid-ass issues with my Dad and I am sure Al did with his, but never when we were in The Muse. The 90 minutes the Ellington band played that day capped off with the speech and the same original arrangement his father had done on his tune proved that point to me in Mercer's case. Oh, I forgot to mention Al's statement just before they ended that gig.

Al took the mike from Clark Terry, who did 99% of the emcee work and said, "I would like to introduce may father, who is sitting right down front" pointing to his Dad sitting right near us. "He is the man who taught me everything important I know, except how to play better than his favorite tenor player" pointing over his shoulder at Zoot. Al's dad jumped up and shouted, "That's MY boy!"

Posted by Fred

Charts

OK, so today I got my second e-mail from somebody I have never met (not even in cyberspace) because of TBOTB blog. This time I paid attention because of this charming question, and I quote, "who the fuck are you and where did all this shit come from" yes, it was all in lowercase without any punctuation.

I directed this interested individual to earlier posts and pointed out the blog's glossary, that was about Noon my time on 8-28-2010.

About three hours later I got another e-mail asking that I "glosserize" (is that a word) at least four other terms; Chart, Book, Jazz and Cool. "She" also explained, in that e-mail, that English was not her first language but she liked Lester Young and would like to see an American Baseball game in Yankee Stadium. (I guess asking "Blogger" not to list you to search engines only goes so far.)

I thought for a moment and realized that it was not within my ability to define Jazz or Cool, if Pops and Duke couldn't who am I to presume, but I will take a shot at "Chart and Book."

Chart is a slang term for Arrangement. An Arrangement is something done by an Arranger generally broken down into one of the following categories: Orchestration (more below), Special (do anything you want) or Lift (AKA, Record Copy).

200, or more, years ago an Arranger would take a piece of music and modify the ensemble, or solo instrument, of the original composition for a different ensemble, or solo instrument, therefore an arranger and/or orchestrator were virtually identical. These early arrangers never intentionally modified any of the original composition's material except when necessary due to the limitations of the ensemble/solo instrument it was being arranged for.

Since the late 1800's, Orchestrators became independent of the Arranger label because they mostly expanded the sketches of lazy-ass composers into stuff people could actually play. At that point, Arrangers became those people who listened to a piece of music and said to themselves, "No, I think it should go like this..." wrote it down and people played it.

So, in the 20th century, an Orchestration was a devout replica of the original composition while an Arrangement may have been a major bastardization of a concept of the original composer.

Perhaps I should have billed myself as a bastardizer? But, there was not an AFSC for that. So in my career in the AF Bands, I did two orchestrations, one on "Pixeland Rag" (from Chick Corea's "Leprechaun" album) and another on some Piccolo Concerto, I cannot remember the composer's name. Everything else I wrote was a Chart.

Book. Well, the Book is a bunch of charts. Kinda... When a Chart is completed, it (the score and individual parts) are normally cataloged in a library, where they are kept together like that, score and parts in a folder or envelope by piece. The Book is different. In the Book the parts are kept together in separate folders or envelopes and the total of those folders/envelops are normally kept in a box, also known as the Book, or road library. So, you can have a Big Band Book, 16 or 17 smaller books, by the part, or you could have a Lead Trumpet Book, Bari Sax Book, etc.

Now that I have bored you to tears, allow me attempt to inspire you a bit with my thoughts on when I finally had made a significant contribution to a pretty good Book which contained some pretty good Charts of mine.

By the mid 1980's, when I was with the AFB East, most of the vocals that were being performed with the Concert Band and Jazz Ensemble were mine, along with a substantial number of instrumentals, both originals or arrangements (both still Charts) and I was feeling pretty good about my competency. So right on up until 1991 I continued to crank out some pretty good material. How? Here's the secret.

One day I sat down to write a Chart and decided that I would not write it for me or the audience, instead I would write it for the individuals in the band. I considered going so far as to label the parts by name, but I decided that would not go over so well so I didn't. During the first read we made it through all the way. It was not perfect, far from it, but that was rare. We added the vocalists next and again, made it through the whole thing (about a six minute number). This time I could see people smiling, there was even some laughter after the cutoff.

I had earned the trust of the band. On the break the lead trumpet player came over to me and made a suggestion about a few bars here and there, and I said, "Go for it, but just mark up the part in pencil, just in case." Moments later the bass clarinet player came over with another suggestion. That one was so good I actually had to change the score and read out new notes to the woodwinds when we went back later.

From that day forward my stuff was treated with the same respect as a new Dr. Alfred Reed or Sammy Nestico Chart. My writing got better and better (until the fizzle of 1992) because of the band, not because of any stroke of genius on my part.

I wonder how many of my Charts are still in that Book?

Posted by Fred

4 comments:

Chris said...

> If they have any sense, a lot of them. Fred, you wrote some of the most challenging charts I ever read, and to this day, I can only remember changing one note of one of them...the end note of the 1st Horn part of "Tomorrow" was originally a pretty lame concert F (C for me) third space in the staff; I changed it in the first rehearsal to the octave higher, just so I could screw with the lead trumpet player who had the same note. I held it as long as he did...

Fred said...

> Mmm... But by then you knew you had Carte Blanche. I was talking about "Modern Broadway" though you and Stephanie had already proved yourself on "Cohan!" "Willkommen" would not have been in that medley if I didn't know you would blow it away. Oh, OK, then there's "Georgia On My Mind" or and those RIDICULOUS horn parts on "WOTGWW" yadda, yadda, yada.

> Soon my friend!

Stephanie said...

> The weaving together of the songs in WOTGWW is some of the most incredible arranging that I have ever experienced, Fred! I asked you once about publishing the medley. Ever considered trying to? I think it would make a great full-blown stage production! Oh, and the "At the Ballet" segment still gives me chills every time!

Fred said...

> Why, thank you, Ma'am! Yeah, I remember you mentioning that. I did check, and three years after leaving the Air Force I then had Publishing Rights (though Uncle Sam retains performance rights forever). Interesting. Maybe an SSAA thing with various soloists? Humm. Even if it didn't make any money, it might be fun to get that music out in public again.

A Jack Of All Trades

Again, with these people I don't know? This time the question was a bit simpler, and I hope the answer will be less boring. "What are your instrument?" Again from the non native English speaking lady. Not knowing if she meant "What is your instrument" or "What are your instruments" I will attempt to answer...

Formally, I had my first saxophone lesson, on tenor - my Dad's horn, on April 27th 1967, at Zera Musicland, Fairfield, CT. I only remember the day because it was my 12th birthday. So, technically, saxophone. But...

Two years later I started taking piano, you know, the Hannon, all that stuff. That wasn't going to work, I would have to practice and all... But, Sax came rather naturally to me and I got good enough to make the JR HS bands and HS bands and all. Somewhere along the way I adopted the Recorder also.

In HS, I rented a flute so I could learn that Jethro Tull tune. I cannot remember the name though. My Dad told me a few days later that if I was going to learn doubles that I should also learn clarinet, so he gave me access to his. By the time I left HS I had done a few musicals covering sax, clarinet and flute. The normal rack...

While off at a summer music camp, I borrowed my roommate's "other" trumpet (or was it a cornet?) and got to the point that I could play my major, minor and chromatic scales, though with limited range, before the summer was out. Oh, that's also where I learned to balance things on my nose...

A few years later I borrowed an oboe and an Eb, transverse mounted, piston valved Mellophonium (what a cool axe) from another friend. I quickly gave up on the oboe (WAY too hard to play) but loved the Mellophonium, wish I had one still...

I dabbled with other instruments, even bass and guitar but nothing really caught my fancy until I got to the AFB Overseas. That's when I realized that the true answer to the above question might just be the instruments I ever played on a gig, at least once. So, here goes.

Obviously I did a lot of gigs on sax, bari was my choice but alto, tenor and soprano too. With that said, flute and clarinet were the standard doubles, along with piccolo (which I suck at) and bass clarinet.

I played piano in public three times. Once in Germany, with the short lived American Patrol band. The second time was a solo gig in a hotel lobby for New Years in the early 90's (just walking music, there was no place for anybody to sit and listen, as if I was that good) and finally a few tunes with that Dixie band I played with in Macon, GA on a night that they wanted to play some standards. So, I guess those piano lessons came in handy.

I did one half of a gig on trumpet while with the band in Germany. Our lead trumpet player was late to the gig because he had to pick up his car at the port and was like two hours late. I covered (if you could call it that) the 4th book and everybody shifted up a chair. Oh, and on the two Don Menza charts we had in the book, I would switch back to tenor. My face hurt for days after that.

I did one chart (if you can call Tchaikovsky's Nutcracker Suite a chart) on one gig on, of all instruments; Eb, transverse mounted, piston valved Mellophonium. I was a substitute for the 4th French Horn part. FUN!

Then came a run of gigs on an instrument I had never really played before, except just like any adolescent kid had done, in the cafeteria on the edge of the table, Drum Set.

We were short drummers at the band in Germany. At a staff meeting the First Shirt asked if anybody could play a Trap Set. I raised my hand (not normally a good idea for a GI to do). Without so much as asking how good was I, he said, "Good, see Supply and check out the Rogers. You have a trio gig at the O' Club tonight." SHIT!

I went and got the set, very cool drums. Old, all wood, small, perfect for a small group drummer. The one problem was that I had never sat behind a drum set for more than a few minutes in my life. I took it to my office (yeah, arrangers got offices there too) set it up and started playing time, the best I could. After about an hour the Chief walked in. He looked at me and asked, "Where did you learn to play drums?" I pointed at the floor of my office. His eyes rolled. I jumped in, "I can do it, just don't do anything too fast and no waltzes, I can't make that work yet."

Well, I have already posted a story about the first set of that gig; the Three Down, Three Up thing, but here is the opening of the second set. "My Favorite Things" at about MM = 200. I hung. Learned how to play waltzes that night.

Coda: Years after getting out of the AF, I moved to California. Once here I took up another instrument that I had dabbled with as a child. But, this time I got really good at it, close to a virtuoso, in my opinion. My new axe, and the one I will for sure play forever is The Radio. Thank you, KKJZ, 88.1 FM!

Posted by Fred

2 comments:

Tom P. said...

> No cello?

Fred said...

> Well, there's always room for cello...

One Of These Things Is Not Like The Others

OK, so this is three days in a row posting something that came to mind because of those two "unknowns" in my e-mail. This time it's back to the person with the initially rude (well, say we say slightly off color) question. This time he (she?) asked what was the oddest chart request/assignment I ever got. Hum, that got my head spinning.

As I started writing this I realized that the strangest charts I ever wrote were actually requested by me. Well, to be more correct, I begged the bosses to let me do them. For example, "The Twelve Days Of Christmas" and my Halloween time medley called "Scary Music," (or was it "Things That Go Bump In The Night"?) which included such favorites as "The Theme From The Blob" and "Attack Of The Killer Tomatoes." But, that would not have answered the question. So here they are in chronological order.

August 1978, AFB West. I have mentioned this before, but my first assignment for the Air Force was a concert band chart on Donna Summer's "Last Dance." Not that a request for an arrangement for a pop (disco) tune for a traditionally stuffy kind of an ensemble is all that unusual. But, considering my aversion to that particular tune, it made the list.

This was while I was still at the AFB West, but a few months later. One of the flute players from the concert band came to me and asked if I would have the time to write something for the Woodwind Quartet. Gee, I didn't even know we had one. I also didn't know, at that point, that I was only supposed to field requests from the commander or requests that were forwarded through my supervisor (which I didn't have yet). So, sure, what tune? She requested "Pixieland Rag" the Chick Corea thing from the "Leprechaun" album. How cool!!! OK, OK, once again, not that strange a request, but considering the people that made up that quartet, five of the SQUAREST people I have ever met, I was amazed.

January of 1993, just after getting out of the Air Force. I got a call one day from a guy who had heard from a friend of a friend of a friend (you know the drill) that I could write Marching Band music (oh JOY) and might need the work (how CORRECT). I told him I could do the music part but not the choreography (the "show"). That worked because that was kind of his specialty. Cool, what's the tune? "When Doves Cry." By PRINCE, that "When Doves Cry?" That's the one... We set the length and key and I quoted what I thought was an unreasonably high price, halfheartedly hoping that he would turn me down. He excepted. His request was for the score only, he said he LIKED doing copy work (I swear, that's what he said). Three days later his check arrived. The next day I mailed him the score.

July 5th 1993. I only remember the actual day because the day before was the first time I had NOT had a 4th of July gig since 1969, so it kind of stuck with me. There was a letter in my mailbox with a request from a String Quintet leader from someplace in New England. They wanted a chart on "Some Skunk Funk" by the Brecker Brothers. I didn't even finish reading the letter or look to see how much they were willing to pay, I just sat down and started writing.

I finished the score that night and the parts the next day. On the third day the package was in the mail. That's when I read the rest of the letter and found the enclosed check for $400.00.

It turned out that the "When Doves Cry" guy knew these ladies (an all female String Quintet) and turned them on to me. I guess he must have liked his chart and I guess he thought my rates were reasonable. By the way, I would have done that chart for free as long as they sent me a copy of a recording of it.

The following week I got another letter for the String Quintet ladies. It was very flattering, they loved "Skunk Funk", and there was another request for a chart on "Four Brothers" with another $400.00 check and instructions that the Viola part get the Woody solo and the more traditional quartet play the part of the saxes.

Once again I sat right down and started writing. Well, I did cheat, I had a copy, two actually, of the original chart so I was transcribing mostly - but I did abridge much of the ensemble stuff. Again my package was in the mail soonest. This time I returned the check and added a note that all I wanted as payment for "Four Brothers" was a cassette of the two charts.

About a week later I got another letter from them. Well, actually it was just an envelope with the same check I had sent back and no note. I never heard from them again.

September 1993 I was working on the Sovereign of the Seas, Royal Caribbean Cruise ship and had one of the dancers approach me with a request for a chart on "There's A Boat That's Leavin' Soon For New York" for the twelve piece house band. OK, OK, this was not an unusual request at all, at least not at that time.

It's one of my favorite songs, especially the Miles/Gill version from "Porgy And Bess" so I was really interested. The guy, a tall beautiful (yeah, that kind of handsome) young black man who was not a member of the "Breeders" (a term used by the gay contingent on that ship to describe people like me and many of my friends) went on to give me an idea of what he was looking for. He told me it was to be a dance number. He was a feature dancer on the ship and had this one number, a slow Latin thing, where he slung around this amazing Australian babe in such a manner as to belie his sexual preferences. He wanted it to be something unlike anything the "Blue Hairs" would be expecting. BINGO (big ships term) Miles and Gill.

This one took a few days but he bribed the band into doing a rehearsal by offering them beer (smart man). So, we showed up one morning to run down the chart. For a change the band was there before the soloists so I had the chance to talk them through it before he even arrived. When he did, I was in for a surprise.

He walked in, in a full 1920's style tux complete with a bowler hat and cane wearing tap shoes. Oops. On the stands was a hardcore late 50's Hard Bop chart and Fred "Mandingo" Astaire (please, I mean no offense by that - that was a name he himself used to describe himself later) was standing in front of me. I was freaked and was trying to figure out what to say when one of the trumpet players shouted something about getting started... Blah, blah, blah, bitching all the way. Our soloist ran down the stairs to the stage and shouted that he was ready as he assumed a classic tap-dancer's frozen pose. I kind of shrugged and kicked it off.

The band started playing (these cats could SIGHT READ!!!) and it sounded pretty much the way I wanted it to. Our soloist slowly unfroze and just looked up at us. I think he might actually have had tears in his eyes. Blew that one, is all I could think. He never moved but when we were finished he asked if he could have a few minutes before we ran it again.

A few minutes later he returned in that same body suit he used for that sexy dance I mentioned above and asked if we could run it down one more time, and he started a cassette recorder. I couldn't watch this time, so I kicked off the tune and sat to cover my part. As I cut off the band, all I heard was a loud, "YES!" from the stage and my dancer was gone.

That night he did run a tab for the band at the crew bar, so everybody was feeling OK about the extra rehearsal. The next night was the "Crew Show." Those were the non production shows that were mostly made up of the Cruise Staff, semi-pros. "There's A Boat..." was first to be performed. It got a HUGE ovation from the crowd. Holly cow?!?

Crew shows were replayed on video over the closed circuit TV system on the ship. That was only the second night I ever watched one. My dancer, Desmond, that's his name - it finally came to me, had made my chart a masterpiece. Well, not the chart (the chart got about a 5, the band an 8 and Desmond about a 22, on a scale of one to ten). I tracked him down later in the other crew bar that was basically frequented by the "Non Breeders." I had never been a part of anything that incorporated dance before. I was exhilarated. Oh, and I was made an official honorary member of the Non Breeders that night...

I ran into Desmond the next day and he was down. He told me that the Cruise Director informed him that he could not do that number on the ship any more. The Captain had seen the replay and called it pornographic. We both smiled. We also attempted everything we could to get a copy of that tape but were not successful.

Coda: So what does the title of this post have to do with the post? Well, of the charts mentioned here, "There's a Boat..." is the only one I ever heard (saw). I was on my honeymoon the night that "Last Dance" was performed (the only performance, as far as I can tell) and nobody ever sent me tapes of the others. Oh, yeah I did eventually cash the "Four Brothers" check. I still would have rather had a tape.

Posted by Fred

Ain't But The One

I was about to come up dry again today when the phone rang here at the house as I was frying chicken for tonight's dinner. After cleaning up the kitchen I plopped down in my office and checked the answering machine. There was a message from a very close friend asking a very strange question. The words were, "When I finally do get back in the studio can we record 'Ain't But The One?'"

I sat there for a while and replayed the message a few times. Then it hit me. I had written a tune by that name way back on May 25th, 1974. It's not odd to me that I can remember exactly the day I wrote it, all the way out to the first version of a big band chart in a single day. What is odd to me is that I can't remember how the tune/chart goes except for maybe parts of the intro.

I was driving down US-1 (AKA The Boston Post Road to the folks in my home town) in Southport, CT on my way to Zara Musicland which was just up the road in Fairfield, CT. On the radio, WRVR, came the news that Edward Kennedy "Duke" Ellington had passed away the day before. I quickly pulled my 1972, baby-blue, Plymouth Duster into the Greek Diner just up the road and started to cry. I didn't even park, I was just sitting there in the lane until somebody honked one of those ever so friendly NY style honks. I pulled into a space. As I parked I remember the DJ saying, "Something, something... Ain't But The One" as he started to play "Come Sunday" the one with Bessie Smith on vocals.

I turned the car around and went back to the house, stopping at the Stop And Shop to buy a six pack of beer with the money my Dad had given me to pick up some reeds for him at the music store. Yes, it was 1974 so I was only 19. But the state of Connecticut, in its divine wisdom, had changed the drinking age to 18 in 1973 (as did the state of Texas) the year I turned 18, so that was kosher. When I got home, well, to the house my folks lived in, not the house I grew up in, where I was riding out my short dropout period from NTSU. I went right to the piano, downstairs in that split-level, and started to write (and drink).

Moments later my Dad came down and asked where his reeds were and if I was planning on going to work as he eyeballed my beer. I just turned to him and said, "Duke died yesterday" tears still streaming down my face. He knocked down the rest of whatever he was drinking and said he would take care of it. Moments later I hear my folks "having a discussion."

My folks never really argued, but they were known to raise a voice or two in discussion. So I ran upstairs, hearing my name mentioned. I was no longer crying when I got to the kitchen, but that was not to last for long, when my Mom turned to me as I entered the room and grilled me: "Your father just told Matt (my boss) that you would not be going to work because of a death in the family." She had this very blank expression on her face. Dad answered for me, "Duke Ellington died yesterday." I burst back into tears, Mom hugged me and they both left me alone for most the rest of the night. I returned to the piano, angry.

After about three hours I had a tune on a lead sheet and about half of a chart written. I had never done anything like that before. I had also killed a six-pack of beer and finished a pack of cigarettes – I had never done anything like that before either. So, I called a friend, who was only 17, but he could drive me to Caleasies (nearby Italian Delicatessen) where I could remedy my shortages, or so I thought. When I got him on the phone I told him I needed a ride because Dad had pulled my keys - which he did after seeing me with a beer. My friend asked why I was drinking to which I replied, "Duke died yesterday." He asked me what I needed from the store and I told him. He said he would be right there.

We he arrived I had all but finished the chart. In he walked, not knocking or anything, he was kin, just not blood, with two six-packs of beer and two packs of Kools. I had no idea how he procured the beer and I also had no idea how I was going to pay him because I had like two bucks on me at the time. He never asked. "What do you have so far?" he said, as he took over the piano bench. He started to play off my lead sheet as I lit a Kool. He commented: "This is not bad;" a major complement coming from him - or any of my musician friends of that time.

A few minutes later my Mom came down. My friend and I were both smoking and drinking beer at that moment. My Mom did her one and only "I'll be cool and not go berserk" moment I can ever remember her having, and she said to my friend, "I will call your Mom and let her know you are sleeping over tonight." As Mom was going away, my Dad came down, this time with one of his Vodkas in his hand. He asked what that was being played on the piano. When I played, it was like a bunch of notes... a stop, more notes... more stops... When my friend played, it was like music - though he was not actually a piano player either. My Dad and I stood behind my friend as he played, and improvised, and made suggestions on how this should go or how that should go. I was not angry any more.

A few years later, back at NTSU, I resurrected that lead sheet and did a chart that I brought it in to the Lab Band I was playing in at that time. Even the second coming of that tune was not anything to write home about. But, that must have been when my friend, who called me tonight with the question was first exposed to it.

I attempted to resurrect that same NTSU version while I was with the AFB Overseas and again in AFB East with no luck; it was just not that good of a chart. Then in the mid 80's a vocalist with the JZ at AFB East, said that she wanted to do a vocal chart on "Goodbye Pork Pie Hat" (GBPH) but didn't like any of the lyrics she had ever heard on that tune, so she asked if I could write some new ones, just for her. Me being me, said of course I could do that (having only written one set of lyrics before in my life, but they turned out OK, on "Central Park West"). Unfortunately, she then went off and sold the chart (not even sketched let alone written) to the band leader as something she wanted to do on the next album we were scheduled to do just a month or so down the line. Oops!

I sat with "...Porkpie..." and felt no words. I sat with it some more, and felt more, no words. I sat with it some more and got really angry. SHIT, that was it! Charles was angry when he wrote that just like I was when I wrote "Ain't But The One." I never knew why I was angry those 10, 12, 14 years before but now I did. I was angry, as I can only imagine Mr. Mingus was, that a genius was taken away from us. I finished my beer and snuffed out my smoke and went to bed. Snuggling with the mother of my two children I fell asleep very peacefully, only to awake a few hours in a panic or was it a muse-induced trance?

I bolted to the kitchen, put on a pot of coffee, grabbed a legal pad and started writing words. "His mother called him Lester, me just Prez, or Porkpie Hat..." That was the opening line. The hook came from the title of a tribute album to Billy Strayhorn ("His Mother Called Him William"). In my head all night had been Mingus, Ellington, Mingus, Ellington... Then it came to me, join the anger that Charles and I felt, but write something respectful, perhaps even melancholy. Less than an hour later I had the lyrics. Less than an hour after that I had a sketch of the chart. Before the sun came up I had parts and a pretty pissed off wife who kept thinking I was sick or something, the way I was acting.

That afternoon I brought home the rehearsal tape of GBPH compete with the first for bars of the intro that were identical to the first four bars of the intro to "Ain't But The One" though fare better orchestrated, and played it for my lady. She liked it. 10 years of frustration vanished in an instant.

Coda: A lot of the stuff in this post happened a long time ago. Fortunately, when I was younger I kept a log (that's a guy's name for a dairy) so much of what I just typed was recounted from notes taken 20+ years ago. I wish I had continued that - but I guess I am now...

I added so many annoying little details to this post only to magnify this: The thing that still drives me nuts about this whole experience is that other than the first four bars of the intro to "Ain't But The One" I still cannot remember anything else about the tune. At this moment...

Posted by Fred

Six Of One, Half A Dozen Of The Other

My buddy Chris reminded me of this in a comment to yesterday's post. Thanks, Chris! Chris was not sure of the name of the tune, and to be honest, I don't remember it either (I am not even sure it was one of mine). But I do remember dubbing the solos. So, here goes...

It was traditional with the AFB East JZ to track all but rhythm section solos, though rhythm section folks were allowed to patch their stuff. So, on the "Comin' At Ya" session the trumpet player had a few choruses on this one tune. So, there he was with his cans on (Fostex T-20's) and a mic in the room, dimly lit. The engineer cued up the tape, gave the trumpet player a warning and rolled tape. Then he, the engineer, said "My bad, not enough lead..." he stopped talking when the notes started flying. He also let the tape roll. Everybody in the booth was gassed!

The engineer hit the talk-back and said something like, "Not much pre, want another shot at it?" The trumpet player simply made this grin and gave a thumbs-up. Somebody interpreted for the engineer,

"Yeah, roll another one." This time the cue started up a few bars earlier. The second take was equally as good as the first, if not better. This time the engineer hit the talk-back and said, "We got it!" and everybody in the booth agreed.

Seconds later, the trumpet player had his lips smooshed up on the window between rooms, with his thumb down. The engineer didn't need any interpreter this time, all he said was, "I got four more tracks to spare, tell me when you are done."

Four more takes, four more gems. The engineer finally told the trumpet player that all the tracks were full and that we still needed to lay the tenor and trombone solos so that was going to be it for him. The trumpet player skulked off as if embarrassed. The folks in the booth were just about speechless. So, everybody went on and on about how good all the solos were. We got everything else we needed and got to the point where we needed to thin the herd - send the players home so the mixing crew could finish things up.

I caught the trumpet player just before he split for Warner Robins and asked if he had a preference of one of those solos on that tune. He said it didn't matter to him, they all sucked, and again walked off as if he was embarrassed. I was astonished. The worst solo I ever heard that guy play was far better than anything I could have imagined, let alone pulled off. He really was that good though.

When we got to the mix down, everything had been decided on except for the trumpet solo on that one tune. We listened to the takes over and over again and still could not decide, I mean like literally, everybody liked ever take best. Finally somebody came into the booth with a pair of those fuzzy-dice that used to hang on rear view mirrors and held on to one and tossed the other on the table next to the board. It came up "Snake-eye." Not everybody from the mix-down team was present for that die roll, but those of us who were decided that we would vote for number one. Yup, we went with the first take. But, none of us ever felt like we had wasted our time either laying the tracks or discussing which track to use. I wish I had a copy of the out-takes...

When the album came out, I asked the trumpet player if he liked the solo we selected (I never told him how we selected it). He said, "Yeah, the first take was my favorite too. But as long as you were gonna let me do takes... I would have played all day." We would have let him!

Posted by Fred

1 comment:

Stephanie said...

> You know, in every way I can sympathize/empathize with our
> "Tracks" of my Tears" friend. I don't think I've ever had a cut
> released, that I didn't want just one more shot...

Military Medicine . . . Is That Like,
Military Intelligence?

Note: I actually wrote this over a month ago, but never got around to
posting it. So the references to recent events, like "Today" or
"Yesterday" are only relative.

Not to this Vet... Every once and a while I lose control of the
symptoms of a condition I have had for like twenty-five years now.
Today was one of those days. It's not a big thing, but it did make me
think about some of my experiences with my GI Doctors, Dentists
and other medical support staff. So, once again in semi-
chronological order:

Lackland AFB, 1978. Just after getting out of basic I was told by the
base dental clinic that I needed to get my wisdom teeth removed.
Never having had a tooth pulled before I didn't have any problem
with that, though Dentists were not my favorite people. Fortunately
for me, in the late 70's it was common practice to over medicate
patients, at least for that one dentist, so after I sat down and took
whatever it was they gave me I became a zombie and the next thing I
remember was laying in my bed at home with my new bride's face
just above mine staring down at me.

My initial reaction to that sight was to become amorous but quickly
realized that I had awakened from my drug induced sleep to relieve
myself. So, I bolted out of bed, fell, slipped, slid, ended up in the
bathroom. After I was finished, I glanced at my reflection in the
mirror over the sink and remember thinking, "Good drugs!" as I

melted into a puddle on the floor.

Berlin, Germany, 1980. I don't remember how/why my wife was allowed to go along on that trip but she was there. I also don't remember if it was after a gig or we had the night off, but I remember that my wife and I had dinner at some Chinese restaurant that night, fish. I also remember what went on in my stomach not long after that dinner.

We were on the Ubahn (Subway) and we looked at each other like, "Ooops! We better get our butts off this car and get near a bathroom." Amazing what you can say with your eyes. So we hopped off, and turned it back around to the base. How we did not defoliate a German subway car that night, I don't know. As soon as we got back to the billets, we ran to our respective gang bathrooms where we spontaneously erupted from both ends, anointing the floor the walls and perhaps even the ceiling with stuff I never figured I would talk about over the Internet. YUCK!

The next little playlet includes a fellow bandsmen of mine. Somewhere along the line he came to a conclusion that he shared with us. "Wow, you two are so cool. I think that if I felt as bad you two look, I wouldn't want anybody in my room talking to me." He looked sheepish, moments later, and left us the F*** alone.

Sometime before sunrise my boss, the NCOIC (AKA: CMFWIC), got involved. He called the base hospital and ordered up an ambulance to take me and my wife to the hospital. We got there and took our place in line. At that time we were informed that all Active Duty Military personnel would be seen first, followed by Retired Military personnel and then dependents (the unflattering term the military used to describe my wife). I think I might have struck the A1C telling me that, at that moment except I had to visit the bathroom once again.

As I returned to the waiting room I realized I was OK. It was over for me, then I heard my name called. I went to the desk and asked that they take my wife instead of me, because I was now OK. I got shot down. A few minutes later, she returned from the restroom and had finished up too.

Time does heal all.

Some base in England, late 1980. We were flying in for some sort of Christmas dance gig with the AFB Overseas. The weather sucked and we found out later that every air field in the country was closed as we landed. Our C-9 hit the runway and we slid, and slid, and turned and slid and finally came to a stop.

I was running the loading crew for that band at that time so I hopped out quickly. I went a few feet and then hit some part of the plane and went down. It may have been the ice on the runway, it might have been what I hit, but either way, I was down. The next thing I remember was being in a Dr.'s office on a British military (RAF) base. The Dr. was explaining to me that I had a "muscle bruise." He went on to say that because I was a "Yank" he could not prescribe anything for me, then he handed me a piece of paper. On his note were instructions to pick up two large bottles of one of my favorite German Apple Schnapps' and how to use them for medicinal purposes.

I made the gigs and will be forever in gratitude to that Major for introducing to a now favorite beverage of mine.

Landstuhl, Germany, late 1981. That was the closest real US GI hospital to where I was stationed. I was there for a blood-test. This particular blood-test was a once and a while variation on the piss-test that somebody from every squadron in the AF had to go thorough in those days to test for "Illegal Substances." I was really kind of used to those tests because I became known to the heavies in my squadron as a guy who did not do drugs. Why? Because I didn't (though I did appreciate the stuff I was given when they took out my wisdom teeth). I got cool with beer at an early age and combined with my fear of spending extended amounts of time in Kansas, against my will, it was easy. So, when tests came up I expected to be picked and showed up.

That particular day I was to be plucked by an enlisted Army med tech named John. I am embarrassed to say I do not remember his last name because I (we, my wife and I) actually became friends with John, his wife (Babette) and their family. Well, anyway, just like I was not a fan of Dentists, I never liked having blood drawn. That day, John set me up with the tube thing on my arm and went to the cabinet to get the stuff and asked me to look away. The next thing I remembered was him sticking a cotton ball on my arm and saying, "You're done."

Here is where my chronological order becomes "Semi." Mid 1980's, AFB East. Rick and I were packing up the PA equipment for a trip to the Azores islands, a protectorate of Portugal somewhere in the middle of the Atlantic ocean, and I fell. I was lifting the top to the box that covered a floor monitor and my back went out. I actually though I was going to die.

What flashed through my head was a childhood memory of my father pulling sheets of lumber through the cellar window of our house in Schenectady, NY when I was bout 5 when he fell. My uncles, Paul and Art, rushed down and took my dad away and I didn't understand what had happen until years later. He had ruptured three disks in his back. My fall, only accounted to a partial rupture of one disk. But, as I said, I was sure I was going to die.

Not having any uncles in attendance, Rick rushed over to me and assumed that, "I will help you as you puke you guts out in the parking lot" position and told me not to move. Somehow, some time later, I was at the Robins AFB clinic. Somehow, sometime after that I was sitting there talking to the PA (Physician's Assistant) holding my bride's hand and felt a little bit better about knowing I was going to die as long as she was there. The PA started barking orders to my wife.

The next thing I remember was in a shower, 122 Victor, ST, Warner Robins, GA Master Bedroom - Bathroom, with EXCEPTIONALLY hot water flowing over me and a fist attempting to rupture my spine, about six vertebra from my tail bone. She, the 100 lbs woman holding her flabby 175 lbs man and attempting to make him feel good said, "Baby, please" there was probably more. But that's all I can remember.

I was back at work 17 days ahead of my Quarters Orders, though I did miss that trip. Thank you Rick. The PA and Susie. Oh, my back is still pretty OK.

Mid 80's, I cannot remember when, but I do remember the place. I was sitting at my house writing something and the phone rang. On the other end was "THE" Chief and he told me that he needed a sub, on Alto in like two minutes. When this man spoke you just did it. There were no questions, except "what uniform?" and I got to the base just in time to catch the bus. Dang?

Once I got on the bus I asked one of the guys, "What's up with Tom?" (the guy I was subbing for) "Dunno, I think he's sick" somebody said. OK. We can't smoke here right (mostly drove the truck, not often on the bus any more)? Yup. F***! Shortly thereafter we, the AFB East JZ, were setup in the parking lot of the Albany, GA, Civic Center ready to play. I think it was like the second tune and my head blew up (almost literally).

I pulled the horn out of my mouth and looked around, everybody else was still playing. I would have sworn I had just witnessed the worst feedback in sound reinforcement history, but it turned out to be just me, it was my left ear. The ringing was so loud it was painful and it made all the real sound around me garbled. I closed my eyes and concentrated on listening to the bass player. A few seconds later I could plainly hear the bass and the ringing was a bit quieter. The band cut off the tune and somebody shook me. I opened my eyes and just made some hand gestures pointing to my ear and looked confused. I then did a hand roll indicating to go on without me, they did. I closed my eyes again and concentrated on the music in front of me. After about a chorus I could hear the band and the ringing was still obvious, but OK. I started to play again. As soon as I did, the ringing got louder. By the end of the tune I was somewhat under control. Fortunately, the gig was just one set, so I made it through the whole thing somehow.

After the gig, I road back in the truck, where I could smoke and concentrate on the rumble of the engine (something that I had learned to love over the years). By the time we got home I was pretty much under control and put off an emergence trip to the clinic.

A few days later I was still having to close my eyes and concentrate a lot to keep the ringing under control, but it was working. I finally saw an Audiologist and he did a bunch of tests. He came up with some term for what I had/have but told me that there was no known cure but surgery "might" be able to help. He then asked how I had managed to get it under control as quickly as I did. So, I told him the little exercise my arranging teacher guru gave us back at NTSU, where we would close our eyes and attempt to listen to only one player in a band or orchestra, amazingly enough, if you concentrate, you can do that. All I did was reverse it. I would listen to the world and concentrate until the ringing turned into just a dull numb feeling/sound kind of off to my left. That is what goes on with my left ear to this day.

For a few days I still had to really concentrate each morning to make the ringing go away. After a few weeks it was just kind of normal. A few days later still the Audiologist from the clinic showed up at the squadron with a bunch of photo-copies of stuff on how to deal with my condition. As I glanced over it he commented that it was basically what I had described to him in his office. I agreed.

For the rest of my time at AFB East, that Audiologist would regularly check up on me and offer any new material he had found on how to make things easier for me, though my original remedy was (and is to this day) the best I have found. He also made it a point to be a part of my discharge physical where he informed me that my condition qualified me for a disability. I jokingly tilted my head and asked him to repeat that in my good ear, pointing to my right ear. He laughed, called me an asshole, shook my hand and that was that.

Coda: Yeah, I had to learn to listen differently, mix sidesaddle, stuff like that, but no disability. I still have my music, still marvel at Mr. Beethoven and those GI medical people who have a damn tough job.

Posted by Fred

5 comments:

Stephanie said...

> I believe it was a combo/pipes? trip to Key West back in 1983. I was supposed to go on the trip. Ken was on the gig and had already left to help load the truck. It was an evening flight I believe. I hadn't been feeling great before Ken left the house, but soon after he was gone, I got really sick. I called Ken and told him that Kat would have to go and sing on the gig.
>
> After a couple of hours, Jack R came and took me to the base hospital. They said I had contracted the Asian flu, (I've got news for them... it came straight from hell!) you know... the kind of sickness where you can't decide if you should sit on the great white throne first or bow at the great white throne first.... I think most of the time I was sitting on the throne and embracing the bathroom trash can at the same time.... I know TMI, right?
>
> I lost 6 pounds in 6 hours. They IV'd me and it took three bags of fluid to rehydrate me. I'd never been sick with a stomach ailment that intense before then or since! I was so grateful there was a first shirt nearby to take me to the Hospital and that it was very close to where I lived on base. I was also grateful for a great medical team in the ER that fixed me up well and quickly.

dlanni said...

> Hey there old friends. Dave (Worst guitar player you ever heard) here. It goes like this, 6 Years of crashing 16 inch marching band cymbals 8 inches in front of my face. Turns out the only difference in DB level compared to standing 20 feet from a jet engine is a couple of pts. Then I do one of the rock bands for two years. Fast forward to 1998 and, pardon the pun, I've got Tinitus in both ears to beat the band. My ears ring and hiss 24/7. All I can say is "Who Knew?" Cheers.

Fred said...

> Welcome to TBOTB, dlanni... Oh, you don't even come close
> on the "worst guitar player..." thing. Sorry to hear (pun
> intended) that somebody I know has a similar problem... But,
> on the other hand I guess that makes it a familiar ring... I will
> stop now.

Chris said...

> Both of you should investigate the VA...if not for the stellar
> medical treatment, then at least for a determination of slight
> disability. Heck, if Sgt Flattop can get one for hurting
> himself playing ping-pong, then tinnitus surely would be a
> service-related injury.

Fred said...

> Well, maybe D should consider it... I am a lousy mooch. I
> was never even comfortable smoking or drinking OP's while
> in... I'm fine, I just need to concentrate some times...

Col. "Kuz" Skis, Sgt Flatop Skis, We All Ski! For Ice-Ski?

The AFB East had a great commander in the beginning of the 80's. I
know because I enlisted in October of 1981 and this Lieutenant
Colonel was in command when I arrived with my spouse after basic
training in November of that year. I truly respected and enjoyed his
soft-spoken manner, his sterling musicianship and his obvious
respect for the Band.

We performed "The Nutcracker Suite" that December at our
Christmas Concerts and I performed the "celeste" solo on "Dance of
the Sugar Plum Fairy". Col. K told the story of Tchaikowsky "flying"
the heavenly sounding celeste, invented by Mustel in 1886, from
Paris back to Russia..... Hmmm..... 1886 - celeste invented.... 1903
...first airplane flight . . .?

It took awhile for the Colonel to live down the "flying" faux pax....
and the Band gave him pokes about it at routine intervals.

Sgt Flattop had a wild and crazy idea of a way to play a practical
joke on and, at the same time, salute this gracious man that we
admired so much on his birthday in 1982. I had the privilege of
seeing this man at a recent Band Reunion. He is 73 years old
(wouldn't tell you that info if he hadn't told me with boldness), and
he looks fabulous may I add (incredible shape... looks early 60's...
maybe!), so I'm calculating that he was celebrating his 45th birthday
that year in 1982.

We each willingly purchased a special name tag to wear in Concert
Band rehearsal on his birthday.

This commander's last name ended in "ski". A very interesting name,
in my opinion, of Slavic origin, Sgt Flattop devised a plan to make
every Band members' surname Slavic by adding "ski" to the end of
their surname, and if their surname didn't quite work with the suffix,
we'd make up a name like, "Snowski, Waterski, Jetski, etc.

Every Band member had a "new" name tag in rehearsal that
morning...We had "Smithski", "Joneski", "Frankski", etc...

The dear Colonel did not notice the name tags... rehearsal went on
for 40 minutes....and he still hadn't noticed.

Finally, Sgt Flattop rose and made an approach to the podium,
flashing the right side of his chest at the commander, who was
looking at Flattop with furrowed brow, like he had lost his mind.

Then, finally, Col. K saw Sgt Flattop's tag....then the woodwinds'
tags... he began to grin...then he saw the second row's tags... a light
chuckle.. then the adjacent rows' tags.... full laughter from him and
all of the sections of the Band! He had been punked and took the
joke in the lighthearted way in which it had been composed. How
refreshing to have an authority figure with a hearty sense of humor!

It was a treasured moment in my most pleasant memories of my
days under the command of Col. K.

Posted by Stephanie

Happy Thanksgiving!

Nothing funny, nothing silly here, just a heartfelt Happy Thanksgiving to all.

Well, then a band related Thanksgiving story.

My lovely bride got to Germany not too long before Thanksgiving in 1979. I had been there since July. We didn't really know anybody, me the arranger, she being very new, so we had no Thanksgiving plans. Somehow the word got out to the Commander at that time. Soon thereafter, an invitation to Thanksgiving dinner came directly from him. Just he and his wife and me and mine. I was so gassed that he would offer I never thought about how that would look, from a fraternization stand point, but obviously he didn't care. So, I graciously excepted without even checking with the boss, my real boss, not my Commander.

I think we were probably a little sheepish that afternoon when we arrived at the K's. But it only took one handshake and a hug (the ladies did that) and we were just fine. The thing I remember most about the meal was the blessing. The Major's wife included us by saying something about us being the newest members of their family.

Many years later, September 18th of 2010 to be exact, I met up with that man and his wife again. As I went up to him, sitting behind the Name Tag Table and extended my hand, he smiled, stood and extended both of his hands and called me "Thanksgiving Boy."

This time the boys hugged.

Posted by Fred

2 comments:

Mike said...

That's truly a touching story. There really is a special bond amongst AF musicians.

Fred said...

TY. Does this particular Mike's last name start with an "S?"

Slay Ride

The AFB East had musicians coming into and going out from the group on a fairly regular basis. I'm pretty sure that I'm thinking of the right person for this particular saga.

She was a vegetarian ("I don't eat animal flesh!"), had serious disdain for smoking ("It's too smokey in here"), thermogenetically challenged ("It's too hot!", "It's too cold"), and was dissatisfied.... well, pretty much with everything! ("When are we gonna eat?" "Are we almost there?" "I gotta go!")... but she was an excellent musician!

She had not been with the Band but a short while, when her day to be CQ (Charge of Quarters) came around. During her duty that day, the NCO in charge of Band uniforms came to her and said he would cover for her. He gave her the keys to the Band's brand new van to go down to the local dry cleaners/alterations shop called "Stratos" to be fitted for her performance uniforms. And the following parody, Slay Ride (to the tune of Sleigh Ride) was inspired by the events that followed:

Slay Ride
Just hear that window jinglin' ring ting tinglin' too
I wrecked the Band's new van and I'm sure that some money is due
It was a boring day, it was my turn to be the CQ
Oh, just an average day until Will J****** came into view
Hurry up, hurry up, hurry up, Will said
Go down to Stratos
They're ready now to fit you in some clothes
Crank it up, crank it up, crank it up, you can

Go down in the van
I parked in the lot in a slot that was next to the Strato sign
Now when I came back out of the store and I got in the car
I put the gear in "R" and I backed up a little too far
I heard some metal clattering, glass was shattering too
Oh no, I had a wreck and I'll write a check and I
Think I'll pass when somebody asks if I'd
Drive that van, I don't think I can
'Cause I'm broke! Oh yes, I'm broke! Oh yes, I'm broke!
Oh yes, I'm broke! Oh yes, I'm broke! (sound of a horn honking)
SLAY RIDE!!!!

Posted by Stephanie

8 comments:

Fred said...

    Cl. or Fl.?

Chris said...

    Played the typewriter part when we performed Leroy
    Anderson...

Chris said...

    Sorry Fred, this week I'm a bit slow... clarinet player...
    redhead, used to be my clerk when I was Librarian.

Stephanie said...

    I must be losin' it Chris. I always thought the strawberry
    blonde flautist was the star of this parody... ;D

Fred said...

    Those were the two I was wondering about... Either C. B./Cl,
    or E. S./Fl, would work for me... lol

Stephanie said...

> I never meant to imply that our Slay Ride star had a corner on the gritch (gripe and.... well you know) market. Just that she frequented the corner more than most... ;D

Chris said...

> Well, it could have fit either, but I remember when the accident happened, and she gritched for a week or two about having to pay for the damage. Now the other one was frequent gritcher; in fact, I think she was the target of Randall H's parody... (in a nasal voice), "It's too SMOKY in here" whenever boarding the bus.
>
> God, I miss his humor...

Stephanie said...

> Randall was our lovable, fuzzy tuba-playin' teddy bear. So many great memories.
>
> He is sorely missed. :(

While The Cat's Away . . .

It was a warm and blissful day in June of 1980 at AFB East.

A certain french horn playing Staff Sergeant and family were going to St. Petersburg, FL on summer leave and asked a certain trumpet player if he would watch the house and cat.

They knew trumpet player's feeling about cats. But he agreed anyway.

He fed the cat religiously and on the 2nd day, much to his dismay, the cat was never to return.

SSgt French Horn never took down his Christmas lights ever. Trumpeter thinks he sold the house with them still mounted.

As the days went by, Trumpeter received a phone call from Headquarters and was told that SSgt French Horn was promoted to Tech, and would no longer be the oldest living Staff Sergeant - but might still hold the record!

So, Trumpeter gathered a few friends to decorate French Horn's house for a special welcome home and congratulations!

They took all SSgt French Horn's furniture and faced it towards the walls. Cellophaned the toilet seats, left the piled high dirty dishes in his sink, and hid his bedroom phone between the mattresses.

They took the paintings of castles in Europe that hung on the wall, and turned them upside down.

Then, they commenced to partake of his fine liquor cabinet as to be prepared for his arrival.

However, after a while, they had had enough, and didn't want to face the consequences, which meant facing the wrath of SSgt French Horn.

When they departed, they illuminated his beautiful June Christmas lights and went home.

SSgt French Horn and family arrived home late that evening to admire the decorator's work. Shortly after, the "decorators" reassembled to congratulate him on his promotion.

They brought back what was left of his liquor to celebrate. They drank until all was gone. To this day, Trumpeter and the guys don't think that, now TSgt French Horn, knew it was his liquor.

His wife didn't care about the cat.

French horn asked at work what had happened to his telephone.

Trumpeter called him later that night.

French horn found it.

All is well.

Posted by Stephanie

10 comments:

Fred said...

> OK, this would have been two years before I got to AFB East
> in July of '82. So did I know the FHn. player as a TSgt/MSgt?
> And the Tpt. player eventually as a SMSgt?
>
> Cool story no matter who they were...

Stephanie said...

> Yes, you knew/know them both in those capacities.... Hints,
> initials are L.W. (aka as An hour and a half....) The target of
> many a practical joke. Star of prior TBOTB post-Furniture
> Clearance... everything must go! Trumpet Player, initials are
> D.E. (CEO of pranks against "an hour and a half" throughout
> the years in the Band) ;)
>
> Hey D.E.!!! Thanks for the memories ;D
>
> P.S. Fred.... This is my recounting of the story as told by D. to
> me yesterday... I got to AFB East in Nov 1981... so I missed
> the fun of this story too! ;)

Fred said...

> Thanks for the clarification. Nice to know I had it right.

Chris said...

> Kiss a fat lady's ....!

Stephanie said...

> LMAO! Chris, I'm sure you remember the story about the Band golf scramble and D. throwing his club in the lake after a Bogey and shouting KAFLD loud enough for the entire base to hear!

Fred said...

> Yup, I even played that scramble. I had a 300, or something. Isn't that a perfect game? Or is that bowling? At least I got my moneys worth.

Stephanie said...

> I'll say you got your money's worth!! LOL!

Chris said...

> I shot a 90 that day... after the third hole, I just drank and walked along... no more golf for me, thanks; I've had enough... I was waiting for D's group to finish that hole when the infamous shot occurred... he hit a tree when the shot hooked like it had eyes, and the ball almost made it back to the tee. That's when the club went whizzing through the air... it was classic!

Stephanie said...

> LMAO! Yep! Better than "Caddyshack" ! Wasn't it Chief, Scooter, D., and Jack? (what a foursome!)

Chris said...

> Yep... AKA the Four Horsemen of the Apocalypse... can't remember which one was Famine, though...

I Hadn't Heard This One . . .

The meat of this post was sent to me simply as a joke. There was no mention of it having anything to do with any GI band, nor any reason to believe that it ever actually happened in real life. But, as soon as I read it all I could think about was the AFB West, in an era slightly before my time, that would be Tom P.'s time (mid to late '70's) where interaction between officers and enlisted personnel such as this was common, therefore legendary. So, please allow me to re-orchestrate the joke for military band. I am, after all, an arranger ...

The Major (conductor) was getting exasperated with one of the drummers at a rehearsal one day and finally said, "You know, when a musician can't really play their instrument, they usually take away his instrument, give him two sticks and make him a drummer!"

Immediately, from back in the percussion section, the band hears, "And if he can't make it as a drummer, they take away one of his sticks and make him a conductor!"

Variations on a theme by: A Friend...

Posted by Fred

Two Of The Coolest Things

I mentioned a trip with the AFB East to Hill, AFB in Utah in another post. Here's a story about the flight there. We got to fly on a KC-135 Stratotanker, you know the in-flight refueling tankers. The tanker was on a return run and would not be loaded with fuel, I would have assumed that they would not take passengers on a refueling mission. It accommodated our small contingent quite nicely.

Along with the traditional USAF Web Seats this plane had one REALLY cool, or should I say COOL, seat. Well, not quite a seat, it was actually a couch, but not a normal couch. This was the place that the boom operator occupied during refueling. During flights where there was no refueling mission, passengers (even unruly bandsmen) were allowed, under supervision of the crew, to take a turn in that seat.

How cool is that! Oh, did I mention it was cold as ice in that cramped little space? It was worth it for the view.

From cramped, though picturesque, quarters to plenty of leg room...

The same AFB East, though the full contingent of sixty or so, had agig at a base in New Hampshire. Chris, Stephanie, help me out with the name? I can't remember. I can remember the ride though. C-5 Galaxy! Whoa, that's a big bird!

I had heard hundreds of them (my apartment in Germany was in the landing path to Ramstein) and seen dozens of them, but always at quite a distance. As we drove the equipment trucks on to the flight line, I remember thinking, "Oh my God. We could just drive both our trucks right inside and not have to even unload." It turns out I had underestimated the cargo area. That plane could have easily accommodated three or four of our 28 foot equipment trucks and maybe have had room for our 60 pax bus. Chris, Stephanie, help again... Did we drive on or palletize like normal?

When I zoomed in on this picture I had from the Internet I realized that in the back left, near the ladder, were two full grown adult males, say six-foot tall? Now take into consideration that the ladder is leading to the upper deck, which contained standard airline type seating for over 100 people, along with a couple full sized bathrooms (remember the $600.00 toilet seats?). How cool was that?

So, while I have gone on and on about some of the cool people I met while working for Uncle Sam, I must also say that Uncle had some pretty cool toys too!

Posted by Fred

1 comment:

Chris said ...

> Pease AFB in New Hampshire; we must have palletized,
> because I can't remember ever driving into a C-5... and given
> the usual wimpy attitude towards driving into an enclosed
> area, I probably would have had to have been the driver...
> nobody else even wanted to drive across Mobile Bay on the
> old bridge during construction because of the barriers on both
> sides, remember?

All You Need Is Love And A Good Ear

After posting so many 10, 20 and 30 year-old recollections, I thought
it might be nice to have something a bit more recent. So, here's one
from the 21st century. Oh, be warned, this is a really long one.

Back in July of 2008 I was fortunate enough to be reunited with a
very close friend, with whom I had spent many hours, days, months,
years (well, only about 2 years) sharing adjoining seats in some
pretty damn good sax sections (OK, some of them sucked too). We
decided to spend one night at a little jazz club in Fullerton, CA,
Steamers Jazz Café (I can highly recommend that place – more
later). Having personally traveled down the DUI path twice it was
decided that we would get a room at a local 1-star motel (though
cleanish, and the free Internet worked) within walking distance of
Steamers.

We got to Fullerton about 5-ish for an 8:00 downbeat. We unpacked
a bit, put reserve beer in the fridge and then we strolled up the hill to
Steamers to grab a bite to eat before the Big Band started. (No-name
band, but worthy of a name – more on them later too).

Because we were so early I made sure to mention to the waitress
seating us that we did want to stay and catch the band. She
mentioned that they most often shared tables at Steamers (very cool
way to meet other Jazz Fans) and pointed to a few places that had
not yet been reserved, all about 20-30 feet away from the band. My
buddy, Gail, asked if we couldn't get anything closer. The waitress
pointed to this one table for two right down in front and said, that's

available. Then quickly, almost apologetically she said, "But that's awful close to the band." The tip of the table was actually touching the Lead Alto players music stand. I would say that was close. Our eyes lit up and we took it!

I had the House Panini and I think Gail just had a salad, that's like good date etiquette, right? We had fun watching the band get setup (and not having to do it), settled back for some Bass Ale and waited for the gig to start.

The band was The Mark Hicks Big Band. They are kind of like an LA kicks band (though kicks players in LA can kick some butt). That night there was only one recognizable (at least to me) name in the band, Edmond Velasco on 4th tenor. The guys wandered in and they started remarkably close to the advertised downbeat time.

The seats were about half full (Monday night Big Band night, and a true LA tradition, show up to a Dodger game in the third inning) but as they played the opener most of the people in attendance adjusted their seats a few inches (feet if possible) farther away from the band than they had been before they cranked it up. Gail and I scooted a bit closer, catching the attention of at least one of the sax players. As the opener was cut off I found my eyes welling up a bit (it had been a long time since I had heard that sound live and never so close without being in the band) and I noticed that my right hand had involuntarily performed a cut-off right along with the lead alto player. Oops, he caught that too.

Sax section observation: Gail and I had already jokingly talked about that short period of time when we were together in Germany, back in the early '80's, when our sax section had three players playing Strathon mouthpieces. On the way to the club that night we also commented on what were the chances that anybody would be playing one of those gimmick mouthpieces tonight. Well, two were. Lol.

The gig went on, and we had a wonderful time. Between sets I would wonder out to the back patio and grab a smoke and our waitress turned out to be pretty bad and adding up the number of Bass Ales we had consumed so the check was a pleasant surprise.

All and all, I would say that between Gail and myself we had played about 80% of the stuff they did that night and heard 10% of the others. These guys were having fun and we did too.

After the gig, I got another pleasant surprise. The owner came over and introduced himself (though we had met a few years earlier – I am pretty forgettable though) and said that his father would like to meet "The wild man that kept directing the band all night." I guess my opener cut-off was not the only involuntary gesture I made that night, but dang it, I was having fun. So, Terence Love Jr. introduced me to Terence Love senior and we shot the shit for a while as the band broke down.

No moral, no Coda, just a comment. That night, for the first time, I felt that the line I had often used on crowd members who wanted to talk to me after a gig "Without listeners, there is no music" was actually true.

Posted by Fred

5 comments:

Tom P. said...

> When I first moved to Hollywood and was "in funds" I would walk almost every night to either Catalina's on Cahuenga or Bob Mark's "Legends" jazz club on the Boulevard a few blocks away. The world-renowned talent played at Catalina's while the studio guys would play Legends. Sad to say that there were nights when I was the only customer at Bob Mark's place and the quality of the music was equal to or greater than what was going on at the packed house around the corner.

Fred said...

> I don't know how a Jazz club can stay in business these days but thank God they do. I have only done Steamers and a few times to the Bakery. I particularly like the room and the vibes at Steamers.

Fred said... (cont.)

> I know what you mean about the local talent. The first time I was taken to Steamers was to see the Jeff Hamilton trio. I had never heard of Jeff (or the big band). I think he had Bill Cunliffe on piano and Andy Simpkins on base (I think Andy went and died on us just a few days later). They were amazing. Jeff is now one of my favorite drummers.

Anonymous said...

> The opener was 'Wind Machine' I remember when they kicked it off the two of us looked at each other with that "Don't we know this chart?" look after only a few bars into the piano solo. That was a great night! We were so close to the band we could have turned the pages for the cats in the sax section.

Anonymous said...

> Oh, BTW, I ordered only that salad 'cuz that was the only veg item they had on the menu. Nothing to do with date etiquette.

Fred said...

> Ahh, you are right on both accounts. You wanna post things?

CODA

A career sergeant looked back on his military band experience and said:

"I'm a taxpayer and I want to know who scheduled this vacation."

Epilogue

The pirates of our tale have long drifted from the field of battle yet our dispatches have sealed their immortality.

Arrives now the time for a new generation of military musicians to forsake the cloak of anonymity that has distanced them from an American civilization thirsting for fresh musical heroics.

The author calls on our contemporary musician warriors to contribute their insights and adventures to the great confluence of an American mind chronicled in the web blog "The Back of the Bus II."

Even so, we mourn for the untapped genius of yesteryear and sound our venerable brethren to assemble and testify to tales still unknown.

We invite you all to fall in and deliver your reports.

http://blogtbotb.blogspot.com/

Glossary

.45: A 45 Caliber, semi-automatic hand gun.

35-10: The number of the regulation governing appearance of all Air Force personnel.

45-15, 45-15 Rule: The number of minutes on and off on a regular GB gig. Often abused by the band when the gig sucked.

4th Book: See Book.

6-8'er: Any musician that is not a Jazzer. AKA: Square.

702: The first three digits of the AFSC for a clerk.

7-Level (Also 3-Level, 5-Level and 9-Level): Skill level proficiencies needed to move up in rank. All Air Force Bandsmen had to be qualified as a 3-Level before entering the Air Force.

8 O'clock: The Lab Band (Big Band) at NTSU that rehearsed at 8:00 PM. The bands started at Noon (the worse band) followed by the 1 O'clock (the best band) on through the 10 O'clock, in descending order of quality. Some times they would have a Friday/Saturday band (really bad) if there were enough students. I spent most of my time in the 8 O'clock, though did make it to the 6 O'clock for a semester.

AFB: Air Force Base. Smaller stations would include AS, Air Station and DET, Detachment.

AFM: The "American Federation of Musicians" or, The Union.

AFRES: Air Force Reserve Command based at Warner Robins, Georgia.

AFSC: Air Force Specialty Code, Job Number.

Air Force Brat: A child of an Air Force member, enlisted or officer, well behaved or not.

ANG: Air National Guard, AKA: Guard. Pronounced like Hang, but seldom pronounced.

Article 15: Severe Nonjudicial Punishment normally accompanied with a fine. Lesser such actions include the LOR, Letter for the Record, or LOC, Letter of Counseling. Bad Mojo!

ATC: Air Training Command. A command within the structure of the Air Force in the last century.

Ax, Axe: Any musical instrument, EVEN an accordion.

B1: A GI issue One Suite, suitcase. B2's are for two suits, though seldom issued to bandsmen.

Bakery, The: Short for The Jazz Bakery. A beloved Jazz Hall in Southern California.

Balls: Intense, as in "Balls-To-The-Wall" or "Play it with more Balls!"

BAND Hat: A special, organizational headgear worn by military bands. The most notable BAND Hats are those that are simply one color with the word band in bold block letters. Other such organizational hats may be called Band Hats or band hats, but never BAND Hats!

Band-wives: I know that should not need an explanation, but it doesn't just mean what it looks like it means. The term Band-wife was also used for husbands, girlfriends and boyfriends. Any non-bandsman who provided exceptional off-duty support.

Bb, B-Flat: A pitch, a major second below C, or in Jazz-Speak: Mundane, ordinary

BBK: Short for Bayerische Brauerei Kaiserslautern, a Pilsner beer. Sort of the PBR of the Rheinland-Pfalz, central Germany.

Beer Tent: What does it sound like? Yes, heaven. Oh, technically it was a common German festival held in a tent (though not always) where they served... Yup, you got it, BEER!

Big Band: Well, they are not really that big, normally 16 or 17 players, but the term often used to describe the types of bands also known as Dance Bands from the 1940's. That would be; 5 saxophones, 4 (sometimes 3) trombones, 4 trumpets and a rhythm section consisting of piano, bass and drums (sometimes a guitar). Expanded versions also existed.

Bird: 1. A Colonel, an Officer with clout, one step below a General and one step above a Lt. Colonel (AKA Lite Colonel or Telephone Colonel). 2. An airplane, most commonly a C-130. Buses are also called Birds, but not that often.

Birthday, Birthday Boy: Something they can't take away from a no-striper or someone who can have nothing taken away from them because they have nothing to loose. As in, "I got nothing to loose. What are they gonna do, take away my birthday?"

Blow, blew: Term to describe the quality of a players skills, normally improvisational, but can also be used to describe the players ability to play the Dots. For example, "That Cat can really BLOW!"

Bluebird, Blue-Bird, blue bird: A utilitarian military personnel bus, not necessarily manufactured by the Bluebird bus company. In terms of charm and comfort it typically ranks a few notches below a prison bus.

BMTS: Basic Military Training Squadron

Book: Term used to describe the collection of pieces of music, parts, that make up the traveling library (also know as "book") for a band. Books are associated to the instrument, for example: there is a 4th Tenor Book, a 2nd Trumpet Book, etc.

Booth, The: The name for where the Recording Engineer sits with all his gear, and producers cut up and stuff like that.

Brick: Motorola Walkie-talkie.

BTZ: Below The Zone. A military system for promoting someone faster than normal.

Butt-can: A container, often covered, for collecting cigarette buts. The two "T" spelling was adopted by the TROGS, so is used here. It can also be used to describe a smoking area, even if there is no container. In that case, the troops would Dress (Filed Dress) their buts.

BX: Base Exchange, the general store on a military installation

C-130 (AKA: 130 or Hurc, short for Hercules): A propeller-driven military cargo plane that can be configured to carry passengers.

C-141 (AKA: 141 or Star Lifter): A jet powered Air Force cargo plane. Larger than a C-130 but smaller than a C-5.

C-4: Not a plane, that's the stuff that blows up...

C-5: A jet powered Air Force cargo plane. The largest plane on earth.

C-9: A military passenger jet, medium-size.

Cachao: A famous Cuban bass player credited with establishing the ultimate Cuban Jazz groove. Therefore it is also used to describe that groove.

Cammys (AKA: BDU's): Camouflage uniforms.

Cans: Headphones.

Career Field: A subset of jobs in the Air Force. Casual Status: Those who had just concluded Enlisted Basic Training or Officer Training School who were awaiting assignments.

CB: Concert Band or Citizens Band Radio (commonly used illegally by Military bandsmen).

CBPO (Pronounced See-Bow): The Consolidated Base Personal Office, like HR for the Air Force.

Cellar, The: A most favored bar in Macon, GA.

Chevron (AKA: Stripes): Rank insignia of enlisted personal either made of cloth and sewn to a uniform or made of metal and attached to a uniform with frogs. (See Frogs.)

Chops: Your lips or may be used to describe a player's ability as in, "That cat is good! Dig his chops!"

Civvies: Short for Civilian. Normally used to describe clothing but can be used to describe people.

Clam, Clams: Wrong notes, either written or performed that way. CMFWIC: Chief Mother F***** What's In Charge -the head dude or dudette.

CMSgt: Chief Master Sergeant, eight stripes, highest enlisted rank. Collar Brass: The insignia of the United States of America, US, worn by both officers and enlisted members of the military.

Combat Pay: Additional monetary compensation given to those in combat situations. Band guys don't get that very often.

Combo 1 (2, 3 and 4): Normal Air Force Uniform Combinations. Combo 1 (AKA: Dress Blues): Blue uniform complete with jacket (blouse) and light blue shirt and tie. Combo 2: A blue uniform with long a sleeve light blue shirt and tie. Combo 3: A blue uniform with a long sleeve dark blue shirt and a tie. (Discontinued in the 1980's.) Combo 4: A blue uniform with a short sleeve light blue shirt with or without a tie.

Commander's Call: A military Staff Meeting that normally is conducted by the Commander, though is sometimes be used to describe a meeting for only enlisted personnel.

Corfams: Shiny plastic shoes adopted by military personnel so they didn't have to really shine their issued leather shoes.

Crypto: Short for cryptography, the code breakers/makers of the military. Note that the word does not have a period after it, well, unless it ends a sentence.

Cutting Contest: In a Jam Session, when one player attempts to outdo another. Can be fun, can be messy...

D-300: A synthesizer with weighted keys (to make the feel resemble an acoustic piano) that was popular in the 80's. It was shortened from RD-300, some just called it a 300. Can also be used to describe just about any portable keyboard.

D. C.: The District of Columbia, or in musical terms: Da Cappo (the head), go back to the beginning.

DE: "Dixie Express." The Dixieland Band of the Command Band of the Air Force reserve (AFRES), Robins AFB, GA.

Dep, Deputy: Short for Deputy Commander. Note that Dep does not have a period, except at the end of a sentence.

Deuce, Deuce-and-a-half: Large Military truck.

DF's: The less polite term for the TROGS. The term indicates the person's potential for engaging in sexual activity with canines. Not that they do, but are capable of it. They are also are very loyal and have cold noses...

DIB: "Dimensions in Blue." The Jazz Ensemble (big band) of the UASF Band Of the West, Lackland, AFB, TX.

Dots: Written musical notation. As in, "Play the DOTS you Lizard!"

Double or Doubles: All the instruments you MUST play (even if you hate them) to get the gig.

Dress, Field Dress: A way of breaking down a cigarette butt to make it a non FOD factor. The burning ember is flicked off, the remaining tobacco is scattered in the breeze and the filter, if any, is either tucked into a pant pocket or tossed in a trash can, when a butt-can is not available.

Dump, The: Term used to describe the road quarters normally procured for military bands. Quality quarters were normally called, "Oh, my God! Who booked this place?"

Dumpster-opening: Term used to describe a worthless activity, at least in the eyes of those who are assigned it, normally a performance.

E1, E2, E3, E4, E5 E6, E7, E8, E9, E10: Either 10 octaves of the pitch E or Military Enlisted Ranks. There is not actually an E10, but the term is commonly used, as in; "What, you think you gonna make E10?"

EFES: Turkish beer. Not bad stuff.

F. L. I. C. K.: The "Federation for the Liberation of Indecent Carnal Knowledge." A fraternal organization dedicated to respectfully archiving Adult Entertainment Materials.

Falc's, The: "The Falconaires." The Jazz Ensemble formerly of the ASAF Academy, now stationed at Peterson (Pete) Field, Colorado Springs, CO.

Farkas: A top quality manufacturer of brass instruments, most noted for their French Horns.

Fasching: In Germany, Carnival or Mardi Gras.

Flight: Not the act of flying but a small unit within a Squadron. The equivalent of an Army platoon.

Flight Cap: Flexible military cap. When looked at from above it distinctly resembled a anatomical region that only women have, therefore it's nickname the C*** Cap. Just sayin'...

Flight Deck: Like a Cockpit, but for larger aircraft.

Flight Line: The runway and aircraft staging areas of an Air Force base.

FOD: Foreign Object Damage. What happens when crap gets sucked into a jet engine. It also is used to describe materials that can cause such damage to an aircraft, including flocks of geese.

Formation: A group of people arranged in ranks and files, as with a Marching Band. It is also used to describe any gathering of GI's or, among bandsmen, a performance.

Fraternizing, fraternization: Inappropriate mingling of Officers and Enlisted personnel.

Frog: Someone from France, and amphibian or those little clippy things used to fasten anything with a spike to a uniform, such as Chevrons.

Gasthaus: German term for Pub.

GB: General Business. Used to describe tunes or the gig itself.

Getson: A well respected manufacturer of brass instruments.

Gitmo: Short for Guantanamo Bay Naval Base, Cuba.

Gold Club, The: A most favored Adult establishment in Atlanta, GA.

GORT!: The name of the robot in "The Day The Earth Stood Still." Also the salute used in "Barbarella" and adopted by the AFRES TROGS, note that GORT is also TROG spelled backwards. GORT!

Groovies: Term for the local currency of the moment. Prior to the Euro there were many and trying to keep up with the names wasn't worth it.

Hamilton: A fine Studio (tall) Upright Piano manufactured by the Baldwin Piano Co. Also and crappy music stand that could be disassembled for easy transport, but far inferior to the Manhasset music stand.

Hancock's: A chain of fabric stores in Georgia.

Hannon: THE master instructional book for beginning piano student. Also uses as a term for getting back to basics. For example; "Man, you are way outside. Pull out you Hannon and go back to school!"

Harry's: A most favored eatery and tavern in Atlanta, GA.

Hats-off, Hats-off Area: Hats-off simply indicates a place, normally outside, where saluting is not required. For example, the Flight Line of all Air Force basses are considered Hats-off Areas. It can also be used as a term for take it easy, for example, "Hats-off, man, it's no big deal!"

Hill: An Air Force base in Utah.

Hit: A popular song or sharp percussive note played played by an individual or ensemble.

Hump it: A term for something uncomfortable, normally a long bus trip, but can be used to describe difficult manual labor.

IZOD: The name of a line of clothing popular in the 1980's or somebody who thought of themselves important or stylish.

Jet-tone, Cheater: A trumpet mouthpiece designed to make high notes easier to play and make you sound like crap. See also, Strathon for sax players.

JZ: Short for the word Jazz but also used to indicate a Jazz type band.

KAFLD: Literally, "Kiss A Fat Lady's DI**" where DI** is an anatomical part a fat, or slender, lady would not possess. Used as a term to describe much displeasure, like DARN, but much stronger. A slightly watered down of KAFLD would be, "Kiss A Fat Lady's Derrière" an anatomical feature she would have. A variant of KAFLD, KAFLP stood for "Kiss A Fat Lady's Patootie" though I am not sure that "Patootie" is actually a word.

K-town: Kaiserslautern, Germany. A large city close to where the AFB Overseas was stationed.

Kaserne: German for Base or Station.

Kit: A drum set.

Lackland AFB: Air Force base located in San Antonio, Texas. Home to the Band of the West and the Air Force basic training facilities.

Lackland Laser: A flashlight with a long conical, yellow shroud, about six inches long, in front of the lens that was issued to all basic trainees.

Last-four: The last four digits of a Social Security Account Number (SSAN) used by the Air Force to help identify unique personnel.

Lifer: Someone who had been in the Military so long it was as if they had lived their whole life there. Normally those people intended on making it to retirement, but that did not always happen.

Lizard: Someone who is bad at something as in, "You Suck! You Lizard!"

Loadmaster: The senior ranking enlisted member of the flight crew. He/she was responsible for the load, including passengers. Oh, and don't be fooled, the plane belonged to the Loadmaster, NOT the pilot!

M-16: Standard issue military riffle. Also a standard issue military gas mask.

Manhasset: The king of all music stands, complete with a hydraulic lift adjuster.

Manumals, The: See TROG...

Mess Dress: The most formal of uniforms. The enlisted version included a tight waistcoat while the officer version sported tales. Kind of a GI Tux.

MM, MM =: "Metronome Marking" or "Meter Marking" indication the number of beats per minute. For example, MM = 120 would indicate 120 beats a minute, a common March Tempo.

Msgt: Master Sergeant, six-stripes

NBC: The National Broadcasting System or to the military; Nuclear, Biological, and Chemical.

NCO: Non-commissioned officer; effectively any sergeant.

NCOIC: The Non-commissioned officer In Charge.

No-striper: See One-striper.

Note, The: "The Airmen of Note." The Jazz Ensemble of the United States Air Force Band, Washington, DC.

NT, NTSU, UNT: North Texas State University, renowned for it's jazz program with jazz lab bands named the One o'clock, Two o'clock, Three o'clock, etc.

O-Dark-30: Any unreasonably early time. For most GI musicians that would be any time before 9:00 AM. Also spelled: Oh-Dark-Thirty.

Oma: German for Grandmother or just an elderly woman.

On Quarters: The Air Force term for doctor's orders not to go to work.

One-stiper (Through eight): The number of stripes that make up an Airman's (the rank, not the generic term) chevrons. There is also a zero striper, known as a No-striper, AKA: Airman Basic.

On the Economy: The military parlance for renting civilian homes and apartments.

Opps: Operations. When used alone in normally indicates the person, or team, responsible for the logistics of a given unit (band). When used in conjunction with a qualifier, such as "Flight Opps" that would indicate the team responsible for the logistics of a given Air Force base.

Orch: Orchestra, either a traditional Symphonic type of ensemble or just a Big Band, even without strings, such as the Tonight Show Orchestra.

OTS: Officer Training School, the equivalent of Enlisted Basic Training. The school was at Medina, AS; San Antonio, TX.

Pain Stick: The name given to the Clarinet by those who had to play them who did not particularly want to, mostly sax players.

Pass In Review: A military ceremony normally called to get some officer's rocks off and piss off the band.

PCS: Permanent Change of Station, going to a new base. As with Permanent Party, permanent did not mean permanent.
Permanent Party: Those Permanently stationed at a given Air Force Base, though to Uncle Sam, permanent usually meant only a few years.

PI: Philippine Islands. There was a large Air Force base there with a band until a volcano blew up in the early 1990's.

Pickle: Term for basic trainees inspired by their unadorned olive green uniforms.

Q: The lookout for a prank or maneuver. Probably a combination of CQ (Charge of Quarters) and "On The QT" do it quietly or under the table. Not used much but we needed a glossary entry that started with the letter 'Q.'

Rack: 1. An array of instruments; for example Sax, Clarinet and Flute is a normal rack displayed by big band sax players. Racks may also include Skills that are not visible, as in "The dude plays a bunch of sax, but dig, he's also got composing and arranging in his rack." 2. A box, portable or built in, containing sound equipment.

RAF: Royal Air Force, British.

Raki: Turkish White Lightning masquerading as a liquorish liquor. Rather like Ouzo.

Ramstein AFB: Air Force base located near Kaiserslautern, Germany. Home to the USAFE band.

Ranger: A US Army Special Forces Soldier.

RCCL: Royal Caribbean Cruise Lines.

REA: Recording Association of America.

Recorder: An electronic instrument designed to record sounds or a Renaissance wind instrument often called a Flute-O-Phone these days.

Road Guard: A basic trainee, Pickle, whose job it was to stop traffic so his or her flight could pass through intersections. This job was normally assigned to the pudgy trainees, as was the case with Fred, because they had to work that much harder than the others. At least the TIs though that was a good idea.

Rogers, the: Fred's beloved drum kit he had to leave behind in Germany and misses to this day.

Room, The: In a recording studio, where the musicians record. There may be a Big Room and a Small Room, but they are seldom called anything else by the players. The room where the Engineer sits is called The Booth (See: Booth, The).

Round Hat: Military hat the resembled a traditional Bus Driver's hat, often called the Bus Driver hat.

Ruffles and Flourishes: Musical stuff added before playing in dignitaries. They went "Dah, dah, dah, dot, dot, dah." You got one of those for each star you had as a general and The President got five.

SATB: A Choir term indicating Soprano, Alto, Tenor and Bass (perhaps Baritone). Also used to indicate simple four part (voice) writing for any instrumentation.

Sgt: Sergeant, three-stripes

Shirt, First Shirt: The Squadron First Sergeant, kind of like an HR Rep., normally a MSgt or above.

SM-58: A well respected microphone of the 1970's and 1980's made by the Sure company (SM stood for Sure Microphone). The SM-57 was also popular at that time.

SMSgt: Senior Master Sergeant, seven-stripes .

Sopranino: An instrumental the term used for a voice higher than a Soprano.

Spitballs: 1. Those tiny wads of paper that were shot through a straw in study hall. 2. A cleaning device that brass players would blow through their horns to help keep them clean on the inside.

Spooks: Members of the CIA, but to the military they were Cryptologists, AKA: Cripto.

SrA: Senior Airman, rank that precedes Sergeant.

SSgt: Staff Sergeant, four-stripes

SSL: "Solid State Logic" mixing console.

Star Lifter: See C-141.

Stinger: The decisive last sharp, short, and loud note of a piece of music, normally attributed to Marches, written or improvised by the band.

Strathon: See Jet-tone, Cheater.

TADMST: Total Active Duty Military Service Time, how long you served in whatever branch of service even if you got out and came back in.

Tarmac: Material used to build landing strips (flight lines - airports, military or civilian).

Tattletales: A most favored Adult establishment in Atlanta, GA.

TDY: "Temporary Duty." I know, it should only be TD but the NFL already used that one. Any road trip.

Telephone Colonel: See Bird.

Three Down, 3-Down, Three Up...: This is actually a System rather than a term. The actual number, of fingers, used can be any number from Zero (a fist) to Five. The fingers indicate the number of Flats (when the fingers are pointing down) or Sharps (when the fingers are pointing up) in the Key Signature. Pretty cool, hu? Oh, if you want to play something in six or more sharps of flats on a GB gig, you should be shot!

TLQ: Temporary Living Quarters, a Base Hotel...

Tomahawk Chop, The Chop: A chopping motion made by sports fans that resembles a Tomahawk in action. It originated at Florida State University but was later adopted by the Atlanta Braves.

Travel Orders: More silly Air Force paperwork required any time you went TDY. (See TDY).

Trogs, The: Short for Troglodyte. The name adopted by the serious party people in the AFRES band. Similar, though perhaps not as deadly as the "Manumals" of the Band Of The West.

TSgt: Tech Sergeant, five-stripes

Turn Around, The Turn Around: The part of a musical phrase just before it repeats. It can also be used to describe the added material used near the end of a piece to extend it, even though it normally would be over. That's normally the III-VI-II-V thingy.

USAF (AKA: AF): The United State Air Force

USAFE: United States Air Forces in Europe

VI: The Roman Numeral for 6 or the Virgin Islands." Also, USVI.

Voicings, voicing, voiced: The actual stack of pitches used in an orchestrated piece of music or by polyphonic instruments such as piano or guitar. For example a C7 (a dominant seventh chord with the root of C) could be voiced C-E-G-Bb, that would be in "Root, Closed." Or it could be something like C-G-Bb-D-E-F#-A that would be "Altered, Open" (and sound much better with the 9, +11 and 13th added).

Vox: See X.

VSI: Variable Separation Incentive. The USAF Early Out program, which Fred took, of the 1990s.

Warner Robins: Town in Middle Georgia location of Robins Air Force base. Home to multiple commands including the Air Force Reserve Command and it's band.

Web Seats: Hammock like seats made from formidable nylon strapping material about two inches wide, normally found on AF Planes. While comfortable for a while, they could produce some interesting patterns on your bottom, known as Web Bruises, on long flights.

Wheels-up, Bows-up: The exact scheduled departure time. Normally used for planes, or boats, but also for buses, trucks, etc.

Write-Pat: An Air Force base in Illinois.

X, Vox: A notation normally added to a piece of written music after it has been performed a while. It indicates the place in the music where the band should go WHEN the singer messes up.

Yearling: A GI who has yet to be stationed over seas, regardless of how long they have been in.

'zids: Residuals, residual payments.

Zoo: An after gig party.

Made in the USA
Charleston, SC
01 December 2011